PRESENTATION COPY

To record the fiftieth anniversary of the first birth-control clinic to be established in the United Kingdom.

Dear Doctor,

Immediately we learned that this history was being written, we commissioned a special edition to present to our physician friends.

This is not a textbook, but a fascinating essay on human behaviour. May you derive as much pleasure from reading it as we have in presenting it.

Sincerely,

Managing Director

ORTHO PHARMACEUTICAL LIMITED
HIGH WYCOMBE, BUCKS, ENGLAND

THE FIGHT FOR ACCEPTANCE

A History of Contraception

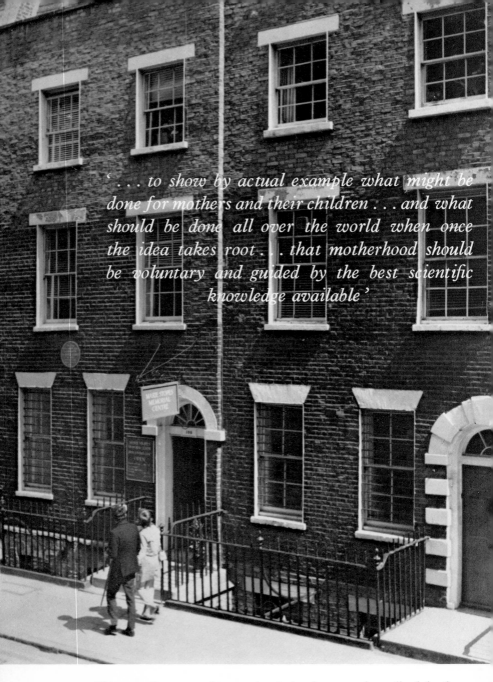

' . . . to show by actual example what might be done for mothers and their children . . . and what should be done all over the world when once the idea takes root . . . that motherhood should be voluntary and guided by the best scientific knowledge available '

This quotation comes from an inscription hung on the wall of the first birth-control clinic to be opened in Britain. The clinic was opened just fifty years ago, on 17 March 1921, by Dr. Marie Stopes and her husband H. V. Roe. The original clinic was at Holloway but later moved to the building in Whitfield Street shown in this photograph.

Clive Wood *and* Beryl Suitters

THE
FIGHT FOR
ACCEPTANCE

A HISTORY OF
CONTRACEPTION

MTP
Medical and Technical Publishing Co Ltd
AYLESBURY

PUBLISHED BY MTP
MEDICAL AND TECHNICAL PUBLISHING CO LTD
CHILTERN HOUSE, OXFORD ROAD, AYLESBURY, BUCKS

SBN 85200022 7

FIRST PUBLISHED 1970

PRINTED IN GREAT BRITAIN BY
BILLING & SONS LIMITED
GUILDFORD AND LONDON

Preface

NOT everyone might agree with Alexander Pope that the proper study of mankind is man, but for those who do it is clear that two aspects of the proper study must receive our special attention, if we are to gain an insight into what distinguishes man from the beasts. The first, of course, is that aspect which deals with man's origins. The long slow process of biological evolution has produced an organism which is unique, at least as far as its ability to order and influence its environment is concerned. And yet, as modern zoologists are happy to point out, much of man's physical and emotional make-up derives directly from his ancestors and may only be properly understood by considering it in this light. Such an approach can be of enormous value so long as it is not allowed to get out of control; it is unwise to allow the tail to wag the ape. The second aspect has to do with the way that man has managed to increase, slowly at first and then so rapidly as to produce a situation that gives (or should give) anxiety to people everywhere. This second approach therefore is concerned not so much with man's origins as with his continued existence, and in particular with his means of reproducing himself.

The course of human history has depended to no small extent upon the ability of mankind to control his surroundings rather than being controlled by them. His success has been measured by his ability to tame a hostile environment which is constantly making his life difficult or dangerous. From the striking of the first handaxe to the launching of the first Earth satellite his technology has been directed towards this end. At the same time much of his science has been directed towards influencing himself. From the bone-splint to the heart-lung machine he has been concerned with curing his diseases (or at least removing their symptoms), with increasing his life span and with ensuring that his children should live to replace him. At least part of his mental activity has therefore been turned inwards rather than outwards and has been directed to ensuring that his species would survive despite its inherent weaknesses.

It is not perhaps obvious that these two activities are closely related. However, even a hunting party must have a minimum number of fast, healthy individuals. The development of an agricultural system requires a lot more, each performing his particular function within the society. Survival, and certainly material prosperity, therefore depend upon the organization of a population of individuals into a group, and immediately we are forced to ask, just as our ancestors did, 'how big should the group be?'. The moment that the emphasis shifts from the individual or the individual family we are forced into a consideration of population size.

But there are only three ways that the size of a population can be altered: by birth, by death, and by migration. The first two of these are exactly the processes that man sought to control when he turned his interest upon himself. With the second he had little success, for the control of death is a very recent advance. The ability to cure epidemic diseases and significantly to increase a man's life expectancy has been achieved only within the last two centuries. The control of birth, by contrast, is a much more ancient activity, and one over which even the most 'primitive' individuals have some measure of control. The desire to influence the number of his children is one of the most fundamental of all man's aspirations.

Indeed, the late Norman Himes, perhaps the best known of the
(relatively few), writers who have considered the subject,
went so far as to declare that: 'Men and women have always
longed both for fertility and sterility; each at its appointed
time and in its chosen circumstances. This has been a universal
aim, whether people have always been conscious of it or not'.
It is our belief that Himes was correct and that the 'longing'
has been finding practical expression for many thousands of
years.

Our focus in this book is on the methods that men have
employed at various periods in history to limit their fertility,
and (just as important but usually neglected), on their reasons
for doing so. Our intention is to trace the history of birth
control – or more correctly of population control – from the
earliest times to the present day, and on into the near future.
The population explosion has already been mentioned once.
It is by far the most serious threat of disaster that has ever
faced our species, and a book like this would be incomplete if
we did not discuss it. However, this is not a book primarily
about that problem. The remarks that we make about the
future of population control (remarks with which some may
disagree), should be, and indeed will be, expanded into a book
of their own. They are included here because they give con-
tinuity with the past and also because any warning note that
can be sounded about population growth must be a timely one.

The book is timely in another sense. It is just fifty years since
the first two major birth control clinics in Britain were opened,
(within months of each other), in different parts of London.
For British workers in the family planning field the anniversary is one worth celebrating—though one must also remember
that even before 1921 similar clinics existed both in Europe
and in the United States. We would like to think that the appearance of this history goes some little way towards marking
that event. It is also timely because it appears within twelve

months of the re-issue of Norman Himes's great *Medical History of Contraception*. It is probably true to say that any book on contraceptive history written since World War II has owed something to this author's pioneering work. The present book is no exception and we are only too pleased to declare the fact.

Himes lived long enough to produce only one of the three volumes which he had planned. In that sense his published work is incomplete. The same charge will doubtless be levelled at this present book. It does not give a complete account of its subject simply because, in the space available, it cannot. The reader will search in vain for a reference to the original Drysdale 'clinic' which opened as early as 1908; he will find no direct mention of the experiments of Ludwig Haberlandt on 'hormonal sterilization' in the 1920s; the work of the Eugenics Society receives no documentation and developments which have occurred in intrauterine contraception in the last ten years are scarcely mentioned.

The last defect will be remedied in the near future, for an entire book dealing specifically with the topic is in preparation. The others however will not. The exclusion of such subjects (and the reader will find more for himself), does not imply that we think them unimportant. It simply reflects the inevitable selection that has had to take place if the book was to emerge at all. Isaac Newton said of his own efforts:-

I do not know what I may appear to the world, but to myself I seem to have been only a boy playing on the sea-shore, and diverting myself in now and then finding a smoother pebble or a prettier shell than ordinary, whilst the great ocean of truth lay all undiscovered before me.

We have seen the ocean: with each year's research its volume grows alarmingly. And we have not taken the pebbles and shells entirely at random. Each, we hope, typifies a different area of the beach, and together they show its full extent. Also, we have tried to thread them. We have tried to describe the development of contraceptive methods and the development of man's attitudes towards them, rather than giving a series of static snapshots. The thread is not a straight one, nor indeed is it a single one. It is for the reader to decide just how strong it is.

CLIVE WOOD AND
BERYL SUITTERS

Oxford and Bloomsbury
September 1970

Acknowledgments

Trustees of the British Museum for permission to use the frontispiece from Robert Dale Owen's book *Moral Physiology* on front cover.

National Portrait Gallery for permission to use the picture of Francis Place.

The Johns Hopkins Press, Baltimore, Maryland, USA, for permission to quote from *Soranos Gynecology* translated with an introduction by Owsei Temkin, published in 1956, on pages 36 and 41.

Jonathan Cape Limited, London, for permission to quote from John Langdon-Davies' *A Short History of Women*, published in 1927, on page 51.

The Belknap Press of Harvard University Press for permission to quote from *Contraception: A History of its Treatment by the Catholic Theologians and Canonists* by John T. Noonan, Jr., published in 1965, on page 62.

Oxford University Press for permission to quote from R. W. Chapman's edition of *Jane Austen's Letters*, published in 1932, on pages 104 and 105.

The Clarendon Press, Oxford, for permission to quote from *The Witch-Cult in Western Europe* by Margaret Murray, published in 1921, on page 70.

Martin Secker & Warburg Limited, London, for permission to quote from *Private Case – Public Scandal* by Peter Fryer, published in 1966, on page 99.

The Joint Editors of *Isis* for permission to quote from *Isis*, Volume 15: 1, an article by Zirkle on 'Animals Impregnated by the Wind', published in 1936, on page 7.

The Editor of *The Practitioner* for permission to quote from its special issue on birth control, published in 1923, on pages 174 and 175.

The Bodley Head, London, for permission to quote from *The Life and Death of Mahatma Gandhi*, published in 1969, on page 192.

In addition to those who have been kind enough to grant us permission to quote parts of their work we would also like to extend our thanks to the following people and institutions who have helped us considerably in producing this book.

The staff and library of the Welcome Institute for the History of Medicine have been particularly helpful, as have the staffs of the International Planned Parenthood Federation, London, and the Bodleian and Radcliffe Science Libraries, Oxford. We are grateful to Mr George Coral and Mr James St Lawrence for assistance with the pictures; to Dr Derek Roe and Dr John Baker of Oxford University, Mr Norman Berry and Mr John Neville of L.R. Industries Ltd, and many others for stimulating discussion. Finally, it is a pleasure to acknowledge the invaluable services of Mrs Yvonne Wood in the preparation of the manuscript.

Contents

CHAPTER ONE

In the Beginning

THE human race has been getting progressively older. According to Genesis the process of creation took a week, although it is not clear in which year the week occurred. In the seventeenth-century that distinguished Irish scholar Archbishop James Usher carefully examined the Old Testament and calculated that the creation of the Universe (mankind included) had in fact taken place in the year 4004 B.C. In the absence of a better estimate this figure was accepted by many authorities for the next two hundred years. However, as techniques of geological and archaeological dating were developed in the nineteenth-century it became apparent that the Earth, and mankind as well, had been in existence for a considerably longer period. The first recorded human fossil remains were uncovered in 1848 and the first of the famous Neanderthal skulls in 1856, but their exact ages were for a long time uncertain. Only in the present century has it been realised that mankind has been in existence not for thousands or tens of thousands but for hundreds of thousands of years.

Within the last decade the origins of man in Africa have been taken back as far as two million years. But he did not appear everywhere at exactly the same time. In some continents he is a comparative newcomer. In north western Europe for example he probably made an appearance only about half a million years before James Usher was born. We can assume that he first adopted agriculture, as well as hunting for his food, some ten thousand years ago. Again this is a date which is open to much speculation and variation from one area to another, but it is a good enough estimate for our purposes. We can even speculate on man's rate of reproduction during this long and distant period and the constraints, either self-imposed or imposed from outside that have limited the rate of his increase.

Since there is so much uncertainty about the length of mankind's existence it surprises many people to hear that we can make a reasonable estimate of the number of people alive at various times and even the total number of people who have ever lived. The figures are the very roundest approximations, but they are probably correct to the nearest order of magnitude —quite accurate enough to demonstrate the striking changes which have taken place as time has proceeded. In the last half million years about one hundred thousand million people have been born. The figure seems colossal, truly astronomical, and yet there are more grains of sand on a piece of beach one hundred yards square and one yard deep. A far more staggering fact is that four percent of all the people who were ever born are alive today. Equally staggering at first glance is the fact that ten thousand years ago there were no more than about 5 million people in the entire world. Indeed during that vast stretch of time that ended with the adoption of agriculture there were probably only ten thousand million babies born. We say 'only' because 490,000 years produced a mere ten percent of the total world population. The other 90 percent have arrived in only one-fiftieth of man's total period on the earth, and unbelievable as it seems, a quarter of them have been born since 1650.

However, our interest in this chapter is not so much in these recent changes in the size of the human population, as in the relatively static and unchanging population of the old stone age. Why did the Paleolithic population increase so slowly, and to what extent was the slowness of its growth the result of a conscious process?

Part of the answer is to be found by considering the death rate among our early ancestors. In 1965 the death rate in the United Kingdom was 11·5 per 1000. In the United States it was 9·4 and in the Netherlands only 8·0. Averaged over the whole world in the first half of the 1960s the rate was about 16 per 1000, but in 1700 even in Europe the figure was twice as high. The advance in medical science that has taken place over the last two hundred years and the consequent increase in the number of people remaining alive has been well documented and calls for no discussion here. The fact which is significant is that during the Paleolithic period the death rate could not have been less than 30 per 1000. In other words, in any given year at least 3 people in every 100 were certain to die.

A death rate of this magnitude severely limited the life expectancy of our stone-age forebears. A hunter who survived to 40 would be an old man indeed. Even more profound was its effect on the life expectancy of the newborn infant. In any group, however advanced their medical science, children under 5 are more at risk than any comparable section of the community. Even until quite recent times infant mortality in Europe was so high that only half the children born survived their first few years of life. In the Old Stone Age the situation must have been at least as bad.

A high level of infant mortality has a profound effect upon population size because it represents not only an actual loss of individuals from the group but also the loss of potential members. If children do not survive to the age of puberty they have no chance of reproducing themselves. Not only the present generation but also the future generations suffer as a result. The converse of course is also true. The very rapid expansion of mankind over the last 50 years has been largely due to the survival of children who have themselves subsequently reached childbearing age. It is not necessary to assume that women now are any more fertile. There are simply more of them, and most of them are having babies.

It would however be a great mistake to think that a high death rate and an initially small population were the only causes of the slow rate of increase of Paleolithic man. Undoubtedly there were several other factors, although few of them have received the attention which they deserve.

The first is sterility. In Great Britain and the United States the number of sterile couples among the married population is placed, somewhat arbitrarily, at about 10 to 15 percent. To a large extent this is a matter of definition. What we really mean is that about 10 percent of married women who want to have a child, who have 'normal' sexual lives, and who take no steps to avoid conception will not have succeeded in becoming pregnant after a period of twelve months. The cause of this sterility may be difficult, even impossible, to establish, but it is not always due to any physical defect in either partner. In many cases it may be due to what, for want of a better term, are called 'psychological factors'. In some instances it may be due to sheer bad luck. As we shall see, conception is a chancy business. According to the probabilities a certain number of quite normal women can expect to remain childless at the end of any particular year. There is no better proof of this than the fact that half of the women who have failed to conceive by the end of the first year are likely to be pregnant at the end of the second although they have received no treatment in the interim.

However, in an unknown proportion of childless couples (one might guess perhaps at a half) there is a real physical cause underlying their childlessness. In some cases it is a failure to produce an adequate number of healthy sperms. More frequently, it is a defect in the female reproductive system. Perhaps the commonest are either a failure of the ovary to release an egg, or a blockage of the Fallopian tube which prevents the egg from ever being fertilised. This latter defect is perhaps the most common of all the definable causes of infertility and is often associated with the presence of disease. Both gonorrhoea and tuberculosis are known to be causes of tubal blockage, and even today some 3–5 per cent of the infertile women in the Western world owe their condition to a tuberculous infection of the reproductive organs.

In some developing nations the problem is much greater. In parts of Africa for example it is estimated that as many as half the women of child-bearing age suffer an impairment of fertility, the cause of which is probably pathological. The condition is associated with poor medical care and poor standards of hygiene. In parts of Asia and the Pacific the figure is lower but it is still in the order of one-third. How much more acute must the problem have been a thousand generations ago? Although our ancestors have left few remains and an accurate picture of the diseases that afflicted them is difficult to draw, it seems quite likely that in addition to a short life span another of the problems with which they had to contend was subfertility brought on by disease.

The stablemate of disease is malnutrition, and it is worth speculating if only briefly, on its effect upon our forebears. It seems unlikely that stone-age man, predominantly a hunter, ever had enough to eat. There would be seasons when game was plentiful but there must also have been lean years, indeed lean centuries, when much of the northern hemisphere was covered by ice. At best he must have existed at a subsistence level. However it is well established that deficiencies of food and particularly a shortage of the amino acids of which proteins are composed can cause a lowering of fertility both in the male and the female. Although the action is often indirect the effect on pregnancy is very marked. Again it seems reasonable to believe that the fertility of our early ancestors was, during certain periods at least, seriously impaired.

To a high infant mortality and a degree of infertility we might have added low population density as a further factor to account for man's slow rate of increase. It is estimated that even 10,000 years ago, at the beginning of the New Stone Age, there was probably only one person to every 15 square miles of land. A tribe might go for a long period without encountering another, and when it did so there was no guarantee that they would be friendly. In some modern primitive societies monogamy is the rule and incest is frowned upon. If this were so for our ancestors then individuals who failed to meet the members of other families would forfeit their right to reproduce. However polygamy is not universally condemned in modern societies, although specialists are not sure what effect it has on the birth rate. In any event it is usually impossible even to guess at the kinship system of our stone-age forebears and such speculations can have no real value. But what is possible, having discussed some of the external factors limiting his increase, is to enquire whether any aspect of man's own behaviour, either conscious or conditioned, was also responsible for the extremely slow build-up in his numbers.

The most obvious way to do so is by considering the behaviour of modern 'primitive' groups, on the assumption that early man behaved in a roughly similar manner. It is also useful, though perhaps not flattering, to review what we know about the breeding patterns of some of man's closer relatives. Both approaches have pitfalls, the former probably more than the latter. In the first place it would be a very brave (or very foolish) anthropologist who tried today to define what he meant by a primitive population. Fifty years ago the science was simpler. Primitive meant, by and large, different to us, and we still retain a few of the misconceptions that arose in those pioneering days when there were still too few facts to refute the anthropologists's preconceived notions.

One of the most important and persistent of these misconceptions is that primitive men do not understand the connection between sexual intercourse and birth. This assumption is one that has in the past misled many biologists. The argument is that the interval between an act of intercourse and the birth of a child is really quite long. During that time all sorts of things might happen—storms, fires, floods or plague —each apparently more significant and more likely to be responsible for pregnancy than its real cause. The argument is supported by the statements that in at least two parts of the world, the Trobriand Islands in the Pacific and North Central Queensland, the inhabitants actually believe that conception has causes other than intercourse.

For a long time this evidence has been debated but today probably the majority of specialists consider it in a different perspective. If a man believes that conception occurs only when some spirit enters his wife's body he will say so. It is magic and hence important. Similarly if his wife conceives because of some charm or as the result of a dream this too is sufficiently out of the ordinary to be recorded. In addition, he may well be aware that an act of intercourse has *also* to take place; indeed in Fiji, one act is not regarded as adequate. But compared to the spiritual causes such an act is so humdrum and so much a part of his daily experience as to be unworthy of any special comment. The sexual act is taken as read. No mention of it is made to the field worker and the error enters the scientific literature. It is nobody's fault, merely the result of a failure in communications.

Even with the legends that we will refer to later—the myths that mares, vulture, hens and women could be impregnated by the wind—they are simply that: legends and myths. They do not imply that their believers thought pregnancy was always and exclusively caused in this way. What they do show is that conception, pregnancy and birth were thought significant enough to construct legends about. Men only produce myths about what they consider to be important aspects of their lives. Not everyone will agree with this analysis, but we suggest that it is valid. No-one has ever seriously maintained that mankind anywhere does not really appreciate the connection between copulation and pregnancy in wild and domesticated animals, even if sometimes they are thought to become pregnant by magic as well. To maintain that men do not appreciate it in their own case reflects the naivety of the anthropologist rather than that of his primitive subjects.

A second misconception is that primitive groups always have as many children as they possibly can. After all, life is hard and there is strength in numbers. The fact that many children die is an inducement to produce yet more. Primitive women must therefore be reproducing to the very limit of their capacity.

Obvious as this notion is it proves to be quite unfounded when the actual figures are examined. In favourable conditions the maximum number of children that can be born during the reproductive life-span of any woman (say from the age of 15 to 45) is usually put at about 20. Obviously not all women marry, and so the average for a whole community would be less than this, though still high. But if we look around the non-industrial societies which still exist in different parts of the world we find that the average number of children is nowhere near this limit. Statisticians talk of the 'total maternity ratio'. This is the average number of live births per woman for all women now aged 45 or over—that is to say for all the women who might ever have had children. For the Ashanti of Africa the figure is about 6, for the Sioux Indians about 8 and for certain groups of Eskimo (who can certainly claim to live in difficult conditions) it is less than 5. It is most unusual to find any group in which the average even approaches 10.

At the same time it is true that almost without exception primitive women have a horror of being sterile. The sterile wife is of little value to her husband and often a social outcast. It is also true that children represent an economic asset. In some cases they provide child labour, in others the future husband pays good money for his bride; daughters in the family are therefore at a premium. But the opposite of sterility is not unrestrained fertility. It is a happier medium—an optimum situation—that can be reached somewhere between no children and twenty children. It seems that many primitive groups in the modern world realize this and act accordingly. If we accept the analogy then we are forced to conclude that for early man too the total maternity was a long way off its theoretical maximum. Paleolithic women did not have to endure the maximum possible number of pregnancies.

Such a situation finds parallels among man's relatives although the motives are instinctive rather than conscious. The gorilla is a species that shows a regular menstrual cycle; menstrual periods occur about every 30 days. The length of pregnancy is also similar to that in man and about half the young die in their first five years of life. It is estimated that during her reproductive life-span a female gorilla gives birth to only four or five young. The parallel is not perhaps a perfect one since a female may not live to be more than 20 and she does not become sexually mature until the age of 7 to 10. Her rate of reproduction is therefore faster than that of her human counterpart, but it is still well below her maximum capacity.

One reason for the greater reproductive rate of the gorilla may be the fact that the female only becomes sexually receptive to the male for three or four days during each menstrual cycle. These are precisely the days during which an egg is maturing and being shed from the ovary into the Fallopian tube, and they are precisely the days upon which conception is most likely to follow mating. In a large number of lower mammals of course mating and ovulation are very closely synchronised. Copulation is always periodic depending upon the reproductive cycle of the female, and often it is seasonal.

In our own species this does not seem to be the case. It has been remarked that man differs from other mammals only in that he drinks when he is not thirsty and makes love all the year round. Now this is not entirely true. Even in Western societies the conception rate does appear to vary somewhat with the time of year—'In the spring the young man's fancy . . .', and census figures bear out the poet's suggestion. One can see good reason why such breeding seasons should have originated. Often they ensured that the young would be born at a time of year when the weather was clement and the food plentiful, the time that would give them the maximum chance of survival, though this is no longer necessary in our own case. Restricting the time of intercourse during any particular cycle ensures the somewhat different aim of increasing the chance of mating being fertile. This synchronisation man appears to have lost. Attempts have been made to correlate human sexual activity with the phase of the menstrual cycle but there has been no convincing demonstration that intercourse is more frequent at any particular stage. And such a loss has important repercussions.

It has been estimated that the probability of conception arising from a single act of intercourse is about 3 percent. That is to say, only three in every hundred acts will result in the wife becoming pregnant. On the basis of personal experience this figure may seem rather low, which proves only what a poor guide the personal experience of any one couple can be. The most basic law of demography is that the fertility of different women varies widely. Other authorities have suggested that in the region of 200 acts are necessary, depending on the age-group of the women concerned. A reasonable compromise figure might be about 50. The single act that does result in pregnancy is of course the one which, by chance, happens to coincide most closely with the time of ovulation.

When the timing of intercourse becomes random the effectiveness of the process is seriously diminished.

Did the breeding pattern of early man vary with the seasons like that of several groups of modern monkey? It may have done. We shall never know. In addition his acts of intercourse may well have been less frequent than those of modern man, and more closely tied to ritual and taboo. For this we do have some suggestive evidence.

Even twentieth century man is less athletic than is commonly imagined. It was only in 1953 that details were published of that most intimate of all vital statistics—the frequency of sexual intercourse in the population. The figures were collected by Kinsey's group and they refer to white American married women. Nonetheless the pattern that emerges is probably not restricted to the United States or to the white races. The number of weekly acts of intercourse was found to vary from 3·7 for the age group 16–20, to only 1·7 for the group aged 41–46. Again the figures may seem to contradict personal experience, and in some cases they undoubtedly do. But as a statistical picture of the whole population there is no reason to suppose that they are unreasonably low.

They are certainly far lower for the male gorilla. He may remain celibate for up to a year. This is because in addition to restricting the timing of intercourse during the menstrual cycle the female is also unreceptive during the later stages of pregnancy and during lactation. This lack of a heat period during pregnancy is not general throughout the animal kingdom. Sheep for example show periods of sexual receptiveness even though they are pregnant, and human beings often show little apparent lessening of the sexual urge until the pregnancy is very advanced. As far as any effect on fertility is concerned it really makes little difference whether the female is receptive or not. Despite some reports to the contrary, it seems extremely unlikely that a pregnant woman, for example, can conceive another child before the birth of the one that she is carrying.

By contrast, a lack of receptivity during lactation will exert a marked effect on the overall birth rate if only because the female spends a fair proportion of her adult life suckling her young. In many human societies too intercourse during the period of lactation is unthinkable. In others, where it is allowed, suckling will also influence fertility, although for a different reason.

The reason is that lactation tends to inhibit ovulation. We say 'tends to' advisedly. The effect is by no means general. Some women conceive remarkably quickly after giving birth whether they are lactating or not. As a means of deliberately trying to limit the size of one's family the method is useless— a fact which cannot be stressed too often. It is far too unreliable for a couple to use it with any confidence. On a statistical basis however, prolonged lactation does have some effect on lessening the overall birth rate, although only when the suckling demands of the infant are heavy. Such a situation is rarely found in Western countries. It is unusual for children to be suckled for a period of years and equally unusual for them to be constantly with their mother and continually receiving milk from her. Elsewhere in the world the situation is different; the baby may be fed at the breast for three years or more, and feeding is entirely on demand. The remarkable facility shown, for example, by some African women, to produce milk almost continuously is in marked contrast to the ability of many of their European sisters, and has been remarked upon many times.

It is probably safe to assume that although not constantly pregnant the women of Paleolithic times were in an almost continuous state of lactation. As one child grew old enough to wean, another would take its place. We do not know whether intercourse was restricted during this time but even if not the effect would have been to limit to some degree the number of acts of intercourse that resulted in conception. The extent of this limitation cannot be estimated, but the fact that some limitation occurred seems indisputable. The interesting question is whether the limitation was deliberate, and whether our earliest ancestors made any conscious attempt to control the number of their children.

The answer is that they probably did. A taboo may be placed on sexual relations for reasons of hygiene, magic or religion. Those who practice the taboo might say that to indulge in intercourse (for example during the suckling period), is simply wrong. They may have no real explanation of why it is wrong. But although the reasons may be only semiconscious the restriction grows up as the result of some preexisting necessity. In other words, the restriction was originally, if only half consciously, intended as a means of keeping the birth rate within reasonable limits. Since this restriction applies widely today we believe that it has applied over many generations. We also believe that other methods of fertility control have been known and used for many thousands, perhaps tens of thousands, of years.

It is always dangerous to argue that because a particular activity is practised today then it has always been practised. It is easy enough to find two different groups of people whose behaviour is quite different one from another. Which of their behaviour patterns (if either) is the old-established one? The answer may not be definable. However if we find that the majority of cultures, though separated both ethnically and geographically, do share certain attitudes then we may perhaps reasonably conclude that these attitudes are ancient and common to most of man's ancestors. A belief in an after-life is one such attitude, though a fear of death is another. The desire to have children is a third, and so, we suggest, is the desire to limit the number of children that one has.

In the non-industrial societies for which figures are available it seems that those which practice some form of population control outnumber those which do not by at least three to one. The methods used include abortion and infanticide as well as migration out of the tribe. This latter means should not be overlooked. By allowing either men or women to marry outside the group the care of their children ceases to be the group's responsibility. Societies which are relatively unsophisticated in other ways are well aware that this is the case. But the control of population also means controlling the fertility of individual couples within the society, although these couples may be experiencing whatever pattern of sexual behaviour is considered to be normal. In short it means contraception.

It is a reflection of our vanity that we tend to think of the use of contraception as being the exclusive domain of Western man, and even that for only the last hundred years or so. It is true that large sectors of the world appear to have relatively little desire to limit the number of their children but it is a mistake to think of this attitude as a 'primitive' characteristic. The attitude results partly from a failure of the population to realise that economic stability and even a measure of prosperity could be achieved if their rate of increase could be slowed down. But to a large extent the type of economic stability that Western organizations and advisers offer is not of a type that the society thinks of as desirable. The great problem here is one of communication. To the peasant in Ceylon two acres of rice paddy are enough. He has no desire for any more, and if another child arrives he just extends his hut. His needs and desires are quite different from those of the people who are trying to help him. The situation is further complicated by matters of caste, religion and the family system. But this is not to say that he has no aspirations, simply that his aspirations are not the same as those of his Western counterpart.

The problems turns on what the two civilizations regard as

being important resources. These cannot always be measured in monetary terms. At least one school of anthropologists believes that many truly primitive groups realise fully the relationship between their resources and the size of their population. As well as employing contraception as a means of avoiding the birth of illegitimate children and for other 'social' purposes, they also attempt to limit their numbers because the things which they value are also limited. As long as resources (and they may be food, living space or simply the symbols of prestige) keep pace with the growth of population, all is well. Attempts are made to maintain this stable relationship by a variety of means, one being the artificial limitation of births. This view should strike a familiar chord, for it is simply a more reasoned restatement of the opinion expressed by Himes over thirty years ago.

It is not even necessary to enquire whether the types of contraception employed by these peoples are really effective. What is important is that they should realise that they have some control (however slight) over their circumstances, and that the prevention of births is one important way in which this control can be exercised. Some of the means of contraception available to non-industrial societies are among the least effective that we know of. We have mentioned lactation. To this we might add douching and the use of certain drugs. However, withdrawal, or coitus interruptus and the simple pessary are known to a number of modern primitive groups. When used correctly they are capable of giving a fair degree of contraceptive protection, and their users may well derive some real practical benefit from their use. Such groups may find that their control over their family size is considerable, without having to resort to abortion of the unwanted foetus or to the deliberate neglect of every second or third child. Our ancestors may well have found the same.

We have ranged widely and speculated widely in this chapter, though much has been left out. We have not considered the age of puberty or the menopause and its effect on fertility in the population. We have not discussed the temporary or prolonged separation of husband and wife. We have not discussed the cave paintings which some believe to depict the use of a male contraceptive sheath, much less the view that all cave art has fertility as its basis. The fertility of our early forebears deserves a book to itself; we have only scratched the surface. What we have tried to show is that our ancestors, even in Paleolithic times, were well aware of the cause of pregnancy, and that they had the desire to influence its occurrence. To a large extent the size of their population was determined by factors beyond their control, but if there is any value at all in reasoning from the present to the past then it is not too much to believe that they also had some knowledge of how births might deliberately be prevented.

We are forced to speculate on these matters largely because there are no written records that we can use to guide us. Once we enter the period when men wrote down their ideas we are on safer ground. There are still problems of translation and interpretation but at least we have a basis to go on. However even the most ancient written documents are little more than five thousand years old—extremely recent in the time scale that we have been considering. Fortunately they often have to do with legends which are far older than the records themselves. Legends of the creation and of the great flood are frequently found, and so too are myths that give us some insight into the way that men since the end of the New Stone Age (and perhaps even during it) have thought about conception.

A concern with fertility is one of the most frequent and recurrent themes that runs through the mythology of many different lands. The idea of the mother—(which is the Earth)—uniting with the father (represented by the sky) to bring forth man and all living things is found again and again. Some anthropologists have even claimed that the whole framework of organized religion has such a concept as its basis. This is to say that the modern religions of mankind spring directly from an earlier, simpler creed in which man worshipped the Earth from which he had sprung. The almost obsessional interest of earlier civilizations and of many modern primitive societies with the death of nature in winter and its rebirth in the spring lent weight to their arguments. To some more modern thinkers this view is now outdated. It is too great a simplification. Nevertheless the importance which our ancestors placed upon fertility, both of their crops, their animals and of man himself is undeniable. Whatever the truth about religious origins a great deal of primitive magic certainly has the control of fertility as its basis.

Gods and man often become inextricably mixed. The Ancient Egyptians believed that their rulers were descended from the marriage of a God, Amon-Ra and a human Queen. Further East, the Buddha was thought to have been born of a virgin, his royal mother having become pregnant when a small white elephant entered her womb. In the Persian legends, Zarathustra was miraculously conceived. In fact, many classical and mediaeval philosophers accepted it as fact that women, birds and animals could be impregnated by wind or water. The Greek and Roman legends abound in stories of all manner of strange births—it seems that almost anything could happen. Women were made pregnant by Gods, who came as good-looking young men, or who could, on occasion assume the form of birds or animals. The Goddess Venus sprang fully-formed from her father's head and no-one seems to have thought that it was particularly strange.

But these legends and beliefs can hardly be taken as a serious explanation of how the people in the past civilizations thought of procreation. Obviously, they had a second set of ideas to

explain human conception, pregnancy and birth. It is quite
possible to accept two sets of apparently conflicting beliefs.
So far as the Gods, heroes and rulers were concerned, like their
lives, which were so different from the experience of the
ordinary man, their births would have to be different too.
In that context, something supernatural and extraordinary
would be the obvious explanation. By its nature, a religious
belief is not necessarily logical. It does not have to conform to
the criteria used to judge other happenings and problems encountered in everyday life. Therefore, most civilizations have
found no dichotomy in accepting one set of facts and terms in
dealing with religious beliefs, and a completely different view,
when dealing with everyday life.

The number of legends involving supernatural forces in the
birth of Kings and Gods is enormous. The beliefs were so
common that many of the founding fathers of the Christian
Church had no hesitation in citing the fact that the wind was
known to have a fecundating power, to show that the claim
that Christ was born of a virgin was a perfectly reasonable
thing to ask people to accept.

So much for the supernatural plane. It shows where man's
main concern lay. But here on Earth for at least four thousand
years (that is to say, for as long as records have been preserved)
he has been trying to influence his own fertility by methods
which sometimes depend on magic but often involve distinctly
'natural' means. To document man's progress in this regard is
the purpose of the rest of this book.

CHAPTER TWO

Egypt and Israel

WE are indebted to the Book of Ecclesiastes for the knowledge that 'there is no new thing under the sun'. Although the prophet was probably not thinking of birth control when he produced the now famous and misquoted text, his words are none the less as true of contraception as of any other of man's activities. There are a very limited number of methods which any man anywhere can use to prevent his wife from becoming pregnant. He may abstain from intercourse altogether, or he may have intercourse only at those times when conception is not possible (assuming that he knows just when such times occur). He may try to arrange that no sperm enters his wife's body or if it does then that it is rapidly removed, obstructed in its path, or killed before it can fertilize the egg. Alternatively he may try to ensure that his wife becomes sterile for a longer or shorter period. She may produce no egg cells to fertilize, or if she does then the fertilized egg may be discouraged from implanting itself in the lining of the womb.

The great armoury of contraceptive devices which we have available today are all intended to achieve one or other of these ends. We are fortunate in having what appears to be a vast number of different means of birth control at our disposal, but in fact there are still less than a dozen different methods of preventing conception. Now, however, every method has a hundred different proprietary products designed to bring it about more effectively. It is mainly in this regard that we have

progressed. There have been few great leaps forward in thinking about what is necessary for the control of man's fertility.
This has been known or at least suspected for many thousands
of years. The advances that have been made are technical advances. Birth control has progressed through the development
of more effective means of doing what couples were trying
to do even in Ancient Egypt.

In Egyptian culture the gods were of great importance in
all human affairs. In the matter of health, a great number of
supernatural beings had power over the body and its functions.
A number of goddesses concerned themselves especially with
obstetrics and gynaecology. One was a general obstetrician;
one had special charge of the birth house at the Temple where
a woman would go when her time was near. A third took
charge of the hot stones over which women in labour would
crouch, and yet a fourth who was in charge of the feeding of
the infant also took an interest in sterile women. Apart from
these deities others had charge of the development of the foetus.
Paintings of the time show that the body and personality were
prepared by different gods before being combined and given
life. The Gods could be pleased or angered, so it was only
natural that doctors should be priests as well. After all it was
as necessary to invoke the goodwill of the Gods as it was to
attempt to make some sort of diagnosis and prescribe whatever
sort of medicine was considered appropriate.

We know a lot about the daily life and beliefs of the Egyptians, since many of their paintings and papyri are still in existence. Medical practices are illustrated, and often women
doctors conduct operations. Midwives are seen with their
patients. Not only is the physical body shown but in some
paintings the soul is shown too. The Egyptians, like the
members of many Eastern religions and some of the early
Christian fathers, believed that the soul was given late in pregnancy and that the foetus became truly alive only when it

1. The Ebers Papyrus. (1550 B.C.) This document contains the first reference to a pessary used with a sperm-killing chemical. The spermicidal properties of lactic acid were not rediscovered until the end of the nineteenth century.

le Falangidi; *A, il comune Phalangium opilio* L.; *B, un Gonyleptes.* Grand. natur.

2. Phalangium. The spider played an important part in folk medicine. Worms from the body of these 'hairy' spiders were regarded by Pliny the Elder as having contraceptive properties. Such a superstition persisted despite the fact that some centuries earlier Soranos had described the means of contraception in altogether more scientific terms. *By courtesy of 'The Wellcome Trustees'.*

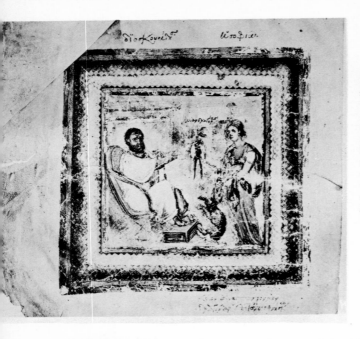

3. Euresis presenting Dioscorides with a mandrake root. One of the greatest authorities on contraception in Greek times was Dioscorides. His *Herbal* listed a very large number of plants, minerals and even stones which were thought to affect fertility.
By courtesy of 'The Wellcome Trustees'

4. In classical times the status of women was often extremely low. The only women who succeeded in achieving any prominence in such a man's world were entertainers and courtesans. The Empress Theodora in the centre of the picture was one of the most famous. From a career as an actress and prostitute she aspired to become the wife of the Emperor Justinian. San Vitale, Ravenna. *By courtesy of Thames and Hudson Library.*

started to move in the uterus. This belief in personality and in
life given by the Gods may have made the society somewhat
opposed to abortion, once the pregnancy had been allowed to
develop. It is difficult to decide precisely how abortion was
regarded and used, because of the linguistic problems encountered in interpreting the papyri. The word for birth and that
for abortion seem to be interchangeable. It seems safe to assume
that medicines were sometimes given both to procure abortion
and to induce or ease labour. But it is also clear from the
existing evidence that contraception was preferred.

It is only natural to enquire why the Egyptians should have
wanted to control their fertility at all. After all they had no
population problem. The Nile Valley is a fertile area, and
there was usually plenty for everyone. Infant mortality and a
short life expectancy kept the population small.

Family life seems to have been one reason; the family was
of great importance, and husbands, wives and children are
always shown as a happy and harmonious group. The Book
of Wisdom of one Pharaoh says that the wise man should
have the house prepared before he takes a wife. Another
equally simple and human reason is that Egyptians used contraception for a cosmetic purpose. Many of the papyri which
mention contraceptive methods talk of the care of the body,
of cleanliness and health, and they describe lotions and oint-
ments to make the skin and hair more beautiful.

A number of papyri have been found which deal specifically
with contraception. The first of these is thought to date from
about 1850 B.C., and it gives information on a number of
female disorders. It discusses how to determine whether a
woman is fertile or not, and if she is, whether she will bear a
son or a daughter. It mentions three different methods of
birth control. The first is simply to sprinkle some gummy substance on the female genitals, allowing the gum to cover the
cervix (the mouth of the womb) and the inside of the vagina.

B

The second is to put honey and sodium carbonate into the vagina, much in the way that jellies and pastes are used today. Honey and gummy substances generally have the effect of lessening motility of sperms and would thus have some sort of contraceptive action. Much of early medicine has been called 'sewerage pharmacology' and not without reason, for dung was often an important ingredient in healing mixtures. The third method in this early document falls into this category. It recommends that crocodile dung be pulverized with a paste-like vehicle. The resulting mass is to be used as a pessary, and placed in the vagina. Aesthetic considerations apart, even this idea had some merit, for the mass would have blocked the path of the sperms, and may also have had some chemical effect, akin to the sponge and spermicide methods used until recent times.

By 1550 B.C. the idea of blocking the vagina with some sperm-killing chemical substance had developed into a more sophisticated procedure. A second papyrus of that date discussed how to prevent conception for periods of up to three years, and it suggests that a lint tampon be used. The lint should be soaked in a mixture made of honey and part of the acacia shrub. Acacia leaves, if fermented, will produce lactic acid, which was used even in the present century as a spermicide. Why the tampon would prevent conception for only three years is uncertain. Probably the writer had discovered the problem that effects most contraceptive methods—the fact that they sometimes fail.

These papyri also quote other methods. Most of them are not very practical, for example, fumigation of the vagina with the smoke of burning drugs. This should be done both before and after intercourse. Alternatively the woman may drink a potion made of grease, herbs and ale. Magical methods were used too. Some of them survived over the years and were still being practised in Egypt in quite recent times. But there is nothing particularly Egyptian about such ideas. Beliefs that burying a certain number of seeds or sitting on a number of fingers will affect the number of children that a woman has, are extremely ancient. They reappear throughout history, and we shall encounter them again many times.

Like women in many countries, Egyptian women used prolonged lactation as a contraceptive measure. They were not expected to bear children more than once in three years and they nursed their children for that length of time. Castration was also known. Men were made eunuchs by removing their testicles. There is also an account of one king who created female eunuchs by removing their ovaries. The Greek historian Strabo tells us that the Egyptians were well acquainted with this practice, as were their neighbours in other areas. The apparent motive for this hazardous operation was to keep women young and beautiful rather than simply to prevent conception.

It is impossible to say how widespread such practices were. The simpler ones, such as prolonged lactation, would have been extremely common. We also know that there were a great many women doctors, midwives, and other attendants. Presumably they would have recommended such methods, especially to patients who seemed to be in special need. But the needs and the motivation for family planning in Egypt may well have been rather different from ours today. The preservation of beauty rather than resources seems to have been of key importance. To some extent this was also true for the Egyptian's neighbours and one-time slaves, the children of Israel.

The Egyptian schools of medicine accepted both men and women as students, it is said that Moses and his wife were both students at the school at Heliopolis. Perhaps it was there that they gained some of the medical and contraceptive knowledge which appears in Jewish culture. Indeed, it has been suggested that Mosaic Laws relating to menstruation were specifically introduced by Moses as a way of controlling the size of the population. These laws forbid sexual intercourse at the time of 'uncleanness', which is to say the days around the time of the menstrual flow. It is of interest to note that the period of fertility was also thought to occur around this time.

Jewish culture is very ancient, and even in their prehistoric past Jewish sources report that people were able to control their own fertility, at least to some extent. The 'generation of the flood' (the people who existed before Noah built his Ark to escape from total destruction) were said to have had two wives each. One of them was for procreation and the other for sexual gratification. The former lived rather like a widow, accompanied by her children, rarely seeing her husband. The latter was given a herbal drink to render her sterile, after which she was supposed to act more lasciviously. This practice is believed by some scholars to be mentioned in the Old Testament. Job 24: 21 reads 'He devoureth the barren that beareth not, and doeth not good to the widow'.

Monogamy, and the other rather special concepts that characterize Jewish culture and family life, developed over a long period of time. Laws and ideas changed and developed over the years. Many leaders and kings described in the Bible had more than one wife, although divorce was not encouraged. David made women his concubines, rather than wives, the reason being that he already had the number of wives permitted by society and was reluctant or unable to divorce any of them. The laws stood as they did for the purpose of promoting family life and encouraging parenthood. The phrase 'be fruitful and multiply' ceased to be pronounced as a blessing and instead became a commandment. Barrenness was regarded as a curse, and fertility was encouraged throughout the troubled times which the race encountered. The dominant idea was that the population must increase. Indeed fertility was also encouraged even when the Jews led a relatively peaceful pastoral life

for two hundred years. This period extended from the Baby-
lonian exile (about 536 B.C.) until the time of Alexander the
Great. It was then that the period of migration known as the
Diaspora began.

The changing conditions brought about by migration meant
that large families were no longer very welcome, and the laws
and their interpretation became subtly altered. Procreation
was required only to preserve the race, and this did not demand
unrestricted childbearing under all circumstances. How many
children would have been necessary to ensure survival at that
time in history is difficult to establish. As at other periods
infant and child mortality must have been high, and life expectancy would not have been long. Of those children who did
survive presumably not all of them would have wanted to
marry, although the law required that marriage and family
responsibility be undertaken by every man. Then too, some
would have been infertile. Each family would probably have
had to produce four or five children to ensure the race's
survival, yet the law only demanded that each man father a boy
and a girl.

A great deal of discussion, both Christian and Jewish, has
hinged on the much-quoted text Genesis 38: 7–10, which
describe the sin of Er and Onan.

Er Judah's first born, was wicked in the sight of the Lord and the
Lord slew him. And Judah said unto Onan: go unto thy brother's
wife and perform the levirate duty, and raise up offspring to thy
brother. Now Onan knew that the offspring would not be his;
and it came to pass, when he went unto his brother's wife that he
would spill on the ground lest he should give seed for his brother.
And the thing which he did was evil in the sight of the Lord, and
the Lord slew him also.

The Christian authorities have applied this story to family
planning within marriage, a decision which has had a far-

reaching effect. Pope Pius XI in his Encyclical *Casti Connubii* in 1930 affirmed:

it is therefore not remarkable that the Holy Writ itself testifies that the Divine Majesty pursued this wicked crime with detestation, and punished it with death as St Augustine recalls . . .

But what might the passage mean in its original sense? Christian writers usually speak only of the 'sin of Onan', and 'Onanism' has become a synonym for masturbation. But what about Er? He displeased God as well. Background sources suggest that Er's motive for practising birth control was that of the Ancient Egyptians. His wife Tamar was known to be a woman of exceptional beauty and his precautions were to preserve her good looks. A later commentator observes too that Er may simply have wished to avoid all the trouble involved in bringing up a family. Even today such individuals have a difficult time if they put forward this idea in our modern society. How much more difficult it must have been when the rule was that everyone had children.

Onan's motives also require further explanation. According to the story, after his brother's death he was to 'perform the levirate duty'. Levirate marriage is a custom found not only among the Jews. Other peoples have made the same provision. When a man dies, if he has a young wife and children they need love and support. Obviously this can be best provided by a close relative who would be intimate with their situation and who would love them already. Therefore the custom provided that the widow should be united with her husband's youngest unmarried brother. Er had died without issue, therefore it was Onan's responsibility to impregnate his widow in order to maintain Er's name and family line. In this rather complicated situation it is open to speculation what the sin of Onan could actually have been. Incest has been suggested. Other commentators have concluded flatly that Onan's sin was his refusal

to do his duty in the levirate marriage, thus avoiding the
problem of a contraceptive act altogether. But the punishment
for this crime is detailed in Jewish Law. It is not death but
public disgrace. It has even been suggested that the story
relates to the unhealthy practice of coitus interruptus. No
thunderbolt issued from heaven to smite down the sinful
brothers—they died of heart attacks brought on by the nervous strain of their contraceptive practices.

Levirate marriage is a complex and difficult issue and the
story of Er and Onan has never been seen by Jewish rabbis as
shedding much light on the principles governing a normal
marriage. But some rabbis have commented on the motives for
practising contraception. Judaism has been said to reject the
cosmetic motive, and also to be opposed to eugenic principles,
since it is not for a man to decide who should be born. King
Hezekiah excused his refusal to marry and have a family on the
grounds that they would be wicked. The Prophet Isaiah told
him that his duty was clear—he should live by the commandments of God. Economic motives were equally suspect. Moses'
father at one point decided on divorce. He questioned the
value of bearing children who would simply be drowned by
Pharaoh. The answer was: 'You are worse than Pharaoh.
Unlike him you decree death not only in this world but also
in the next.' He was forced to change his mind, and Moses was
born.

However, the Talmud and other authoritative works do
offer guidance and suggest that contraception is by no means
forbidden, even for the orthodox. A text which appears
several times says that there are three classes of women who
should use contraceptives. These are young girls, pregnant
women and those who are lactating. From these three examples
other cases can be judged. Rabbis have been known to con-
done or even recommend coitus interruptus in the case of a
lactating woman where a second pregnancy would diminish

the supply of milk available to the existing child. The important principle which is often considered is that seed should not be spilt 'uselessly', and in this case the well-being of the existing child is seen to be of paramount importance.

A device which the three categories of women were recommended to use was called *Mokh*. The word seems to be a generic term for cotton, and is used particularly to mean a tampon. Apart from this simple barrier, the literature contains references to a potion to be taken orally. From the way it is spoken of it seems that such a drink was fairly well known, and that it was thought to be effective. The drink was permitted to many women, especially those who had completed a family. Reports of the use of such a potion continue almost up to modern times. Exactly what the ingredients were is harder to say. One rabbi who died in A.D. 279 left the following prescription:

Alexandrian gum of the *spina aegypta*, liquid alum and garden crocus, each in the weight of a denar, are mixed together. Three cups of wine with this medicine are good for gonorrhoea, and do not sterilize. Two cups of beer with this medicine cure jaundice and cause sterility.

Whilst is is doubtful that the above medicine could be in any way an effective oral method of contraception it certainly seems to have been a reality as far as the rabbis were concerned. As late as the seventeenth and eighteenth centuries there are reports that rabbis allowed women who had difficulties in childbirth to take such medicines and so prevent further dangers. An eighteenth-century Italian Jewish physician reported that Jewish doctors ordinarily gave women a substance called *trifera* or other agents which caused them to become sterile. In the nineteenth and early twentieth centuries though, doubts were raised about the safety of such a course of action, and eventually the idea seems to have been forgotten altogether.

An oral contraceptive is not generally seen to be contrary to Jewish law. Indeed such a method, offering temporary and safe sterility would be more welcome than other means, especially since it does not transgress the positive commandments, the aims of which were to produce a happy, well-spaced family and sexual pleasure for both partners. Pleasure was not seen as sinful. Married couples were supposed to enjoy their relationship.

A striking difference between original Jewish ideas and the way that they were interpreted by Christian teachers is found in Psalm 51: 5 where we find the main support for the Christian view that original sin has a sexual basis and is transmitted from one generation to the next. 'Behold,' it says, 'I was shaped in iniquity, and in sin did my mother conceive me.' Few texts have been so badly misinterpreted. The psalm is concerned in fact with the rhythm of conception. It is actually a rather terse comment on the safe period. It has nothing to do with sexual pleasure if that is what original sin is. In the verse, iniquity has to do with the time of iniquity, that is, the time when menstruation begins and coitus is forbidden. The Jewish laws are both strict and lucid on this point. A woman is 'unclean' for seven days after her 'separation'. On the eighth day she must go to the Temple and make sacrifice in atonement for the issue of her uncleanness. Sin in the psalm refers to this purging of the sin of impurity. The time after purification is quite near to the time when conception is most likely to occur. This interpretation lends a new perspective to the Catholic Church's fostering of the rhythm method—a point to which we shall return in a later chapter.

Apart from using tampons to block the vagina, using drugs to induce sterility, and using coitus interruptus, other attempts to limit fertility were practised by the Jews at various periods in their history. They believed that semen could be removed from the vagina after intercourse by twisting the body and performing violent movements. This was a practice used by many people in antiquity and the idea persisted until quite recent times. Semen could also be removed by wiping out the vagina but not apparently by using a douche. The douche was not mentioned in any of these early writings, and when it did become a popular method in the nineteenth century, was rejected by most of the rabbis of the time. They realized that the available methods for controlling conception after intercourse had taken place were extremely unreliable.

Pregnancy could be interrupted though, and it was thought permissible to remove the foetus when the mother's life was in danger. The basis for a decision on the use of any contraceptive or abortive method seems to be the health and well-being of the couple and that of the children who had already been born. Indeed, many rabbis actually suggested supplementing the safety of the period of lactation by practising withdrawal at the same time. From the records it seems clear that these people were interested in being neither excessively fertile nor completely sterile. Their aim was that of a happy and stable family unit. But such an aim was not always to be found in the Ancient World.

CHAPTER THREE

Greece and Rome

IN Ancient Greece attitudes to life were in complete contrast
to the Jewish ideas which we have been discussing. Ancient
Sparta is notable for an almost total absence of family life.
Every Spartan was compelled to marry, but not for compan-
ionship or the gratification of any personal desire. Marriage
existed simply to provide an adequate supply of young citizens
which the State required to continue its existence and to wage
war. Despite this aim marriages do not seem to have been very
fruitful. Spartan fathers who produced three or four sons
were publicly rewarded. Other city-states, especially in
peacetime when the population started to grow, took to
limiting their number in a drastic manner. Newly born
children who were sick or deformed were simply left to die.
This was also intended to have the dual role of physically and
mentally improving the stock, and of avoiding the impoverish-
ment both of parents and of the State. Athens was slightly less
rigid in its regulations than Sparta. There were laws against
celibacy, but late marriages were acceptable, which limited the
number of children born to any couple. The Athenians also
relieved the pressure of population by colonization.

The Greeks were really the first people to give much serious
coherent thought to population problems. So far as the city-
states were concerned a stable population was regarded as
desirable. Plato suggested that reproduction should be legally
regulated, and that men should father children only when they

were between 25 and 35 years old. Women would get a slightly longer spell—from the age of 20 to 40. He specified these age ranges as part of an overall programme of eugenic improvement. In a perfect State the government could even regulate the pairing of couples. Plato's ideal State consisted of exactly 5,040 inhabitants. Numbers would be carefully controlled. Over-population would be checked by infanticide and abortion, and underpopulation would be solved by stimulating fertility when required. If there were any real problems, immigration and emigration would also be used. Perhaps it is only fair to point out that these ideas were put forward with regard to an ideal situation—a small communistic community in which everything would be carefully regulated. Citizens would even be prepared to surrender all their individual rights and ideals to the common good of the community.

Aristotle took a rather more cheerful view of marriage. He realized that people do not marry simply to procreate, but to spend their lives together and to share both joys and sorrows. However, he also was emphatic that fertility should be controlled. His idea was to regulate the number of children according to the family resources. Some philosophers thought that one child was enough, and others considered that even that was too many. Hesiod thought that if women and marriage were not actually evils to be endured, then they represented good but tempered largely with evil. Greek attitudes strike us as being curiously inconsistent in this matter. To die childless was a humiliating misfortune, and yet mysogony was an almost national attitude. Many of the celebrated classical philosophers were celibate all their lives, and although Socrates did have a wife no one seems to have found a good word to have said about her.

The very life-style of the people acted to some degree as a form of population control. Ther was a common acceptance of homosexual love. This was so widespread that the position of the wife in society reached a very low ebb indeed. Normally a youth became the lover of an older man, and only after some years would he grudgingly marry and do his duty to the State in producing children. After this he himself would fall in love again, this time with a younger boy. The 'respectable woman' was of scant interest except when she brought a sizeable dowry. By about 594 B.C. marriage as an institution had become so unpopular that it was in danger of dying out altogether. The Athenian leader Solon was obliged to produce a set of marriage laws designed to penalize bachelors. He also produced several other laws concerning women, legalizing prostitution and regulating the position of the heiress.

There were three levels of prostitute, the highest being the 'intimate female companion'. Such women held enormous influence in what was otherwise very much a man's world, and some of them achieved positions of great status in society. Apart from their obvious role they gave advice, discoursed on philosophical topics. and were skilled musicians and dancers. They were respected, accomplished and wealthy. In fact they had a great many reasons to try to avoid becoming pregnant. Pregnancy was encouraged for heiresses though. Their husbands were obliged to have intercourse with them at least three times a month, and if they failed then the woman was justified in asking her father's next of kin to father her child. This was simply to ensure that there was someone to inherit the family's possessions.

But even the heiress played a fairly humble role. According to classical ideas about procreation the woman was thought to be relatively unimportant. Maybe the remains of this idea have continued to influence man's attitude towards women throughout the centuries. The man was seen as the active partner providing the all important 'seed'. The woman simply provided a place for it to grow. Some Greek thinkers attributed conception to a mingling of the seeds. The male seed—natur-

ally enough—was semen, and the female seed was the menstrual blood. Usually the semen was thought to cause the blood to
curdle and hence form the embryo.

Ideas about the structure of the womb were not clear either.
The school of Hippocrates thought that it had two chambers,
and that males were conceived on the right side and females on
the left. By the time that the great Roman anatomist Galen
came to describe the uterus he was able to pronounce quite
confidently that it had seven chambers. We can only suppose
that Galen never actually saw one. Such muddled ideas were to
achieve a long-standing though perverse importance since
classical medicine was in use and its basis was generally accepted
until well after the Renaissance.

The uterus was even regarded by the Greeks as a separate
animal. Plato in his dialogue Timaeus said that:

That part of the woman which is called the womb, being an animal
desirous of generation, if it become unfruitful for a long time
turns indignant, and wandering all over the body stops the passages
of the spirits and the respiration and occasions the most extreme
anxiety and all sorts of diseases.

The uterus therefore had a life and desires of its own. Travel-
ling upwards it would approach the heart, liver and stomach
causing any number of diseases, nervous, cancerous and sys-
temic. The 'extreme anxiety' caused in this way was given the
special name of 'suffocation of the womb' or hysteria. This
condition was most common in virgins, for their wombs were
supposed to be lighter than those of childbearing women, and
such lightness enabled the organ to wander more freely. In a
hysterical fit the uterus was supposed to have been drawn up
near the liver by some unexplained attraction. There it would
remain for some time until eventually it pumped itself full of
blood and descended again. In order to draw the womb back
into position rather faster than it would descend if left to its
own devices, the woman should be given vile things to sniff at,

while her vagina was fumigated with sweet and pleasant smelling substances. The rationale is obvious. The independent uterus is attracted by the sweet smell and repelled by the evil one. It will therefore descend forthwith into its proper position and stop creating trouble elsewhere. This theory of the wandering womb is another incorrect notion that was accepted for many centuries. Even 300 years ago some textbooks of medicine recommended types of treatment which were based directly on the idea.

We now know that the uterus is fixed firmly in the pelvis and that it has little chance of ascending into the chest. It is, however, quite possible for the uterus to descend from its position. The Greeks recognized this condition in which the uterus bears down heavily upon the vagina. The condition is called 'prolapse', and is often caused by excessive childbearing. Greek physicians dealt with the problem by pushing the organ back into its normal position and supporting it with a ball of wool tied round with string, which was placed in the vagina. The smelling procedure was also employed, but this time in reverse, to make the uterus move up rather than down. Inflammation of the uterus and heavy uterine bleeding were treated by a similar method.

In addition, however, Greek doctors appear to have used a device which may have a rather different function. The Hippocratic book on Diseases of Women describes a hollow lead tube which is filled with mutton fat and partially inserted through the cervix into the uterus. In the context in which it is described the device intended to keep the mouth of the uterus open. This seems a very curious treatment, and it also seems to be the first time in history that such a device is mentioned. The tube itself is of great interest. It may have fallen out of favour during Medieval times, but it reappears in Europe during the fifteenth and sixteenth centuries. After going through a number of changes and a good deal of redesigning it finally emerges as a contraceptive. It is just possible therefore that intra-uterine contraception dates from the time of the Greeks. We now know that any foreign body introduced into the uterus will prevent conception from taking place, although we are still not sure exactly how it does so.

Unfortunately we do not know exactly how the Greek physicians themselve regarded the device. From the context it seems as though such a tube was actually intended to promote fertility, perhaps by opening up a route for the passage of sperms. Certainly similar devices employed in the nineteenth century were intended for this purpose. But one may speculate that the doctors, assistants, midwives and other engaged in medical work must have known that pregnancy was not likely to occur whilst the devices were in place. Such people were far from stupid. Even the midwives had to conform to high standards for their day. Soranos, the greatest of all classical physicians, demanded that the *obstetrix* should be literate, free from superstition, have good sight and hearing, a sharp intellect, strong arms and legs, soft hands and long thin fingers with short nails. She must be clean and understand anatomy, hygiene, therapeutics and the normal and abnormal conditions of the body. She must love her work, keep secrets, and have considerable practical experience. It is difficult to believe that such women would not be aware of the results of using an intra-uterine device. But apart from such speculations we have a wealth of well-documented text that show quite clearly the nature and extent to which other contraceptive practices were employed during classical times.

The Greek and Roman civilizations produced a large number of medical works. The major part of Roman medicine was derived from the Greeks, and later Greek doctors often worked in Rome. By the time of Christ, physicians had a great volume of traditional medical texts on which to draw. Soranos cites no less than 39 previous authorities in the course of his own work on gynaecology. Contraception and abortion were subjects which received much discussion. In a recent study of the period Keith Hopkin mentions 22 medical writers, 11 of whom suggested actual contraceptive methods. Of the same 22 writers, 18 discuss the various ways of aiding conception and conversely of procuring an abortion.

At best, however, we have only a limited selection of original works on the subject of fertility. Pliny mentions 146 Roman and 327 Greek medical writers, most of them by now only names, for their works have been completely lost. Some of the writers were women. Aetios of Amida writing in the sixth century A.D. mentions one very interesting lady called Aspasia. Aetios obviously admired her. As a contraceptive she recommended a wool tampon soaked with herbs, pine bark, nut galls, myrrh and wine. But the writers whose work still survive show quite clearly that the methods in use in classical Greece and Rome were as sophisticated as most of those which appeared in Europe before the early nineteenth century.

The first Greek writer to mention contraceptive methods seems to have been Aristotle. He and his wife Pythias worked and studied together. They were interested in all aspects of biology. They collected eggs from many different animals, birds, insects and spiders. From these specimens they even deduced a theory of generation, as far as was possible without the aid of a microscope. As a means of birth control Aristotle recommended the use of oil to cover the cervix and coat the inside of the vagina. He seems to have thought that its smoothness was its important feature. In fact, oil does reduce the motility of sperms. If it also blocks the entrance to the uterus then it makes it even more difficult for the sperm to gain access.

One of the most famous names in the history of medicine is that of Hippocrates. However, there prove on examination to be few, if any, surviving works that we can say with certainty

have been written by him. In contrast, the works of his followers, the so-called Hippocratic school, were numerous. We have
already mentioned that the Hippocratic writers, either by
design or accident, may have used an intra-uterine contraceptive method. The same writers also mention a contraceptive drink. It contains an unidentified substance called *misy*
which dissolved in water is supposed to prevent conception for
a year. A number of guesses have been made as to exactly
what misy might be. Suggestions include sulphur, copper
sulphate, iron sulphate and alum. Dioscorides, who wrote his
famous *Herbal* several hundred years later, was in no doubt,
although his account does not help us very much. He described the substance in his fifth book, which deals with vines,
wines and metallic stones. We are told of misy that:

. . . the Cyprian is to be chosen looking like gold, hard and in the
breaking of a golden colour and glistering like a star. It has the same
faculty as burning Chalcitis. . . . That of Egypt in respect of others
is the best, being the most effectual.

Chalcitis itself is mentioned as being 'good for fluxes of blood
which come from the womb'. Any modern scholar who is
both chemist, historian and classical specialist, can have hours
of amusement attempting to unravel this particular problem.

The Hippocratic writers also knew that semen was essential
to conception and they reintroduced the suggestion that it
should be 'removed from the vagina' or 'shaken out with
bodily movement'. Unfortunately this advice is rather too
ambiguous to be of any great value. They also observe that fat
people are less fertile than thin ones, and suggested that
putting on weight might help those who wanted to avoid
pregnancy. The Latin poet Lucretius made similar observations and noted that diet was an important factor of infertility.
He suggested that sterility was caused by 'thickness' or 'thin-
ness' of semen, and hence that fertility might be aided by the

right sort of food. He felt that certain positions for intercourse were more conductive to conception than others, and he supported the idea of violent bodily movements to shake the semen from the vagina after intercourse. Pliny the Elder was distinctly less objective. He tells us that the best way of preventing conception he had come across was to wear as an amulet the worms taken from the body of a hairy spider.

Of the Greek authorities who discussed contraception three are particularly outstanding. We have already mentioned them briefly. They are the herbalist Dioscorides and the physicians Soranos of Ephesus, and Aetios of Amida.

Dioscorides lived in the first or second century A.D. and was an enormously prolific author. His *Herbal*—a treatise on botany and pharmacology—was a standard work until the sixteenth century. It was translated into many languages and copied out by hand until the invention of the printing press. It was not available in English until 1655 when the first translation was made by John Goodyer, but it was certainly available in other European nations and it was well known to the Islamic physicians. It was read by both Jewish and Christian doctors in Spain.

Dioscorides had knowledge of several different kinds of contraceptive. He thought that there were substances that could be taken orally to cause sterility. These included the fruit of the 'Chaste tree' which seems to have been both a contraceptive and an abortifacient. Willow leaves, beaten small and taken in water also caused 'inconception'. Asparagus had the property of making a person sterile but it was not necessary to drink it. The plant could work quite as well tied up and worn as an amulet. If none of the methods seem to be very promising perhaps the medicated pessaries Dioscorides mentions are more hopeful. These are prepared from a great array of material, including herbs, pepper, 'sword-shaped sickle wort', and peppermint juice. Most of them were mixed with honey and 'laid before conjunction to the mouth of the matrix'.

Like previous writers Dioscorides mentioned viscous substances like cedar gum, and he also recommended alum in various forms. Animals which are themselves sterile, such as the mule, and trees which apparently bear no fruit have traditionally been thought to effect human fertility. His version of the story was that the kidney of a mule, taken with white poplar bark caused sterility. Dioscorides seems to have been among the first to record such ideas, which were found all over Europe in the Middle Ages, and which have persisted until modern times. Indeed his work is of particular importance because of the continuous influence it had on medical practice for many centuries, especially during the so-called 'Dark Ages' when real knowledge fell into disuse and superstition took its place.

Of the early writers Soranos was admittedly superior in his discussion of contraceptive techniques. But his books were lost for many years. His work dates from the first half of the second century. It was obviously known to Aetios of Amida who wrote in the sixth, and who described him as a great master. Soranos was interested especially in gynaecology and obstetrics but he wrote on most aspects of medicine known at the time. His style of writing was simple, and his books are well illustrated. They were intended to be easily read and memorized, and the knowledge in them was for the practical use of doctors and midwives.

The commonsense account of the qualities that a midwife should have is typical of his approach. His discussion of birth control is equally sensible. He began by discussing contraceptives and abortifacients, and he described the difference between the two. He considered in particular how these things should be used. Abortion was not to be entered into lightly. It was certainly not permissible simply to hide the fact that adultery had taken place, nor merely for keeping the female form beautiful. If abortion were necessary for health purposes, then it could be employed, but even so contraception was to be preferred.

Soranos seems to have been alone in making these fine distinctions. Dioscorides, for example, thought that pepper is an abortificient unless used after intercourse when it is a contraceptive. Soranos in contrast, mentions some medicaments recommended as contraceptives and then says that they 'not only prevent conception but destroy any already existing. In our opinion, moreover, the evil of these things is too great.' He was perhaps the first openly to suggest that people should abstain from intercourse at the time when conception is most likely to occur. Unfortunately he believed this to be about the time of menstruation so that his idea is not very helpful. He suggests in addition that the woman should 'hold back' emotionally to prevent semen from entering her womb and that she should then get up, sneeze, wipe out her vagina, and drink something cold. His ideas for vaginal barriers are perhaps more valuable. The list includes oil, honey, resin, juice of the balsam tree ('alone or together with white lead'), myrtle oil and woollen tampons. His list includes a selection of other substances with instructions on how they should be used. Particularly interesting is the use of fresh acidic fruit pulp such as the pomegranate. Undoubtedly such a substance would have a spermicidal action, assuming of course that a couple could be prevailed upon to use it. It is to Soranos' lasting credit that he rejected the majority of magical contraceptives. For example, his commonsense approach made him totally opposed to any kind of amulets—he had no faith in them at all.

The work of Aetios of Amida, written in the sixth century, is very similar to that of Soranos. Aetios also commences his discussion by considering the difference between contraceptives and abortifacients, and then describes many of the substances that Soranos mentioned. But in a sense his work is a retrograde step. He mentions several magical methods, including amulets, such as a cat's liver worn in a tube on the left foot, or the testicles of a cat worn in a tube around the navel. Part of the womb of a lioness encased in an ivory tube is described as being 'very effective'. Towards the end of his account he produces the new and interesting idea that a man should wash his penis in vinegar or brine. Both substances have a spermicidal action. They would of course have been more effective if they had been diluted and placed in the vagina. Nevertheless Aetios was at least on the right track. Neither substance seems to have been mentioned before and neither were to reappear until 1832 when Charles Knowlton was to suggest them as possible douches. Less helpfully Aetios resurrects the old superstition that the burned testicles of a mule drunk with a decoction of willow makes an excellent male contraceptive.

It is impossible for us to tell exactly how much effect the knowledge recorded by Soranos and Aetios would have had on the lives of the people who read their work. But certainly in Roman times there was much talk of depopulation. In the Roman view, marriage existed primarily for the purpose of raising children, but even so marriages do not seem to have been very fruitful. Many patrician families became extinct. By 164 B.C. the population of Rome seems to have been steady or even in decline, and the census returns were recorded with regret. The Censor, Quintus Metellus urged that laws be passed compelling citizens to marry. He is reputed to have been a happily married man himself. At the same time however he is quoted as saying, 'if we had the power of living without wives we should all be free from that trouble; but nature has so disposed it that we can neither live very commodiously with them, nor without them exist at all. We must therefore provide rather for perpetual security than for transient pleasure.' One wonders what his wife must have thought about such an utterance.

Both Julius and Augustus introduced laws to encourage procreation. Such laws rewarded those citizens who produced large families and penalized those who never married. Julius, it is said, prohibited women over 24 who were unmarried, from wearing precious jewels. Augustus was more thorough and persistent in his population policy. In 18 B.C. he introduced the first of his laws, but people were so opposed to it that it was not enacted at the time. Basically his idea also was to try to bring marriage into fashion. Since his modest target was only three children per family, it seems certain that the average family size was below that number. Tacitus refers to the Julian laws and declares that they were unsuccessful. Despite the fact that the State demanded higher and higher penalties, the celibate population preferred to pay and live without children. The extravagance of Roman life made child care a burdensome expense.

Since those Romans who married usually did so at an early age their family size would have been greater than that demanded by Julian unless some means of limitation had been employed. Records show that abortion was widely practised and it has been suggested that infidelity and debauchery were two other limiting factors. It looks as though the faithful husband was a non-existent creature. But then Roman wives were not noted for their fidelity either. They had intercourse both with equals and with slaves. There was some moral condemnation of such practices, but they were certainly condoned in a great many cases. By contrast, certain undesirable elements in the population were apparently prevented from ever having intercourse at all. Celsus describes the practice by which such men were 'infibulated'. This operation consists of drawing the foreskin forward over the end of the penis and making two openings in it through which a ring was placed and sealed in position.

Roman society was certainly not without infanticide, although the practice was more common in Greek times. Roman women preferred to avoid the pain, danger and inconvenience of childbirth as far as possible. Indeed society was well organized as far as health services were concerned. There were slave doctors and more highly trained doctors too. The latter would have been aware of the work of Soranos and others, since they trained at well-established medical schools. Oribasius, the court physician to the Emperor Julian, cited both Soranos and Galen.

But although there existed this tradition of practical working knowledge of birth control, Roman literature hardly mentions the subject. Perhaps those writers who describe their fears of depopulation and whose works extolled the joys and virtues of parenthood and the desirability of a larger population in the State, were reluctant to offer any possible clues to those who disagreed with their ideas. It seems surprising that the advice in Ovid's 'Art of Love' includes not a word on how to avoid pregnancy—especially when the advice is directed to the attractive courtesan. Horace's 'Odes' contain only one line (I. 2, 23) which has been thought to refer to birth control, but which may equally well relate to the heavy casualties of the civil war: '*vitio parentum rara iuventus*' ('the evil of the parents makes children scarce'). Juvenal has another possible reference when he remarks, 'So powerful are her arts and medicines that she makes women sterile and brings about the killing of infants in the womb'.

Perhaps the practice of contraception is not mentioned because the writers failed to understand the difference between contraception and abortion. Unlike the Greeks the Romans did not have a very specific word for it. If this was something which puzzled the medical practitioners, it is not surprising that even well-educated members of the community failed to appreciate the distinction. Even in modern times, those involved in campaigns to spread information about family planning often come across people who cannot see the difference in preventing conception from taking place and removing the embryo at a later stage. Aulus Gellus thought that a child could be born after 7, 8 or 10 months of development, but certainly not after 9 months. For some reason he had the idea that during the eighth month the foetus is smaller and weaker than it is during the seventh. Such ideas would have made it difficult to calculate the time when conception took place. In consequence the confusion between contraception and abortion would have been even greater. Pregnancy must have been fairly difficult to diagnose. This is clear from the large number of pregnancy tests which are described. In addition the number of remedies recommended to 'restore the female flow' suggest that irregularities in the menstrual cycle were common. Thus it would have been easy for a less fertile couple to decide that an amulet of asparagus was the operative factor in saving them from pregnancy, even though their own sub-fertility or abstention during the crucial time may in fact have been the real reason.

There seems to be no mention of the practice of withdrawal during Roman times, nor is there any real evidence that the condom was used either. There is one story, though, which has been cited as evidence for the use of a sheath, and it is worth retelling even though it may not stand close scrutiny. According to Antoninus Liberalis who lived during the second century, Minos, King of Crete had a problem. His semen contained serpents and scorpions which injured the women with whom he cohabited. He married Pasiphae, the daughter of the King of the Sun, who was immune to this 'infection' yet the union was sterile. A remedy was found when a goat's bladder was placed in the vagina of a second lady. Into this bladder Minos proceeded to spend his serpent-ridden semen. Afterwards he could cohabit with Pasiphae who was

then able to conceive. Whether this story illustrates the use of a
real sheath, either male or female, is highly debatable. If it had
occurred to one man that an animal membrane would make a
protection against either infection or pregnancy then it is just
possible that others had the same idea and that animal bladders
had a more general usage as contraceptives. It is just possible—
no more.

It is often said that the sexual excesses of Rome were responsible for its downfall. For the next thousand years the idea
sexuality became almost anathema, and the notion of controlling fertility was condemned from many sides. Yet it persisted
and eventually re-emerged. Although the period is not well
documented it is still possible to trace at least a few ideas on
birth control through the Dark Ages and to see veiled but
unmistakable references to it in Medieval Europe.

CHAPTER FOUR

The Middle Ages

THE 'battle of the sexes' has been a continuing theme through-out European history. A woman's place has almost always been alloted to her by a man, and whilst it is often said that religions such as Christianity have given woman equality, in earlier centuries the status of women could scarcely have been lower or more debased. At times when men are wrapped up in philosophical speculations, and when they desire eternity and the highest place in heaven for their immortal souls, then wo-men tend to be seen as a source of temptation and one to be guarded against.

Women have been despised and feared because of their physical make-up in a great many civilizations. We have already seen that in pre-Christian time the status of women was not high. Christianity took this fear and added its own peculiar emphasis on chastity and death, which were made to appear as a gateway to sublime happiness. The early Church Fathers spoke of the 'tumefaction of the uterus, and the care of yelling infants', and thought that any lady should be 'filled with shame at the thought that she is a woman'. And women of course were unclean.

The obvious sources of this uncleanness are the menstrual periods, defloration and childbirth, all of which involve some loss of blood. Blood has great significance in many religions, including Christianity. It is a symbol of life itself. But men-struation has been considered important in many different cultures. Women have been sent to stay in special places during the period; some are restricted to specific diets; taboos have been placed on using instruments, utensils, bed-coverings or linen touched by a menstruating woman. Some have even insisted that the woman should be kept out of sight altogether. Older marriage customs, some of which are very complex, have left their relics to this day. The meanings are often forgotten yet the original idea was to protect the husband from the dangerous but much-desired wedding night.

Because of this fear of uncleanness, at certain times—before going to war or to hunt, for example—some early civilizations practised a form of chastity. But this was radically different from the Christian ideal. Tribal chastity was not supposed to be either good or virtuous. It was merely a means of avoiding sexual contamination, which was thought to be dangerous and augur badly for the venture. It was also a way of preserving sexual power and strength, which could be sublimated into the struggle of war or the chase. At other times, such people would have thought that chastity was unnatural, rather stupid, perhaps even wicked. Usually fertility was of the highest importance and special ceremonies were performed to ensure fecundity and ripeness. Christianity differed from such beliefs. Its ideals were unworldly, and it strived after spiritual values. But it was a religion for men; left to themselves very few women would have found that it had much to offer.

St Paul's attitude to women is found in several places. In I. Timothy 2, where he demands plain dress, good works and subjection, we read:

Let the woman learn in silence with all subjection. But I suffer not a woman to teach, nor to usurp authority over the man, but to be in silence. For Adam was first formed and then Eve. And Adam was not deceived but the woman being deceived was in the transgression. Notwithstanding she shall be saved with childbearing, if they continue in faith and charity and holiness with sobriety.

An Epistle to the Corinthians also contains some observations on marriage:

It is good for a man not to touch a woman. Nevertheless, to avoid fornication, let every man have his own wife, and let every woman have her own husband. Let the husband render unto the wife due benevolence: and likewise the wife unto the husband. . . . Defraud ye not one other, except it be with consent for a time, that ye may give yourselves to fasting and prayer; and come together again, that Satan tempt you not for your incontinence. But I speak this of permission and not commandment, for I would that all men were even as myself. . . . But if they cannot contain, let them marry; for it is better to marry than to burn . . . but if thou marry, thou hast not sinned; and if a virgin marry, she hath not sinned. Nevertheless, such shall have trouble in the flesh. . . . He that standeth steadfast in his heart, having no necessity, but hath power over his own will, and hath so decreed in his heart that he will keep his virgin, doeth well. So then he that giveth in marriage doeth well; but he that giveth her not in marriage doeth better. The wife is bound by the law as long as her husband liveth; but if her husband be dead, she is at liberty to be married to whom she will; only in the Lord. But she is happier if she so abide after my judgement: and I think also that I have the spirit of God.

There are a number of other comments in the same vein. Nowadays they are regarded as a call for a chaste and pure life; but they were taken to mean much more by the early Christians. These people, who viewed themselves as surrounded by immorality and wickedness and who expected Christ's immanent return, leapt into what seem to be immoderate excesses in seeking chastity and defeating the sexual devils. To be fair, such attitudes were not restricted to the Christians. Many of the rival sects who were struggling for supremacy and attempting to gain converts preached the same anti-feminist message. Christianity was simply the most success-ful. But the opinion that marriage was unclean and less desir-able than celibacy was not an idea which found universal agreement, even within the Church. In fact it took hundreds of years to create a completely celibate priesthood.

In the early days, those who trod the path of Saint Paul often took up strange practices in order to maintain their chastity. They tried living in remote places, never washing their bodies, and squatting on the top of high pillars (which had the added advantage of keeping them nearer heaven). They also scourged themselves continually. Curiously enough the new creed attracted a vast number of prostitutes. Downtrodden women were quick to learn that whatever dreadful acts might have befallen their earthly frames, their immortal souls were more important, and still intact. There is even a patron saint of reformed prostitutes—Saint Mary of Egypt. She, like many others, took to living in the desert, repenting her sins.

But relatively few Christian were hermits. Many felt that attitudes should be less severe, and viewed marriage as a necessary institution. Some went so far as to say that in order to be a good Christian one should first be a good Jew, and they were well attuned to the traditional Jewish ideals of family life. Others by contrast saw forms of monasticism as offering the answer. However, even St Paul appears to be a liberal when viewed against another body of opinion which postulated that marriage was so utterly wicked that it should not be allowed. Sexual intercourse in any circumstances was beyond redemption—self-mutilation was to be preferred. Opinions were growing increasingly severe. In the early days, the clergy did marry, but the teachings of the Church Fathers made marriage sound so inferior that it would be difficult to imagine anything less desirable. The most liberal did not reject marriage completely, but is was certainly better to refrain from it.

Tertullian, the founder of 'Latin Christianity' declared that he 'savoured spiritually' when away from his wife. He wrote to her, saying that on the occasion of the resurrection 'There will be no more resumption of voluptuous disgrace between us'. He was opposed to people marrying for the sake of having children.

Further reasons for marriage which men allege for themselves arise from anxiety for posterity, and the bitter, bitter pleasure of children, whom when we have them we desire to send before us to glory (in respect, I mean, of the distresses that are now immanent); desirous as we are ourselves to be taken out of this most wicked world and received into the Lord's presence. Let the well-known burdensomeness of children, especially in our case, suffice to counsel widowhood—children whom men are compelled by laws to have, because no wise man would ever willingly have desired sons.

What has the care of infants to do with the Last Judgement? Having breasts, the qualms of childbirth, and whimpering brats will make a fine scene combined with the advent of the Judge and the sound of the Trumpet. Ah, what good midwives the executioners of the Antichrist will be.

Tertullian had ideas about birth control and abortion too. He knew that abortion was common and that some women made a living as abortionists. He hurled invective at female practitioners of any kind—doctors and midwives as well.

If a child is extracted dead it verily was once alive. It is your tubes, your speculums, your dilators and hooks are to blame for causing this destruction.

One thing is abundantly clear—he thoroughly agreed with the views of St Paul. Indeed most Church Fathers denounced women as prone to sin, unreliable, unstable, and generally low in thought and action. By the time of the Nicene Council of A.D. 325 general agreement seems to have been reached. The doctrine that emerged was that although marriage and celibacy were both valid states, the latter was infinitely preferable.

However, in the early years of the Christian era these views put forth by the Fathers had little effect on anybody. The religion was illegal. Its adherents were subject to persecution and were often in grave danger. The probability of being disgraced or killed would have made many decline from taking up such a faith. Those who did accept it viewed the hazards as offering a speedy path to God, but such believers would not form a very representative section of any population. Roman Catholic ideas were therefore of small importance. Only in the long run were they to affect a vast number of people, ironically enough only after Rome had ceased to be the most important city in the world. As well as attitudes to women and sexuality, the Church's views on medicine, and particularly on the control of fertility were to exert a great influence upon the society of later centuries. We have already traced the ideas on birth control that were current during the Roman Empire, but what were the sources of knowledge about contraception that the Church saw fit to react against once the Empire started to disintegrate?

The decline of the Roman Empire is a phenomenon that historians still cannot fully explain. The reasons are complex and the self-indulgence to which we referred earlier is at best only a minor contributory factor. We do know, however, that several centuries before its final downfall the effective centre of the Empire moved eastwards. In the fourth century Constantine—the Emperor who finally accepted Christianity as the Empire's official faith—built his new capital at Constantinople. In A.D. 527 Justinian acceded to the position of Byzantine Emperor, and we know that Aetios was a physician at Justinian's Byzantine court. Medical knowledge, including a knowledge of contraceptive methods, was therefore moving eastwards, like so many aspects of classical culture, and in the process was being lost to Europe. Its reintroduction was the result of conquest, and a conquest from an unexpected direction.

Although the Persians had been at war with the Empire for several hundred years it was not they who were responsible for the downfall of Byzantium. In a period of only ten years the

5. In Medieval times and afterwards the midwife was often the witch, or at least was accused of witchcraft. At this imagined witches sabbat a meal of baby's flesh is being eaten (bottom right), whilst another group of witches (bottom left), prepare the baby fat that will go into the 'flying ointment'. *By courtesy of Bodleian Library, Oxford.*

6. Albert the Great, 1193–1280 was a Dominican philosopher, teacher and theologian who was also perhaps one of the greatest alchemists of the Middle Ages. Here he is seen teaching his most famous student, Thomas Aquinas at the University of Padua. *By courtesy of 'The Wellcome Trustees.'*

Persians were themselves conquered by the armies of Islam. By A.D. 664 Syria, Persia, Egypt and Libya were all under Moslem control. Although the Moslems never succeeded in taking Constantinople itself they rapidly overran the Empire of which it was the head, and in A.D. 711 they crossed the Straits of Gibraltar. Only in A.D. 732 was their advance halted at at Poitiers by Charlemagne's grandson, Charles Martel.

This invasion by the Arabs is perhaps one of the most momentous events in European history, and different specialists evaluate its importance in different ways. To the medical historian its prime importance lies in the fact that emerging from the Dark Ages, Europe was able to profit from the medical knowledge that the Arabs possessed. Some of this knowledge derived from the Greek and Roman sources and some of it also came from Persia, Egypt and the other areas that the Arabs had conquered. The first European medical schools started in the eleventh and twelfth centuries were Mohammedan foundations. The definitive medical texts were also Arabic. The spread of knowledge about birth control, like most other aspects of medical science, was therefore almost entirely due to the Arabic sources. Unlike Christianity, Islam was not opposed to birth control, nor even early abortion. The Prophet himself, when asked if withdrawal was permissible in certain circumstances, had replied that it was, since if God willed a child to be born, any precautions would fail. The Koran also commended women to breast-feed babies for two years and to abstain from intercourse throughout the period of lactation.

The two best-known Islamic writers on medicine were undoubtedly Rhazes and Avicenna. The former, who died about A.D. 923 was born in Persia and spent much of his life in Baghdad. His best-known medical book which is variously called either *The Quintessence of Experience* or *The Book for Almansor* was translated into Latin by Spanish scholars in about

C

1150. Rhazes had a wide-ranging medical knowledge. As well as gynaecology and obstetrics he was also interested in, for example, the well-being of the eyes, and in diseases such as measles and smallpox. In Book 24 of the *Quintessence* he concerns himself with the means of preventing conception. He starts by discussing why contraceptive methods should be used, and he echoes Soranos in saying that sometimes, when pregnancy is likely to endanger life, it is most important that semen should not enter the womb. It is interesting to note that both Greek and Islamic physicians were familiar with these medical indications for birth control, although even as late as the nineteenth and early twentieth centuries pioneers in this field were finding it difficult to have such ideas accepted.

There are several ways, according to Rhazes, whereby the sperms can be prevented from gaining access. He describes withdrawal and even the prevention of ejaculation—'a method used by some'. He also describes a whole range of occlusive pessaries, including cabbage, pitch, ox-gall and elephant dung, which may be used 'alone or in combination'. Rhazes is clearly indebted to Soranos for the idea that after intercourse a woman should stand up, shake herself, sneeze and jump backwards to dislodge the semen (jumping forwards assists its entry into the uterus). He suggests either seven or nine jumps, and the point has frequently been made that these are of course magical numbers. There is obviously nothing to prevent a method which has some rational explanation (even if wrongly founded), from being reinforced by supernatural agencies. Alternatively, a woman may sit on her toes and rub her navel with her thumb. If such a method fails there are substances such as sal ammoniac or potash which can be applied to the womb. It is probable that Rhazes is here describing a type of astringent pessary which is to be inserted after intercourse. Rue juice or pepper will have the same effect. The smelling of foul odours is mentioned, (reminiscent of the wandering womb), and so is fumigation of the vagina. This latter method, curious and barbaric as it seems to us, has a long history and undoubtedly originated not as a contraceptive procedure but as a means of easing labour. Elsewhere in the book Rhazes mentions the application of cedar oil to the organs of either partner before intercourse—a notion handed down from the time of Aristotle.

If contraceptive methods fail then abortion may be necessary. One procedure is to insert a probe made of wood or tightly screwed up paper into the uterus. No force should be used, and there should be no hurry. The similarity of this procedure to the modern surgical method of abortion by uterine curettage is striking, although Rhazes envisaged that the probe might have to remain in place for several days. 'This procedure causes no harm,' he tells us. In the hands of the physician possibly not. In the hands of the unskilled it could have been disastrous. Perforation of the uterus and infection are two of the complications that immediately spring to mind. Again the parallel with modern methods of abortion is marked. In skilled hands the surgery is routine. Without proper medical supervision it can prove fatal.

Rhazes also considers it possible to induce an abortion by the use of drugs, either internally or externally. Whilst she is waiting for the menstrual flow to return the woman should engage in violent movements and vigorous intercourse. The old idea of jumping downstairs to dislodge the foetus clearly has a very long history. 'Joking too is useful.' he adds, although whether to raise the girl's morale or simply as another form of shaking is not clear. He perhaps overlooks the difficulty of finding anything funny at such a time.

The two other approaches to contraception that Rhazes considers have to do with other orally active substances. In the first category are those plants such as cedar which would prevent conception directly. In the second group there are a number of anaphrodisiacs—substances which so take away sexual desire that they can be classed as indirect methods of birth control. Lettuce, he tells us, falls into this category.

Perhaps the greatest of all Islamic thinkers was Avicenna, born in A.D. 980. He was concerned with many different aspects of science, of which medicine was only one. His medical encyclopaedia known as the *Canon of Medicine* contains, (according to Norman Himes) nearly a million words and is according to another authority 'a codification of the whole of ancient and Muslim knowledge'. It was translated into Latin at about the same time as the translation of Rhazes, and it was to remain the standard work on the subject for over 500 years.

Avicenna also was interested in the medical indications for birth control. Pregnancy is to be avoided for small women for whom it might be dangerous, and for those suffering from diseases of the uterus or from weakness of the bladder. He is also quite clear about the distinction between contraception and abortion. Many of his suggestions are similar to those of Rhazes but his account also contains other ideas. For example, two notions derived from Soranos are that the partners should avoid reaching a climax at the same time, and that intercourse should be avoided altogether at the time when conception is most likely. The first suggestion requires no further comment, but the second, relating as it does to the notion of a safe period, is far more interesting.

The idea that menstrual blood and a woman's 'seed' were one and the same thing had led Soranos (and presumably other Greek physicians too), to the idea that conception must be most likely when intercourse occurs close to the time of menstruation. Although Avicenna does not state when he considers the safe period to arise we can assume that he also had the same time in mind. These ideas are of course the exact opposite of the truth. An egg is shed from the ovary roughly midway between two periods of menstrual bleeding, but one can hardly blame the physicians of the Classical and Medieval period for making such a mistake. The real nature of the human egg was not appreciated until the nineteenth century, and a properly based understanding of the female menstrual cycle was not achieved until the mid-eighteen-hundreds. Even then it was not appreciated, and it had to await independent rediscovery in the second decade of the present century.

In addition to what we now call the rhythm method, Avicenna also recommended spermicides, potions and substances which take away desire. Cedar oil is said to be a useful spermicide, though it must be used both before and after intercourse. It can also be applied directly to the penis. Balsam has the same spermicidal effect. As a pessary Avicenna reintroduced the use of pomegranate pulp. Cabbage or willow leaves are also valuable for this purpose. As a contraceptive potion a concoction of sweet basil in water is recommended, and to take away sexual desire many different substances can be used. Coriander, lettuce and the water lily are all supposed to be effective.

In fairness to Avicenna it must be said that he did not necessarily believe in the value of all the substances he mentions. His aim was to produce an encyclopaedia of medicine containing all the knowledge, ideas and opinions then current. For example, he records the use of amulets to be worn on the body, but he himself probably had little faith in them.

Apart from the transfer of medical information, the clash of Romano-Christian civilization with that of Islam had far-reaching effects and shaped many of our ideas, concepts and institutions. Our numbers and mathematics, and the form of our universities date from this meeting. Another less direct consequence but one worth mentioning here is the effect which chivalry had on what was an almost entirely feudal society.

Although it has the image of romantic love, chivalry was, like many modern 'western' films, more concerned with the relationship between a man and his horse than a man and his wife. When the Church sanctified war a large number of husbands vanished to fight the Crusades. The position of the woman in all this was wretched. She was left alone with her chastity belt for as long as he was away. If he never returned, she was just the pawn of a feudal overlord, to be bestowed along with the property and title deeds upon any man who deserved a reward for services rendered. The land and deeds were the important part—she was just another chattel.

In fact, the 'wife' might even be a child. Although the Church did try to lay down an age of consent—fifteen for a man and a full twelve years for a girl—when the barons found it feudally more convenient in the administration of properties, they arranged marriages among themselves involving five-year-old girls. One author bemoaned that times were changing for the worse—at one time men only married at thirty or later and the bride would be of age. Now they arrange marriages between youngsters of twelve. He adds 'Beware, lest they have children!'

In theory, the principle that both parties should consent to a marriage had been established. Most of the women of the time are recorded as agreeing, with enthusiasm, to any suggested match. It seems unlikely that young and dutiful daughters would have dared to disagree with anything which their fathers had arranged. Of course, this applied only to the upper classes. The serfs were in the same position as farm animals and were supposed to marry among their fellows on the same estate. Any movement to another estate was discouraged, for the lord wanted to retain couples and their children to increase the labour force.

But for the ruling families the choice of suitable partners became a complex affair. Not only were there considerations of lands and titles and the duty toward overlords, but there were also laws prohibiting marriage between members of the same family. Today one may not marry immediate relatives, but according to Pope Gregory I, Canon Law decreed that immediate relatives consisted of people who were as much as seven degrees related. This meant that if there were any common ancestor during the past seven generations marriage was not possible. If, after a first marriage, a widow or widower wanted to marry again, the choice of a partner was further aggravated, since the first marriage had made the couple 'one flesh'. All of the relatives on both sides gained an equal and close affinity. This would mean that marriage was banned with anyone as remote as the dead partner's third cousin. A similar closeness was created between baptizer and baptized, confirmer and confirmed, god-parents and god-children—and those were all treated in the same way as blood relatives. Checking back into history to establish where any such complex problems existed was almost impossible and must have been a great delaying mechanism, if not an actual deterrent to many marriages.

The ladies of the time sought and found a number of paths offering release. It was not uncommon for a lady to become a 'Bride of Christ', and enter a convent. Some took vows, but in the early days this was not always required. A great many found more freedom in a convent than in their own homes. Religious celibacy would have been a device which (indirectly) prevented a good many people from having children. However, the Church did not manage to create a completely celibate priesthood for many years. As late as the twelfth century, compliance on the part of the priests was sluggish, and the villagers encouraged them to have a resident woman, even if the pair were not married, in order to keep their own women from the temptation of desiring a man who was more educated, and elevated above their ranks.

After the second Lateran Council of 1139 some priests did begin to separate from their wives, but when the flesh was weak they resorted to mistresses and prostitutes. In certain convents the nuns were not blameless in those things either, and it is recorded on occasions the local prostitutes complained that the nuns' activities provided too much competition. The size of the problem may be indicated by the trouble the Church had in dealing with the illegitimate offsprings of the priesthood. When such children wished to become priests themselves special dispensations had to be obtained from the Pope. As many as 484 of these documents were issued in 1342. A far greater number of these children would have taken other jobs, and of course, a great many of them would have been girls.

But Christ was not the perfect husband for all the ladies of Medieval Europe. For some an earthly, though clandestine, lover provided the consolation for their loneliness. Those who did take to illicit affairs desired the means to prevent conception, and to judge from the instructions given to the priests of the day, they were using both rational and magical means to try and achieve their desired aims. It is doubtful whether the wisdom of Rhazes, Avicenna and the Classical writers was generally available. Inevitably, in the wake of the great men there follows a train of less talented and less original workers. The history of contraception suffered from such confusion every bit as much as any other aspect of medical science in this respect. Constantinople and the citadels of Moslem culture were the centres of advance in art and science, but the seaports such as Salerno and Alexandria were the centres where much information was actually exchanged. It is not surprising that medical schools were centred in such cities. Salerno, for example, was a stopping place for pilgrims and was also famed for its medicinal springs and hospitals.

One of its medical teachers who was especially highly regarded was a woman called Trotula. She was a wife and mother, and specialized in gynaecology and obstetrics. She produced many chapters on the subjects of menstruation and sterility. These subjects seem to have presented some problem since she dwells on them at such length. Contraception, however, cannot have been as widely discussed, for her short chapter is not very useful, relying as it does on magical methods. In the main, all that emerged were superstitions—women should remain passive and use amulets. If a pregnancy occurs despite these 'precautions', the mother is advised to avoid dysentery, anger and unhappiness for fear of aborting.

By 1300 Arnold of Villanova, famous in his time, and physician to two Popes, made no distinction between substances which were directly contraceptive and substances which took away sexual desire. An imitator of Arnold's was confidently stating some years later that the juice of willow leaves together with the dust from a mule's hoof was an excellent means of preventing conception. John of Gaddesden considered that a mule's heart was a effective contraceptive. It was not necessary to eat it, but simply to wear it upon the body. An agate had the same effect. Indeed, yet another contraceptive charm, this time of plant origin, did not have to be worn at all. It was simply hung over the bed. A hundred years later Chaucer's Parson in the *Canterbury Tales* warns against the drinking of herbs to prevent conception. He also mentions withdrawal, anal intercourse and abortion.

There is little to be gained from a catalogue of confused ideas, but there is one other author whose views we must consider, as much for their originality as for the fact that he expressed them at all in such detail. Albert the Great was a Dominican, a bishop, and the teacher of St Thomas Aquinas. He was born in 1296 and died at the (for the time) advanced age of 74. He was an outstanding intellectual figure and wrote two encyclopaedias both of which contain information on birth control. In the first he followed Avicenna in stating that lettuce, coriander and rue will all diminish sexual desire. In the second book he discusses the process of reproduction and makes some interesting observations on why it should fail. Apart from anatomical defects, it can fail because of 'human errors'. One error is a failure to achieve orgasm simultaneously. Another error is an error of position. If the partners lie either side by side or with the women on top then the semen is likely to pour out of the vagina. A third error results from the woman rising after intercourse, jumping or urinating—all of which effects tend to dislodge the semen.

Now it is hard to imagine that a man as shrewd as Albert could consider these errors to arise naturally, in the same way as say a congential defect of the vagina is a natural error preventing conception. He was clearly describing deliberate methods of birth control, and he was well aware of the fact.

His account is important for two reasons. First it shows clearly that such means were being employed in the Europe of the thirteenth century. It would have been pointless to describe 'errors' that no one had practised, or even thought of— they would have been almost uncountable. But it also raises the interesting question of whether Albert himself approved of such practices. Almost certainly he did not. He included them, without comment, because in an encyclopaedia it is necessary to include everything that is relevant. In a different context, the same was true of Avicenna. John T. Noonan Jr. as a result of his own extremely thorough researches concludes that:

No one who reads his (Albert's) theological treatment of contraceptives could doubt that he considered contraception a serious sin, yet in his scientific work he abstains absolutely from moral judgement.

But the question which must then be asked is why would Albert have regarded the use of contraceptives as being so sinful. Indeed, why does the Catholic Church still regard most forms of birth control as a serious sin? Equally important is the question as to whether this had always been so. We are not primarily concerned in this book with the history or the present attitudes of any particular religion. But at the same time the Catholic Church's attitude has so coloured the history of contraception (as well as other aspects of sexuality) that any account that ignored it would be incomplete. We must therefore make some sort of answer, if only a superficial one. In so doing we have found the work of Noonan an authoritative guide which should be studied carefully by anyone more deeply interested in the problem.

It is probably true to say that birth control within marriage has not always received the Catholic Church's direct condemnation, in the same way as abortion and homicide have always been condemned. During the first three centuries of the Christian era the early Church Fathers do make reference to birth control, but their comments also extend to other sinful actions of which contraception forms only a part. The use of sterilizing potions by couples engaged in fornication was condemned for example, but then fornication itself is regarded as a grave sin. No comment is made on the use of such potions by lawfully married couples who already have a number of children and desire to have no more.

The first clear statement of the sinfulness of birth control, even among the married is found in the works of St Augustine. Like so many of St Augustine's other statements it formed the definitive basis for the teaching of the Catholic Church for well over 500 years. Like Aristotle and Avicenna, St Augustine was regarded, in retrospect, as the greatest thinker of his century. His conclusions, as theirs, were to become dogma, and it was for a long time inconceivable that his views could even be challenged. The point has been made that the Church's ideas on marriage and its purpose might equally well have come not from Augustine, but from one of his contemporaries who held a rather different view. Had this happened then Catholics today might hold a very different set of beliefs about whether birth control is a serious sin, or even a sin at all. It is worth while wondering why Augustine reached the conclusions that he did, for the answer is perhaps surprising.

We have seen that for the first few hundred years of the Church's life its beliefs were challenged by a number of heretical religions. One such creed was Manicheanism, founded by the prophet Mani in about A.D. 250. The Manichees had an elaborate doctrine in which the universe was divided into 'light' and 'dark' regions, together with a complicated story of creation and the origin of man. Their religion distinguished very clearly between sexual intercourse and procreation. Sexual activity was good and desirable, almost an end in itself. The creation of children, by contrast, was not desirable and the Manichees made deliberate efforts to avoid conception, curiously enough by the use of the safe period. The Catholic Church reacted violently against these Manichean ideas. It was well prepared to denounce the heresy in very strong terms.

Foremost in this denunciation was St Augustine, and there were few better qualified than him to do so. For eleven years he had himself been a member of the Manichean Church. Until he was almost thirty he had lived with a woman, by whom he had had one child. However, on his conversion to Catholicism he set out to correct the errors of his former faith, particularly in relation to the purpose of marriage. In his most famous work on the subject, a book entitled *Marriage and Concupiscence*, he roundly condemns the use of 'poisons of sterility' (contraceptives), even when used within marriage. Those who use an 'evil deed' or an 'evil prayer' to prevent conception are married in name only. He also mentions abortion, and there is no confusion in his mind about the difference between the two. He regards them as quite distinct and he condemns them both. Interestingly enough, in Augustine's view, the foetus does not receive its soul and become truly alive until it has been forty days in the womb. Nevertheless, to obstruct it at any stage is wrong, but he does agree that abstinence from intercourse is not in itself a sinful act.

Although the teaching of Augustine is one of the most important statements of the Catholic Church on birth control, it is not of course the only one. By 1230 the Augustinian view was being restated, and the emphasis changed somewhat. A decree issued by Pope Gregory IX states that:

If anyone to satisfy his lust or in meditated hatred does something to a man or a woman or gives something to drink so that he cannot generate or she conceive, or offspring be born, let him be held a homicide.

It appears that the sinfulness of contraception is not now primarily to do with the use of marriage, but rather with a type of murder which results in preventing the birth of an as yet unconceived child. Contraception as a form of homicide is therefore another, later rationalization of the Church's teaching. Yet a third has to do with the fact that birth control is 'contrary to nature'. This is a view expressed by St Thomas Aquinas among others. Since the 'natural purpose' of intercourse is procreation, then deliberate interference with this process results in an unnatural and therefore sinful act. By the same token, intercourse in any position other than the 'natural one'—in which the woman lies on her back— is also a sin, and a serious one. However, the 'natural' argument breaks down somewhat when the woman in question is sterile or beyond childbearing years. Is intercourse against nature in these cases? The school of St Thomas finds answers to this question, but only after much thought and discussion. It would be easy for us to find analogies between this type of reasoning and the legendary debates of the Schoolmen about how many angels can dance on the head of a pin, but as late as 1930 in the Encyclical of Pius XI entitled *Casti Connubii*, to which we have already referred, the idea of contraception as contrary to nature again appears.

It is not our purpose to analyse the Catholic Church's opposition to birth control any further. Suffice it to say that contraception has been viewed as either equivalent to murder, contrary to nature or detrimental to marriage (or all three at once). And we might also note that within very recent years we have seen no fundamental change in the Church's view, though what we have seen is the development of organized resistance to these well-entrenched ideas, arising from within the ranks of the Church itself. Although we shall in our final chapter attempt to predict the future of contraceptives, to predict the future attitudes of the Papacy towards them would be rash indeed.

Birth control is not the only aspect of human life that the Church has sought to ban in its long history. Another is witchcraft, and it is more than a coincidence that for many thousands of years witchcraft and sorcery played an important part in shaping man's ideas about his fertility.

The Catholic Church has always been opposed to the use of any form of sorcery. It has never been lawful to employ magic to achieve any end, even if the intention is a good one. There is no such thing as 'white magic' as far as Catholicism is concerned. But sorcerers, unlike priests, have always been with us. Much of the cave art of Paleolithic times probably had a magical purpose. By drawing a picture of a man capturing a bison the intention was to will the event to happen again in the future, not just to record it as a happening from the past. Throughout many centuries men thought to be endowed with special powers have been venerated. Their help has been sought and they have been asked to use their magic to achieve some desired aim. Such beliefs are clearly contrary to any form of Christianity which teaches that it is the will of God and not the intervention of man which makes things happen.

Particularly interesting from our point of view is the connection between witchcraft and infertility, and the way that the Church regarded it.

Since the Devil is more powerful than man, and a man can obstruct the generative powers by means of frigid herbs or anything else that can be thought of, therefore much more can the Devil do this since he has greater knowledge and cunning.

This sentence appears in a work published in 1486. It was written by two Dominicans, one the Dean of Cologne University, and it clearly shows that in the late fifteenth century, at least in Germany, contraceptive methods were known and used. However, the work from which it comes is not a medical text, nor is it a guide to moral conduct. It is a handbook for the discovery, trial, and punishment of witches.

It was in about 1260 that the Church began actively to punish those engaged in sorcery, and then only those sorcerers who also preached heresy came under attack. By 1451 the situation had changed, and Pope Nicholas V decreed that sorcerers could be punished even though they were not obvious heretics. Seventeen years later it was decided that sorcery (or more correctly witchcraft) was so serious a crime that the ordinary legal rules did not apply, and in 1484 the final condemnation was forthcoming in the form of a Papal Bull issued by Pope Innocent VIII. It deplored the spread of witchcraft in Germany. The Bull states that:

It has come to our ears that members of both sexes do not avoid to have intercourse with demons, incubi and succubi; and that by their sorceries and by their incantations charms and conjurations, they suffocate, extinguish and cause to perish the births of women, the increase of animals, the corn of the ground, the grapes of the vineyard and the fruit of the trees, as well as men, women, flocks, herbs and other various kinds of animals, vines and apple trees, corn and other fruits of the earth; making and procuring that men and women, flocks and herds and other animals shall suffer and be tormented both from within and without so that men beget not nor women conceive; and they impede the conjugal action of men and women.

The year of the Bull's publication is a famous one in European history, for it marks the start of a relentless and hysterical campaign to exterminate witches wherever and whoever they may have been. The fight was waged for two centuries, during which tens, perhaps hundreds, of thousands of innocent people were tortured, forced to 'confess' and then executed in any one of a number of ways, of which burning was by far the most popular.

Within twelve months of the issue of the Papal Bull there appeared the most famous of all the works ever to be written on witchcraft. It is a book called *Malleus Maleficarum* (*The Hammer of Witches*), and from it comes the earlier quotation. It is a comprehensive guide for inquisitors, and it lists all of the evils that witches are known to perform. The Malleus is littered with references to sexual intercourse, both natural and unnatural, that the accused were supposed to indulge in. Intercourse with the devil comes very high on the list. The blasting of fertility, both of crops and animals, but more especially of human beings, is another of the witches' most common occupations. There are several different ways in which this might be brought about. One of the witches' supposed powers is the ability to make the penis disappear altogether by casting a 'glamour' over it. Only the witch herself can restore normal sexual activity by making it reappear, and only rarely is she inclined to do so. As well as rendering a man's penis invisible, she could also apparently prevent its erection. In addition, witches could render women sterile. The Malleus tells us that:

It is to be noted also that impotence of the member to perform the act is not the only bewitchment; sometimes the woman is caused to be unable to conceive, or else she miscarries.

Taking the Malleus and the Papal Bull together it seems that the clergy of the late fifteenth century regarded witchcraft as evil first because of its rejection of God and worship of the Devil, but also (and only slightly less important) because of its very strong sexual overtones. But if an interrogation is sufficiently long and unpleasant most people can be induced to confess to anything that the accusers have in mind. Certainly many of the inquisitors involved in the trials of European witches seem themselves to have been obsessed with obtaining every last detail of, for example, the experience of having intercourse with Satan. To a large extent the confessions seem to amount to the accused agreeing to, and indeed enlarging upon, suggestions put to them by their inquisitors. Thus it seems that many witches confessed, not to what they had actually done, but rather to what the sexual fantasies of their celibate accusers imagined them as doing. When viewed in this light witchcraft seems to be a psychopathology—a sickness sometimes of the witch, but more often of the inquisition. Once the normal process of law is suspended and imagination is given a completely free reign, the possible consequences are almost unlimited.

The so-called production of impotence by the witch can be explained in terms of imagination. We now know of many reasons, both physical and psychological, why a particular man might be sterile. How easy it would have been for the sufferer to blame, for example, his failure to achieve an erection, not on his own mental state but on some neighbour with whom he had quarrelled and who was obviously bewitching him. The same is true of a woman who has never been able to conceive, or who has suffered from a series of abortions. It would be easy enough to look around and find a scapegoat—a witch who had a grudge against the family and was deliberately restricting their fertility. If the crops failed or the hens failed to lay the same explanation would also come to mind.

Is this then the true explanation of a belief in witches; is it simply the attributing of one's own physical shortcomings and an externalizing of one's own sexual fantasies on to some unfortunate and often half-witted recluse, who because he or she was 'different' (usually old and living alone), was therefore a natural target for distrust and suspicion? Many modern historians do see the two-century-long witch-craze in these terms. To them the witches who were killed had little in common with each other except that they were obvious targets for ridicule and persecution.

However, there is another school of thought, founded largely by the late Margaret Murray, which points out that not all confessions were extracted under torture. Some were given voluntarily. The striking feature of so many of these confessions is that their details are all very similar. The sexual acts which are described, though performed at different times in widely differing areas, all follow the same general pattern. From this and other evidence Margaret Murray concluded that Medieval witchcraft actually represented the last traces of an extremely ancient religion which had the worship of fertility as its basis. As she herself says:

Looked upon in the light of a fertility cult, the ritual of the witches becomes comprehensible. Originally for the promotion of fertility it became gradually degraded into a method for blasting fertility, and thus the witches who had once been the means of bringing prosperity to the people and the land by driving out all evil influences, in process of time were looked upon as being themselves the evil influences and were held in horror accordingly.

This view was originally put forward in the nineteen-twenties, and there are few historians or anthropologists who would today accept it without reservation. It is too all-embracing, implying as it does that one religion lies at the basis of all witchcraft's many aspects. Even if there were independent evidence for the existence of such a cult, it would have to have been enormously widespread and have covered the greater part of Europe. In addition, the transition from fertility magic, which had good intentions, to witchcraft (an activity which is always evil in its objectives) is not at all convincing. Margaret Murray's view is unacceptable largely because it goes too far.

Almost certainly there was no single, ancient religion responsible for the widespread worship of fertility, but what there does appear to have been are a large number of independent European fertility cults, which in a sense were no less important in shaping men's views and beliefs about fertility and its control. Indeed 'cult' is perhaps the wrong term for it suggests a belief or religion distinct from man's everyday experience, But nothing could be further from the truth. Concern about fertility must have had a profound influence on our ancestors' day-to-day living, and ways of trying to ensure it must have formed an integral part of all their normal daily activities.

We referred in the first chapter to the widespread worship of the Earth and the sky. The rain falling on the ground makes the crops grow, and it was perfectly natural for prehistoric man to liken this process to the fertilizing of the Earth mother by the male god of the sky. Paleolithic men were no less concerned with human fertility. From many different parts of Europe we find small, exquisitely carved female figurines— Venus figures as they have come to be known. In all of them the sexual organs are accentuated, and in most cases the figure is that of a pregnant woman. Here art and magic are fused into one.

Phallic worship was also extremely common before the birth of Christ. From Assyria to Scandinavia there is evidence of the existence of phallic cults. The Cerne giant, a male human figure 200 feet high carved out of the chalk in Dorset suggests that phallic worship was also practised in Britain during the first few centuries A.D. Many psychologists see male symbolism in less obvious sources. The Scandinavian gods

Thor and Odin were warriors. One carried a hammer and another a spear, both of which have been regarded as phallic symbols by some authorities. In addition, although there is much controversy over the origin and real significance of the maypole (which was very commonly found in Europe until quite recent times) it is not difficult to imagine that it too originally had phallic overtones.

When faced with such beliefs the policy of the Catholic Church has always been to assimilate and alter them. The month of May became dedicated to the Blessed Virgin Mary. There was still cause to celebrate but the purpose of the celebration was completely altered. With witchcraft, however, there could be no compromise, no assimilation. By its very nature witchcraft was held to be evil. And yet it seems very likely that many of those burned as witches served a useful purpose in the community. This is true not only of the scholars, doctors and lawyers who were indiscriminately accused and killed, but of the much greater number of ordinary people, many of them old or middle-aged women, who were also made to suffer.

Some, for example, were midwives. In the Middle Ages the profession had fallen a long way from the respected position that it occupied in the time of Soranos. The midwife was badly paid and often ridiculed. And the profession was a dangerous one. If a child was stillborn then the obvious reason was negligence on the midwife's part. In the sixteenth century when the craze to destroy witches was becoming frenzied, the charge was not one of incompetence but of deliberately bewitching the mother to make sure that the child would be born dead or malformed. The midwife was thus in danger of the accusation of witchcraft at every birth that she attended.

But why should she want the child to die, before or shortly after birth? Apart from sheer vindictiveness she could be accused of a commercial interest. The body of an unbaptized child was considered to be a valuable commodity. The fat from the body formed the basis of a number of potions, amongst them the famous "flying ointment" that the witch could use to annoint herself before flying off to the Sabbat. There are on record cases where an innocent midwife has been bribed to obtain a baby's body. There is also the famous fifteenth-century Spanish story of *La Celestina*. . .' a past mistress in the concoction of cosmetics, and in patching up the troubles of maidens, and also a procuress and something of a witch'; and Celestina's friend Claudine who had practised for sixteen years as a midwife and who ran a flourishing business in corpses. So great was the fear that the midwife might interfere with the child that licenses issued in 1675 to allow the practice of midwifery stated specifically that the midwife should exercise no form of witchcraft, charm, sorcery or invocation contrary to the law of either God or the King.

The reference to Celestina who patched up maiden's troubles is an interesting one. It is clear from the context that she was an abortionist, and it can be inferred that as well as aphrodisiacs she also supplied contraceptive potions. Though no details are given they probably consisted of herbal mixtures which might also have contained magical ingredients. The recipes may have owed something to Avicenna, but it is impossible to tell. Almost certainly they would have no real contraceptive value, but what is important is that women should be prepared to buy them and use them. At a time when the Church was vocal in its condemnation of contraceptives they were still being obtained from illicit sources. As well as acting as midwives, some of the women later to be accused of witchcraft were also supplying potions against pregnancy. We can therefore see them in something of a new light. The blasting of fertility that they produced might often have been in response to a specific request from a client. The 'wise woman' with allegedly supernatural powers may have played an important role in the history of contraception in Medieval Europe.

It is clear from the Malleus that the Church realized that such activities were going on. However, Church authorities distinguished between natural and supernatural means of limiting fertility. The use of witchcraft to induce sterility was regarded as even more vile than its induction by more natural means. We read in the Malleus that 'A man can, by natural means such as herbs, savin for example, and other emmena-gogues procure that a woman cannot generate or conceive. . . .' We are also told of those 'loose lovers who, to save their mistresses from shame, use contraceptives such as potions or herbs that contravene nature, without any help from devils. And such penitents are to be punished as homicides. But witches who do such things by witchcraft are by law punishable by the extreme penalty.' Again a sexual basis for the persecu-tion of witchcraft becomes apparent.

Having said that medical men in the fourteenth century would have been familiar with the works of Rhazes and Avicenna, and that Albert the Great discussed birth control in his theological works in 1150, does not necessarily imply that a knowledge of contraceptive methods was widespread among ordinary people. On the contrary, knowledge of any form was slow to spread in Europe even amongst scholars. Even longer did it take to percolate down to the level of the ordinary man in the street. The writings of Arnold and Gaddesden bear witness to this fact. Although the desire to prevent the birth of children may have been strong, the means of doing so would have been in the hands of very few. We have suggested that as far as the common people were concerned the local wise woman played a more important role than the doctor or the scholar in providing the information and the means of birth control. Indeed early in the sixteenth century Paracelsus said that he had learned more medicine from these women than from the recognized authorities on the subject. It was not until later in the sixteenth century that the situation started to change. It was only then that ideas about fertility and the prevention of fertility started to go through their own long-awaited period of renaissance.

CHAPTER FIVE

The Renaissance and After

THE sixteenth century was important in the development of many areas of human knowledge. It was a century of awakening. The explorers, the Cabots, Magellan, Columbus and Drake, found new routes to the East and a new continent in the West. Arts, science and philosophy all flourished. Trade and manufacture boomed as never before. And printing was invented. Soon the Caxtons and the Gutenbergs were followed by the Aldines and Elseviers. But beneath the surface in this new and seemingly glorious era, things did not change so fast. Poverty, misery, ignorance and superstition remained. This is something which is often forgotten, for history usually gives more consideration to the aristocracy and the merchants, whose lives were rich and luxurious. So far as population policies were concerned, it was, of course, this élite who considered the question and created the policy.

Thomas Malthus produced his *Essay on the Principles of Population* at the end of the eighteenth century; and he has often been credited with having done something quite unique, in giving consideration to the problems of population growth. In fact, his ideas were not new—and he admitted as much. The number of writers who discussed population during the seventeenth and eighteenth centuries is very large. Many had ideas which could be termed 'Malthusian'. That is, they worried about overpopulation and the misery it caused, and they considered ways in which the growth might be checked. However, more writers were concerned with how to stimulate growth, for it was a time when nations were expanding, and every one of them wanted to be larger, more glorious and ever more populous. They began to equate people with wealth—and came to the conclusion that the wealth of a country *is* its population. At the beginning of the period most ideas were based on traditional theology, rather than any new thought. It was agreed that God, in his wisdom, would provide. The Catholic Church continued to extol celibacy, and the Reformation, also basing its decision on theological grounds, commended marriage.

Many writers put forward ideas not unlike those found in Greece. As Plato had favoured population control in his ideal State, so it was with Sir Thomas More who had population firmly in check in Utopia. Families there were to have between ten and sixteen children each—and any surplus or diminution would be taken care of by a system of migration. Machiavelli, hundreds of years before Malthus, had commented that excessive population would be diminished by war and disease. But political conditions, endemic diseases and sometimes their own nationalism brought the writers of the day to think more about possibilities of stimulating population growth. At a national level no one seriously needed to think about population control at a time when war and disease were such common occurrences. This explains why war, pestilence and migration were the only ultimate checks to gain serious recognition.

So great was the apparent danger that classical policies were reintroduced. There were rewards for fecundity and disincentives to celibacy. Henry IV of France observed, with remarkable perception, that the strength and riches of kings consists in the number and opulence of their subjects. His Government therefore encouraged population growth and sought agricultural development and improvement, further to strengthen and enrich the country. In 1666 France enacted an adaptation of the old Roman law. Most European countries encouraged marriage and taxed the unmarried. Royal and noble families celebrated their joys and satisfactions by providing dowries for poor women. As late as 1796, Pitt urged aid for large families in England, in order to make the large family a blessing and to 'draw a proper line of distinction between those who are able to provide for themselves by labour and those who, after having enriched the country with a number of children, have a claim upon its assistance for support'.

This attitude was fairly typical, in a world where expansion and growth were the keynote of the age. It was not always an attitude typical of the English, however, In the Elizabethan era a great dread of overpopulation manifested itself, and in the late sixteenth and early seventeenth centuries the English went through a phase of worrying about how many people the islands could sustain. Perhaps the general wretchedness of the population was more apparent at that time than ever before or since. The Elizabethan poor law was enacted, and although colonial expansion had begun it affected but few people. One writer at the time recorded that some men already thought that England was overpopulated, and that young people marry too early and fill the country with beggars 'to the hurt and utter undooing of the commonwealth'. Some 'also do grudge the great increase of people in these daies, thinking a necessary broode of cattell farre better than a superflouus augmentation of mankind'.

By the time of James I, the bishops were ordering their officers to delay the issuing of marriage licences. By the time the parish had taken its time dealing with the banns, a long period had elapsed. The intention was that a couple should not marry until the man was at least 35 and the woman 30 years old. But these rules were laxly enforced and teenage girls still produced broods of sickly children to the concern of those who were worried about the problem.

However, increasing colonization and prosperity slowly brought a change in attitude. There were periods of enormous sexual licence at the end of the seventeenth century, and until 1754, when the Marriage Act was introduced, pre-marital sex was the rule, rather than the exception. The attitude toward illegitimacy changed too. There had been punishments for women who became unmarried mothers, and in some countries they were extremely severe. But some humanitarians counselled for the modification of such punishment. After all, they argued, to bear an illegitimate child is bad enough. In time the penalties were made less severe and in some countries they were removed altogether. So eager were the upper classes to see the growth of the nation, that they took the unusual step of providing foundling hospitals. In a reaction against Calvinism and Puritanism, they even tacitly approved of the games connected with the maypole and the chalk figures on the downs—games which gave occasion to great sexual excesses.

It was in the seventeenth century that the science of demography made its first appearance. By the reign of Charles II, 'political arithmetic' had begun to develop, and birth and death rates were calculated and compared. The exercise gave rise to problems, and controversial issues. Among the early discoveries was a reason to oppose celibacy on statistical grounds. Every man who remained celibate denied some woman the chance of having a husband. This lack would lead the left-over women into promiscuity and vice, which in turn would lead to abortions and secret murder. It was the same author who investigated the birth rate in London, and discovered that the population of that city doubled every sixty-four years. At this rate of increase, he decided, one couple '. . . Adam and Eve, doubling themselves every 64 years of the 5,610 which is the age of the world according to the Scriptures, shall produce far more people than are now in it'. However, he rejected the idea. His conclusion was more theological than demographic: 'The world is not about one hundred thousand years older, as some vainly imagine, nor above what the scriptures make it.'

Although English practices and ideas did not vary greatly from other European countries in methods of encouraging population growth, the rules seem to have been less strict, possibly because the limit to population was seen in relation to the relatively small land area available. Few Englishmen emigrated, except to the colonies, and England has never had a problem in attracting sufficient immigrants. One writer who took a long view of the situation was Sir Walter Raleigh. In his *History of the World* he observes that the Earth would be full to overflowing, were it not for the effect of hunger, pestilence, crime and war, and of abstinence and 'artificial sterility'. He also noted that some men marry rich and older women—another factor that would limit the fertility of the marriage. Elsewhere he noted that Spain had not become depopulated despite having many colonies. It contained as many people as before—as many as the land could nourish.

But demography was only one of the subjects which was to influence Renaissance man's view of himself. Another was medicine. It is generally said medicine's own renaissance dates from 1543, the year in which Vesalius published his work *On the Structure of the Human Body*. For medicine, it was not the rediscovery of ancient learning that brought greater understanding, it was new investigation. Practically no advance had been made in the study of anatomy from the second to the sixteenth centuries. Corpses were hard to obtain and dissection was forbidden by the civic authorities. There seems little evidence that religious prejudice, which is usually blamed, really had very much to do with difficulty of study in anatomy. In Bologna the students were responsible for collecting cadavers and for paying any expenses incurred. In 1442 the city assumed the burden of responsibility, but even so, the only available corpses were those of criminals born at some distance from the city. At best there were only one or two dissections a year, and virtually all of them were on male bodies.

Even on the occasion of a dissection, very little knowledge was gained. The Professor sat aside, and read aloud from Galen, whose authority was accepted without question. The Professor would expound hypotheses which he had culled and learned by heart from the Classics, but of which he had no personal knowledge. Whilst he talked, the dissectors would go about their work. They had no way of knowing what they were doing, in fact, as they knew no Latin, and it was impossible for them to follow what the Professor was saying. Thus he would be discussing one organ whilst they were demonstrating another. The grossest errors were possible – and the errors that Galen and the other ancients had made were nourished and kept alive.

A picture in Guy de Chauliac's *Chirurgia Magna* shows a group of students gathered about their professor. He points to a normal uterus and holds a book in his other hand. Perhaps the cause of their amazement and the prayers being offered by one of the group, is that the uterus is lacking the seven horns which Galen assures them it should have. It is clear that for many years doctors simply did not believe the evidence seen by their own eyes. A professor of anatomy working in 1430 was so astonished when he found a uterus without horns, that he recorded it as an anomaly.

It was the development of printing that was largely responsible for the circulation of new medical ideas, but the process was not a rapid one. With the invention of movable types, books became more widely available. Various estimates have been made as to how many books were printed in the fifteenth century. It is thought that some 800 medical and scientific volumes were published. At first, the approved ancients were prepared and circulated, but even these were edited, and when there was a dicussion of some controversial topic, such as contraception or abortion, it was often censored. Changes slowly began to come about, and some brave souls tried to force new knowledge into circulation, but the upholders of the *status quo* did not give up easily. Might was on the side of the upholders of tradition. Paracelsus was not forgiven for insisting on lecturing in his own language, German, rather than the scholarly Latin. He became even more hated when he burned the works of Galen and Avicenna. Vesalius, for his audacity in asserting that the uterus has but one cavity, was subjected to such strong opposition that he burned his own notes and papers and for a time gave up his studies of anatomy altogether.

Anatomists made various discoveries about the circulation of the blood long before Harvey was born, but they did not dare to say much about it. Indeed, when Harvey made his own study of the subject, even he dared not publish it during the reigns of James I and Charles I, as he knew only too well that nonconformists were usually misunderstood, often persecuted, and if the offence was thought serious, they were imprisoned, banished or killed. Medievalism continued to exist as a real force in the minds of men. Even the innovators, trying to think independently and to record facts, were themselves hard put to it to combat the effect of work which had been established for hundreds of years and which formed the basis of their own training and education. Even they could not free themselves from some superstition, and beliefs in astrology and numerology persisted. In addition the dread of an accusation of witchcraft flourished as never before.

The effect of the enormous power wielded by the older

order was that many workers refrained from publishing what they knew, for fear of the retribution which would have followed. The result was that many books which were published at the time do not present a true picture of the state of the knowledge of the time. It was safer and paid better to write about all manner of inane but safe topics. Many important works remained secret, whilst work of a more popular and acceptable nature became the best-sellers of the age. These were often written in question-and-answer form, and very seriously set about answering such burning questions as " Why is man the only laughing animal?" and " Why do babies have blond hair?"

Guy de Chauliac's *Questionary of Chirurgeons* discusses anatomy in a question-and-answer form. Apart from locating the genitals, it gives a very vague description of their structure and does very little else. De Chauliac wrote his book in the fourteenth century. Two hundred years later, Culpeper used the same style. He adopted (or was credited with) the pseudonym 'Aristotle' and *Aristotle's Book of Problems* deals with as many questions about the process of reproduction as he could think up. Much of what the has to say dates back to Classical and Medieval authorities, and his work was still popular throughout the eighteenth century. Whores, he informs us, are never pregnant because 'diverse seeds corrupt and spoil the instruments of conception for it makes them so slippery that they cannot retain seed, or else 'tis because one man's seed destroys another'. Perhaps he was unfamiliar with that short but eloquent word that defines a prostitute's illegitimate offspring. The reason why twins are born is given strictly according to Galen. The several receptacles of the womb are the cause. The trio of uterine horns on the right side engender boys, and the left, girls. He goes on to explain that the seventh horn is the source of hermaphrodites. The conclusion he draws is rather quaint. Instead of questioning any of these statements he observes that 'If a woman should have more than 7 children at once, it should be rather miraculous than natural.'

For the various reasons, political, moral and conformist, writers in the seventeenth century avoided writing about contraception, and in the eighteenth 'manners' began to forbid it. A great many books contain discussions of how to ensure conception, rather than how to avoid it. Some of the causes of sterility which were documented are rather curious. 'Bleedings' or 'letting blood' was a very common medical practice, and seems to have been used to combat all sorts of conditions. Culpeper advised against bleeding young girls before puberty, as he thought this practice led to barrenness. Another author was more worried about the practice of bleeding men, and in *De Morbis Foemineis; The Womans Counsellour: the Feminine Physitian etc.*, which was published in 1686, he observed:

But amongst other causes of barrenness in men, this also is one that maketh them barren, and of the nature of eunuchs, the incision, or cutting of their veins behind their ears, which for a disease many times is done.

This, saith Hippocrates, causes barrenness in them, whole veins behind their ears are cut, to which Galen agrees; for he saith that especially more than from any other part of the body the seed flows from the brain by those veins behind the ears, which also Aristotle confirms. From whence it probably appears, that the transmission of the seed is impeded by the section of the veins behind the ears, so that it cannot at all descend to the lower parts of the body, or else very crude and raw.

One cannot but help wonder how many libertines would have tried this novel form of vasectomy. The passage also demonstrates the continuing reliance on the ancients, and the disregard for the newer scientific discoveries.

The moral aspects of contraception were considered by a great number of writers. Many were unable to separate contra-

. Galen dissecting a pig. During the renaissance traditions died hard, especially traditions in medicine. Galen, the greatest of classical anatomists had flatly declared that the uterus had seven chambers.

. The Doctors and medical students in Guy de Chauliac's illustration of a post-mortem seem to be aghast to find that this particular uterus has only one chamber. What are they to believe— five hundred year old tradition or the evidence of their own eyes? *Both pictures by courtesy of 'The Vellcome Trustees.'*

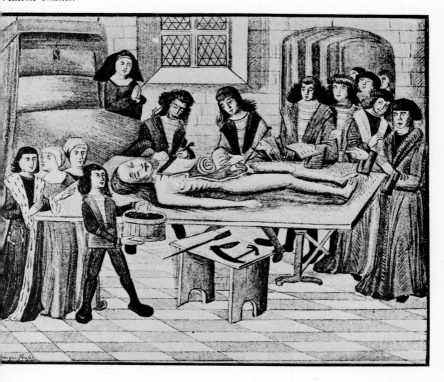

9. Revd. Thomas Robert Malthus
Malthus has been described as the unwilling father of the birth control
movement. Malthus was not a 'Malthusian' but he diagnosed the evils of an
excessive and uncontrolled birthrate. However, he proposed an impossible
solution in his reliance on late marriage and abstinence.

ception from abortion—and of those who could see the difference, it seems that they had no great desire to draw any fine distinctions. If a process prevented children from being born, however it may have acted, it was generally regarded as murder. In Spain, an exceptional writer called Diego Matheo Zapata produced a *Dissertacion medico-theologica*, which discussed the theological aspect of administering contraceptive drugs to a woman in danger of death from a fourth pregnancy. But sympathetic treatments of the subject are rare.

The moral aspects of contraception received very full discussion in a work by Daniel Defoe, entitled *Conjugal Lewdness, or Matrimonial Whoredom. A Treatise concerning the Use and Abuse of the Marriage Bed*. Defoe said that this book was written over a period of thirty years. Its main theme is the achievement of perfect marriage through a blend of sexual and intellectual love—without which there is merely 'matrimonial whoredom', a kind of legalized prostitution. Defoe takes to task those who, as Raleigh had mentioned, marry older women. He has entire chapters on the evil of 'Marrying at unsuitable years' and on "Unequal matches, as to the disproportion of age, and how such, many ways, occasion a matrimonial whoredom". Another chapter is devoted to the dangers "Of Marrying, and then publickly professing to desire they may have no CHILDREN, and using Means physical or diabolical to prevent Conception." '

Defoe points to the error of such ways, and refers to childless wives as 'Barren Does'. He mentions 'a merry club, called The Assembly of Barren Does'. We do not know whether such a club existed or whether it is just a literary device but Defoe recounts a supposed conversation between a 'barren doe' and her cousin, who had been married for seven months, and had so far avoided pregnancy. The cousin was anxious to remain childless. They discuss abstinence, which the barren doe seems to favour, though the young wife rejects. They

D

then have a long chat about potions which may be taken by mouth and act as abortifacients. The barren doe seems reluctant to part with any real information, and keeps pointing out that contraception and abortion are murder. Eventually, she reveals the 'medicine' but omits to include the 'main and most dangerous ingredients'. According to Defoe, 'It was indeed a devilish one'. It must have been, for on taking the less-dangerous ingredients, the lady became very sick, 'and in a word, set her a vomiting and purging most violently, and that threw her into a high fever'. Conscience stricken, and at death's door, she repented, and gave up her ideas on family limitation.

In his disapproval, Defoe lists some of the practices which women use to avoid childbearing. Apparently they even go as far as diabolic means, not confining themselves to 'the human art, to the help of drugs and physicians, whether astringents, diuretics, emetics, or of whatever kind, nay, even to purgations, potions, poisons, or any thing that apothecaries or druggists can supply'. If drugs and medicine fail, 'she will call to the devil for help, and if Spells, Filtres, charms, witchcraft, or all the powers of hell would bring it about for her, she would not fail to use them'. He goes on to quote the instructions given by quacks, offering medicines by which women may miscarry at various stages of pregnancy, and another potion, by which a man may ensure that the pregnancy is preserved, even at the cost of the life of the mother. Writers of the period were taking a new view of women—and of the possibilities of ideal marriage. Defoe stands out in his time as a man who faced the issues and actually discussed the problems of childbearing. Even though he was opposed to its prevention, he had given the matter a long period of thought.

More typical were writers like Culpeper, who was also opposed to birth control, but who wasted no time in discussion. His books are simply devoted to how to ensure conception. *Aristotles Compleat Masterpiece* remarks:

Tho' there are some that desire not to have children, and yet are very fond of nocturnal embraces, to whom these directions will be in no way acceptable, because it may probably produce those effects which they had rather be without: yet I doubt not, but that the generality of both sexes, when in a married state, have such a desire to produce the fair image of themselves, that nothing can be more welcome to them than those directions that may make their mutual embraces most effectual to that end.

He goes on to discuss ways in which conception may be assured; and gives details of how to recognize when conception has taken place, for it seems that many women do not recognize the early stages of pregnancy and rush to the doctor for a strong dose of medicine, which brings about an abortion. He warns the husband against withdrawing too quickly after intercourse, as this made it possible for 'cold to strike into the womb'—a most dangerous occurrence. The woman should rest on her right side, and avoid sneezing, coughing or making any violent movement. Nor should intercourse take place too often—'grass seldom grows on a path that is commonly trodden'.

Apart from general fitness, a good diet and contentment, regular and healthy menstrual periods were thought important. This is easy to understand, since it was commonly supposed that conception was likely to occur at about the time of menstruation and most people thought that the best chance of conception came one or two days after the bleeding stopped. If anyone had seriously taken all of the advice, they could have remained childless for years. Infrequent intercourse, occurring mainly around the time of menstruation would have raised the odds against conception to a very marked degree.

The number of books giving advice on how to conceive suggest that conception was perhaps difficult. Possibly, as in Roman times, irregular menstrual bleeding was common. There are many recipes for medicines to bring on menstruation and such recipes were not restricted to medical works. *The Compleat Housewife: or Accomplish'd Gentlewoman's Companion* which was in its third edition in 1729, advises:

To procure menses: Take a quarter of an ounce of pure myrrh. Make into a fine powder. Mix with three-quarters of an ounce of conserve of bugloss flowers. Two days before your expectation, take this quantity at four times, last at night, and first in the morning. Drink after each time a draught of posset-drink made of ale, white wine and milk and boil in it some pennyroyal, and a few camomile flowers.

The next recipe, with unconscious humour, is headed 'To stop flooding'. Sir Kenelm Digby headed his recipe 'To bring down a woman's courses in an instant'. This sure-fire and speedy method involved using a sediment to fumigate the uterus. Doubtless some of the medicaments described would have effectively caused an abortion but one wonders how many women were burned, scalded or otherwise injured by the use of these and similar methods.

Culpeper's only direct discussion of ways to achieve child-lessness comes in his *Directory for Midwives* in which there is a chapter headed 'Of Barrenness against Nature'. He observes that:

It is not our physicians opinion alone that many women are made barren by diabolical means. I do not call them diabolical because they cannot be acted without invocation of evil spirits, but because they are done by abuse of nature; for as the right use of natural things is from God, so the abuse of them is from the devil.

The next paragraph is very obscure, and seems to suggest that the clergy are in some way to blame in bringing about this barrenness. However, he tells us, other authors have left ways in which such mischief may be prevented. These include a lodestone, the heart of a turtle dove, or a piece of St John's Wort, carried as an amulet; or a 'whole squil' hung over the bed. But if the mischief has already been done, 'the cure is easy, and was done by the man only making water through his wives wedding ring, so there was one superstition helped another'.

One could go on multiplying the examples in which superstition and an insistence on retaining established ideas held up real scientific progress. But there were innovators and a few accurate notions were coming very slowly to the fore. We have already traced the origin of the rational approach to the work of Vesalius. Although his investigations were not the last word in the detailed and accurate study of human anatomy, he had made a beginning, and he had laid a basis on which others could build. One of those who followed in his footsteps in this new, systematic study, was his pupil, Gabrielle Fallopius.

Fallopius was the first person accurately to describe the human oviducts—which eventually became known as the Fallopian tubes. His other observations were equally important. He gave the first precise description of the clitoris, and the skeletal system of the foetus; he introduced the anatomical use of the term 'vagina'. He may also have originated the term 'placenta'; certainly he was among the first to use the word. Apart from his studies on the reproductive system, he was interested in certain features of the digestive tract, and he did a vast amount of original work on the ear and nervous system.

But Fallopius was more than a man who simply studied corpses and described structures. He was also a practical man, and a working physician. It is not surprising therefore, that he concerned himself with the diseases that were both dangerous and widespread in his day. The trio of diseases responsible for the short life-span of Renaissance man were leprosy, plague (the 'Black Death') and syphilis. We cannot say how many people suffered and died from the effects of syphilis. But we do know that the other two diseases were responsible for a massive number of deaths. In the two years 1348–50 it is estimated that a quarter of the population of Europe died: about 25 million people. Boccaccio, describing the plague in Italy, estimated that 40,000 died in Genoa, 60,000 in Naples, and 96,000 in Florence.

So far as syphilis was concerned, the doctors of the day had little knowledge of ways of preventing its further spread, nor of doing much to cure those already infected. The origin of the disease, it was generally agreed, was a punishment meted out by Apollo, on a shepherd called Syphilus. When Syphilus begged for forgiveness, the god saw fit to grant him a cure in the form of 'guaiac wood'—a remedy as mythical as the alleged origin of the disease. The quacks became prosperous, providing 'cures' for the complaint. One of them is said to have knelt before a statue of Charles VIII of France, remarking to a surprised priest 'To me, Charles VIII is a true Saint. He put 30,000 francs in my pocket when he brought syphilis to France'. The effect of the disease on fertility may be judged from a consideration of the life of Henry VIII of England. Despite having six wives, who managed to produce 11 pregnancies between them, only three resulted in living children. Of the three, Edward VI survived only into his teens, before dying of tuberculosis and the effects of congenital syphilis; Mary was apparently infertile, and only Elizabeth was apparently healthy.

Fallopius' method of fighting syphilis was in the nature of preventive medicine. He described an invention to guard against the infection—a simple linen condom. The condom was cut to the shape of the end of the penis (the glans), and Fallopius suggested that the man should wash himself first, if possible, and then place it in position. The inventor pointed out that it had the advantage of being small and very portable, and would be no great inconvenience, carried about in the trouser pocket. A clinical trial which had been conducted with 1,100 men had been successful. None had become infected.

Very few writers have been inclined to give much credence to Fallopius' claim that he invented the condom. Most have spent considerable time proposing alternative origins for the device. Although Fallopius was certainly the first to mention the sheath it does seem possible that it is one of those objects which could have been 'invented' a number of times in different civilizations and in different circumstances. Fallopius' invention was a guard against syphilis. Today, we know that condoms have many forms and uses. We regard them mainly as a contraceptive device: but we also have condoms which are roughened, and intended to heighten erotic pleasure. The ancient Egyptians regarded condoms as a garment—sometimes the only thing that they wore. Today, penis sheaths are in use for many non-contraceptive purposes. They may have an enormous number of functions and differing significances to the wearers. They can be worn for protection against disease or injury; used as badges of rank; or even worn for some reason of modesty. They appear in places as geographically remote as the Himalayas, New Guinea, the South Pacific, Latin America and Africa. They are not necessarily discarded when 'civilization' reaches these areas, but may continue to be worn, but under the trousers. They seem to be a universal answer to a variety of needs, which very different kinds of peoples have found. The vast distances which separate the appearance of this phenomenon would suggest that the discovery has been made anew and in isolation, rather than just being a copy of what has been seen elsewhere.

In 1597 Hercules Saxonia recalled that Fallopius had invented the linen condom. He further suggested that it could be improved by soaking it in a chemical solution several times, and allowing it to dry in the shade. Several other authors discussing syphilis mentioned the sheath and its impregnating solution during the seventeenth century, and thus it passed into the medical literature concerned with the prevention of the disease.

In addition, however, it also became known as an extremely valuable means of birth control.

Previous writers have expended an enormous amount of time and ink in their speculations on the origin of the condom as a contraceptive. One problem is that no one has found any satisfactory way of explaining how the word was ever derived. It seems to have originated in England. Some have looked for Latin and Greek roots, and even Persian origins have been brought into the discussion. Others have looked to a town called Condom in France. However, it seems unlikely that the British, who first used the term would have been aware of the existence of the place. Many authors have decided that it must have been a proper name, and at some point the story became established that the contraceptive had been invented by a man named 'Condom' who was a soldier, courtier or doctor, at the court of Charles II. The device was a great boon to the King, who was at the time somewhat put out at the number of illegitimate children he was managing to father. The stories usually go on to describe the joy of the King, who was so pleased that he promptly knighted 'Condom'. The latter, however, suffered so much infamy that he was forced to change his name. Despite an enormous volume of research, no one has ever found any evidence either to support or deny this story. Some have managed to complicate it, and have suggested all sorts of alternative spellings. Indeed, there was no agreed way of writing the word in the early days of the condom's history. But whatever the spelling, its popularity was assured.

One witness before the first English Birthrate Commission testified that condoms were in use in London at the time of the Great Fire (1666), although no one knows on what evidence the statement was made. The glans sheath was certainly used in Paris in 1655, and the French sources of that time also refer to a number of alternatives, such as withdrawal, and other forms of incomplete intercourse. The contemporary literature begins to abound in references to the new invention. But not everyone was carried away with enthusiasm. Madame de Sévigné is said to have described the condom as 'armour against enjoyment and a spider web against danger'. Whether or not it was she who said it, it became an often-quoted saying, and one with which many seem to have agreed. Birth control was a matter which she took very seriously. She was alarmed at her daughter's health, and worried about the ill-effects of bearing too many children. Her letters contain a good deal of advice, and some warnings to her son-in-law. One letter contains a puzzling reference to something she simply calls 'les restringens'. These are apparently quite unknown in Provence, where her daughter is living. They seem well known in Madame's circle, though. The news that they are not available in Provence seems to have come as a great surprise, and Madame wonders how the poor husbands manage without them. It is possible that she may have meant some kind of potion, or an astringent solution to be placed in the vagina in order to contract the mouth of the cervix.

Linen condoms were mentioned by a notorious quack in London, in the first decade of the eighteenth century. He omitted to give the exact recipe for the solution in which the sheath should be soaked. However, his advice cannot have been of great value by that time, for condoms made of gut were by then also available.

Much of the early description of the condom is in the form of poetry. Several poems as early as the first decade of the eighteenth century discuss them, and their opinion is favourable. The first poem is entitled *A Scots Answer to British Vision* and it mentions the 'sirengue and condum' for preventing and curing venereal disease. *Almonds for Parrots: or, a Soft Answer to a Scurrilous Satyr, call'd, St. James's Park: With a Word or two in Praise of Condons* welcomes the happy invention, which is already being retailed in London Streets, including the Mall and St James's Park.

By 1716, Joseph Gay's *The Petticoat* mentions that:

> The new Machine a sure defense shall prove,
> And guard the sex against the harm of love

However, some feel that this could equally well refer to the hooped petticoats. Less ambiguous are *The Potent Ally* and the even more famous *Panegirick upon Cundums* which says:

> Happy the man, who in his pocket keeps,
> Whether with green or scarlet ribbon bound
> A well made c——m.

For more than half a century the poets happily versified in this fashion. Though little great poetry emerged the results are mildly amusing. One such poem, *The Machine* published in 1744 is of more interest for its frontispiece, which shows a shop where the devices are manufactured and sold. One is being inflated, presumably to test it for holes. The poem also mentions a lady who made a fortune by collecting up the used items laundering and re-selling them. Our forefathers do not seem to have been very particular in these matters, and another cartoon, dating from 1773 shows an auctioneer selling off a young man's effects, including a quantity of condoms 'not the least the worse for wear'. The auctioneer mentions the name of the manufacturer and retailer of the condoms. She was a certain Mrs Philips. Mrs Philips's 'machines' were the subject of several cartoons. One by James Gillray shows an auctioneer in the East Indies. His papers and equipment rest on a large parcel, stamped with her trademark, and reserved 'for the use of the supreme council'.

There were a number of ladies involved in the condom trade in eighteenth-century London. In fact, it seems to have been an exclusively female occupation. There may have been more than one Mrs Philips. Indeed, it has been suggested that there could have been as many as three of her namesakes in the business. They are certainly difficult to sort out. One may have been working as early as 1701. Another must have started trading in about 1731, and after thirty-five years, she seems to have retired for a decade, and then re-entered the trade, because her former customers were not so well satisfied by the other sales ladies. On returning, she opened a shop near Leicester Square. Either she or one of her namesakes had a shop for many years at the Green Canister, in what is now Bedford Street, off the Strand. The street was called Half Moon Lane originally, and the Green Canister was advertised as being the seventh house on the left, entering from the Strand. This particular business was later taken over by Mrs Mary Perkins.

All of the ladies ran advertising campaigns, and produced handbills. The Mrs Philipses seem to have been great exporters, and sent goods to France, Spain, Portugal, Italy and other foreign climes. They also built up a wholesale trade, supplying chemists, apothecaries and druggists. They welcomed 'ambassadors, foreigners, gentlemen, and the Captains of ships'. The handbills circulated by Mrs Philips all ended with a little jingle, which they assured the reader was very applicable to the goods:

> To guard yourself from shame of fear,
> Votaries to Venus, hasten here;
> None in my wares e'er found a flaw,
> Self preservation's nature's law.

To which she adds 'Letters (post paid) duly answered'.

Some condoms of the kind that the ladies sold were found in recent times in a large English country mansion. They were examined by various experts. They were found to be of three different sizes and were wrapped in packets of eight. They were very thin—only 0·038 mm, as against 0·060 mm for a modern, thin rubber sheath. They were rather stiff and would have needed softening before use. However, we know that the users dipped them in water first. Boswell, on one occasion mentioned that he dipped his in the Serpentine. The sheaths were made of the caecum of a sheep, and this information is in accord with earlier authorities who described the manufacturing method.

An account from *A new description of Merryland* by 'Roger Pheuquewell Esq.' describes them as being made of an 'extraordinary fine thin substance, and contrived to be all in one piece, and without a seam, only about the bottom it is generally bound with a scarlet ribbon for ornament'. The process of manufacture has also been documented in other sources. It involved soaking the membrane in water and various chemical solutions for some time, and then careful scraping, to extract the mucus membrane. The remaining peritoneal and muscular coats were then exposed to the vapour of burning brimstone. Finally, they were washed with soap and water, blown up, and dried. They were then cut to length and suitably ornamented.

Many of the eighteenth-century 'experts' on venereal disease had things to say about the sheath. The earliest seems to have been Daniel Turner, who in 1717 mentions that the condom is 'the best, if not the only preservative our libertines have found out at present'. However, it was not entirely popular, since many 'say it blunts sensation', and 'acknowledged that they often chose to risk a clap, rather than engage "with spears thus sheathed" '. Others did not hesitate in damning the device. Joseph Cam thought that it was merely propagating wickedness to tell men to 'use *machinery* and fight in *armour*'. Such things should not be allowed in a Christian country.

It seems that the majority of medical opinion did not welcome the invention. Some said that they opposed it because it was ineffective as a shield against infection. Others took a

moral tone, and opposed anything that allowed pleasure without penalties. Some give the impression that they would rather
men became infected. Perhaps they feared a depletion of their
patients. The great contemporary authority Girtanner said that:

'they diminish pleasure and annihilate the natural end of cohabita-
tion: they are insufficient to ensure immunity, for the least hole
will permit contagion, and again, it may happen that during coitus
the membrane may tear by a strong strain'.

He was outraged that the condoms were sold 'openly, in
London, Paris, Berlin and St Petersburg. The negligence of
the police, who do not seek to prevent the sale of an invention
so shameful and so detrimental to repopulation, is, in truth,
inconceivable'. One is left wondering how it was that if the
condoms were so frail and useless they managed to present
any problem to anybody's programme of repopulation.

The doctors had their say—and recorded it all. One wishes
that some of the libertines and 'lewd persons' had commented
a little more. There are the poems, of course, and a few other
humourous accounts, but in the main, the Restoration rakes
and the aristocracy seem to have had little to say on the subject.
Neither, for once, did Samuel Pepys. His French equivalent,
Bachaumont, quotes from a letter written by Linguet, an
advocate, who apparently became infected in a brothel. The
Madam reproached the 'lady' who was a former ballet dancer,
for not using the condom as she had been taught. Madam
ended her diatribe with the words: 'You know the use of the
condom. The condom, my daughter, is the law and the
prophets.'

A writer who used condoms and was not ashamed of the
world knowing it, was Casanova. He writes of the 'English
overcoat . . . that wonderful preventive against an accident
which might lead to frightful repentance' and of 'the preser-
vatives that the English have invented to put the fair sex under

shelter from all fear'. How eager the French and the English
are to shift responsibility on to each other, especially when the
'responsibility' is for something not quite decent. For years,
syphilis was the 'French caries' and the condoms are still
'French letters' to many of their users.

Casanova makes it clear that his motive in using the sheath
was to protect his partner from pregnancy, rather than to
protect himself from infection. One edition of his *Life* has an
illustration which shows him inflating a condom, one of the
best ways to check if it had any holes. On this occasion, however, he seems to be doing it to amuse the onlookers. On All
Saints Day in 1753 he stole a Viennese nun's 'provisions' from
her secretary, and substituted a poem. But he was sufficiently
moved when she begged him to return them, and gave back:
'That which is so precious to a nun who wishes to make
sacrifices to love'. In a Marseilles brothel he refused the proffer-
red condoms because the quality was too ordinary. Superior
ones were brought—the kind sold only in dozens. He bought a
dozen and seems to have been quite satisfied. The worst he
can find to say about them is that he does not 'Care to shut
myself up in a piece of dead skin in order to prove that I am
perfectly alive'.

Boswell similarly describes his encounters, which took place
in the London Parks, and once, rather incongruously, upon
Westminster Bridge. His use of the condom seems to be much
more for his own protection, however. He reported being
very worried the day after he had encountered a young lady
who assured him that she was perfectly safe, and begged him
not to use his 'armour' as 'the sport was much pleasanter
without it'.

The Marquis de Sade said that the vaginal sponge, the
condom and anal intercourse were three well-known ways of
avoiding pregnancy. Naturally he expressed a preference for
the latter.

The vaginal sponge seems to have made its first appearance in the seventeenth century. In this case it seems that we really can blame (or credit) the French, from whom the idea seems to have been borrowed. The satirist Mathurin Regnier mentioned finding one, along with a collection of other contraceptive and protective devices, in a whore's room in the year 1660. It seems to have taken a hundred years for the first written reference to appear in England. Around 1690 a collection called 'The Duchess of Portsmouth's Garland' attacks a lady unkindly called 'our Monarch's whore from France' and refers to the import of richly wrought dildoes and 'new fashion'd spunges to clear her twat from slimy sperm and whites'. A New Description of Merryland also mentions it, in 1740. By 1786 a French aristocrat explains that it should be wetted with a mixture of water and brandy. The liquid, he explains, acts as a spermicide. Finally, it was advocated by Jeremy Bentham, who seems to have been told about it by his friend, the Reverend Joseph Townsend, a Methodist minister who was widely travelled. Bentham writing of the increase of the poor wrote:

Rates are encroaching . . . You . . . are, I think, for limiting them . . . but how? Not by a prohibitory act . . . not by a dead letter, but by a living body; a body which, to stay the plague would . . . throw itself into the gap; yet not . . . be swallowed up in it. When I speak of limitation, do not suppose that limitation would content me. My Reverend friend, hurried away by the torrent of his own eloquence . . . let drop something about a spunge. I too have my spunge; but that a slow one, and not quite so rough a one. Mine goes, I promise you, into the fire, the instant you can shew me that a single particle of necessity is deprived by it of relief.

Himes, who discovered this passage, suggests that by 'dead letter' Bentham meant the condom. Although the use of the sponge would be a very slow remedy for widespread pauperism, it would not be such a strain as abstinence. At the end

Bentham says that if anyone can show him a better way of reducing poverty, he is quite willing to discard this remedy.

Although the sixteenth and seventeenth centuries saw the introduction of the two principles which were to offer the major means of birth control—male and female barriers—it is strange that the idea of trying to kill the sperms by some chemical means seems to have been lost. There were none of the herbal pessaries, so popular with the ancients, to block the path of the semen, and kill it by chemical action (unless of course, such recipes were kept secret and passed on through families in an oral tradition). When herbs and medicines are considered at all, they seem to be potions and decoctions to be taken orally. Ben Jonson's question, in the year 1609, received a very direct if uniformative answer. 'And have you those excellent recipes, Madame, to keep yourselves from bearing children?' brought the reply: 'O, yes, . . . how should we maintain our beauty else? Many births of a woman make her old, as many crops make the earth barren.' Certainly the respondent seems assured that they have a safe method, but we have no way of knowing what it involved. Most writers indicate that such medicines as there were, were taken by mouth. The Jewish 'cup of roots' had not died out, and reports during the eighteenth century show that it was still given to Jewish women when medically indicated.

With one exception conscious attempts to kill the sperm by chemical means were not made until later. This is not so surprising when one considers the painful slowness with which scientific investigation proceeded. Sperms may possibly have been seen by Roger Bacon in the fourteenth century. He seems to have studied a variety of cells through a system of simple lenses. However, his revelations were not received with enthusiasm. His colleagues simply refused to believe him, and also omitted to check the truth of his statements by making their own investigations. The whole subject was dropped until 1677 when Leeuwenhoek, or rather one of his students, discovered the 'little animals' in semen. He described and drew pictures of both normal and abnormal sperm, and by 1678, a year before this news had been published, discovered that the addition of rain water deprived the sperms of motion. It took almost a full century before Spallanzani added the information that vinegar also inactivates them quite effectively.

In early days little credence would have been given to the power of water to kill sperm. Many thought that water either had a fecundating power of its own, or that it could form a medium for sperm transport. Sir Thomas Browne commented on a case in 1646. The story was told by Averroes of a woman who 'conceived in a bath, by attracting the sperm or seminal effluxion of a man admitted to bath in some vicinity unto her'. 'I have scarce faith to believe;' says Sir Thomas, 'and had I been on the jury, should have hardly thought I had found the father in the person that stood by her. 'Tis a new an unseconded way in history to fornicate at a distance. . . .' Clearly Sir Thomas himself thought that sexual intercourse was necessary for any conception. He also thought that distance and water would kill the male seed. But others were less critical, and still repeated the stories that women had been made pregnant by nocturnal emissions from men sleeping nearby; or that one woman had been made pregnant when caressed by a female friend, who had just come from having sexual relations with her husband. When Spallanzani began to work on these things, he chose to study toads and the confusion became even greater, since of course, toad spawn is fertilized in water.

Although serious medical scientists had long since stopped believing in the fecundating power of the air, during the eighteenth century a clergyman produced one of the bestsellers of the age, which postulated an aerial origin for spermatozoa. This theory does not seem to have been taken seriously by many biologists, but the writer was not alone in producing such ideas. A contemporary put forth the intelligence that 'the whole extent of the air . . . is full of the seeds of everything that can live on earth'. The theory was used in a devastating attack on the Royal Society, when Sir John Hill produced a parody of the style of their *Philosophical Transactions*. The parody describes how a machine was built—'a wonderful cylindrical, catoptrical, rotundo-concavo-convex machine . . . hermetically sealed at one end, and electrified according to the nicest laws of electricity. It was erected facing west, in a convenient attitude to intercept the floating Animalcula, which were prolific in that direction.' The result was that he caught a number of tiny men and women, and fed them to his Chambermaid in a chemical preparation. Astonished, she became pregnant. Some people were able to treat such things as a joke. Many, however, took it all very seriously. Poor Sir Thomas Browne felt that he had to deny the possibility that the incubus and succubus devils were able to take sperm from sleeping men and use it to impregnate women.

In general, scientific progress was slow from the sixteenth to the eighteenth centuries, but at least a scientific basis was created on which work would eventually proceed. Of paramount importance was the creation of a vocabulary in which these subjects could be discussed. Apart from the terms coined by men like Fallopius, words such as 'Gynaecology' appeared, around 1600. At the same time descriptions of the female genitalia were revised to begin with a consideration of the external organs. Previously, the description had begun with the "matrix" and moved down. The ovaries were seen to be part of the system, and were named in 1662, when van Horne decided that 'ovary' was a more satisfactory term than 'female testicle'. Soon, it was also found that the ovary contained large numbers of ova, and many more specific studies then began. Although these were innovations that had little immediate impact, they were to be of tremendous significance for the later development both of gynaecology and of birth control.

CHAPTER SIX

Nineteenth Century Advances

JANE AUSTEN used to stay at 64 Sloane Street when she came to London to visit her married sister. If her spirit had returned to the house in recent years she would probably have been surprised, and yet have approved of the changes which had taken place. No longer a private house, the building has been in turn the Headquarters of the Family Planning Association and the International Planned Parenthood Federation. She said of the house that she liked to stand on the first floor landing, a position which offered her a fine view into the sitting-room, as well as the stairs and entrance hall. The sitting-room has for some years now been a library and one would imagine that today, she would certainly have gone in to discover a little more about what can be done to improve the health of mothers and their children.

She herself was quite certain that having too many pregnancies was damaging to the health of the mother. 'Poor woman! how can she be honestly breeding again?' she once wrote. In a letter to her niece, she commented on a friend's pregnancy 'poor animal, she will be worn out before she is thirty'. Although she remained a spinster, the number of children born to her friends was something in which she took an interest. Like Malthus, she saw late marriage as beneficial, and was glad that the niece did marry late. 'You will be quite young in constitution, spirits, figure and countenance,' she told her, 'since confinements and nursing make women grow old'.

Apart from late marriage, the only other measure she knew (or cared to specify) was abstinence. 'Good Mrs Deedes!—I hope she will get the better of this Marianne, then I wd. recommended to her and Mr D. the simple regimen of separate rooms'.

Jane Austen described the problems of women in her time, and yet she seems to have known only those remedies which were neither easy nor very acceptable. She was writing in the early nineteenth century and even now it seems difficult to look back at this era of comparatively recent history and understand the great problems which have beset the progress of birth control from that time.

The medical history of contraception during the last two centuries, that is to say the study of the development of the methods themselves, is an area which has lacked very much close consideration. Most writers have turned rapidly to an examination of the social philosophers and the propagandists who favoured birth control and we too shall discuss these people in the next chapter. It is important to recognize that they had an enormous effect on society and they did change the whole way of life and outlook of many people. But it is equally important to recall that it was during the nineteenth century that effective means of contraception were first mass-produced, making them sufficiently widely available for the majority of people to benefit.

The struggle for the universal acceptance of birth control is still progressing. The subject has been an almost continuous source of controversy for the last 170 years and one begins to doubt whether it will ever really end. Much of this discussion could be categorized by saying that never have so many found so much to say about a subject on which they knew so little. Unfortunately such a statement also refers to a large sector of the medical profession. Looking back, it seems amazing that anyone could have ever thought of contraception as a medical subject until the last few decades. It was a medical concern during the lifetime of Soranos and Rhazes but from then on, until the twentieth century, a very small minority of medical men ever had anything to do with it. It was only occasionally that the topic was mentioned in the medical press and when it was, opposition was usually very strong.

We have already examined the comments of eighteenth-century medical writers on the use of the condom. The nine-teenth-century doctor was an equally firm upholder of tradi-tional morality, and the British Medical Association took the line that the least said the better. Birth control was therefore ignored as much as possible, but whenever it did gain such ground as to call for some comment, the attitude was almost invariably hostile. When, in 1879, Dr C. H. F. Routh came to write an introduction for the reprint of a paper he had given at Bath the previous year before the Obstetrical Section of the British Medical Association, he found it necessary to explain quite carefully how it was that he ever came to speak of such a subject in the first place.

It was desired by some distinguished members of the profession to open the discussion, so as to offer them a public opportunity of condemning, with no uncertain sound, baneful practices which they knew had been making their way into this country. A disreputable work had been largely circulated and was producing a curse upon the land. It was felt by several of our profession that it was unwise to remain silent when vice, clothed in a misnamed Malthusian garb, and so transformed to deceive many, was put forward as a new virtue to be practiced. I confess I felt somewhat diffident in taking the duty upon myself, not that I ever doubted that the evil prevailed and should be put down, but because there was not want-ing some good men, who thought it was impolitic to speak openly, and especially before a meeting of the Association on so indecorous a subject. . . .

Too indecorous for the obstetricians; one wonders what terrible vices were sweeping the land.

Onanism was a crime, was sorely punished in consequence, but now-a-days, science has devised other fraudulent aids. Nor will I dwell upon them. Suffice it to say that Onan's crime is imitated; coverings are used by the males, plugs and injections by the females to complete their shame. It is almost defilement even thus cursorily to allude to this vile practice.

The vices then are exactly those which are used today— withdrawal, the condom and some form of occlusive pessary, methods in fact all known and used in the sixteenth and seventeenth centuries. But the nineteenth century saw vast improvements in the design and production of these last two forms of contraception. In addition the earlier part of the century saw the introduction of the vaginal douche, a method of rather dubious value, that was first described by the American physician Charles Knowlton. Two other means of contraception, neither of them new, were also to receive much fuller consideration than they had in the past. One was the concept of the 'safe period' and the other was the intra-uterine device, known more generally today simply as the IUD. To take up this last topic we can do no better than refer to Dr Routh.

It has been reserved for some of our own people to discover a fifth method. In a debate before the Medical Society of London, last session, on the use of intra-uterine stems, devised originally for uterine disorders, we were credibly informed that they were also used by some ladies of high position and continually worn by them with a view to *prevent* conception . . . to find them placed in proper position and with this intent implies the assistance of a person of some skill, and shows to what a degree of degradation some men have fallen. The question presents itself—Who put them there?

The method, of course, was far older than Routh knew. Indeed, it is far older than most people today suspect, for the story of intra-uterine devices serves to show how well buried the history of a method can become. It also shows the importance of developing a precise vocabulary, and defining the terms in which these subjects are discussed.

In 1959 the IUD was greeted as a new idea—a device virtually without a history. The new development came about after the publication of two papers describing the use of the method in Israel and Japan. The investigators in those countries had been using the method for thirty years. Prior to that time, it was recalled, a similar device had been recommended by a German doctor called Graefenberg. He in turn had developed his device from an earlier instrument, called a 'stem pessary' which was supposed to have been invented in the nineteenth century, and was also supposed to have been very dangerous.

Examination soon reveals that 'stem pessary' is a generic term, rather than a description of any one particular instrument. In fact there were hundreds of stems, of slightly differing shape and size. This could be explained in terms of the use made of them. As Routh stated, they were originally used for curing uterine disorders. They were supposed to encourage fertility in some cases, and were inserted to offer the sperm easier access to the cavity of the uterus by 'opening up the way' and holding open the cervix. The position of the uterus was thought to be very important to fertility, and some stems were inserted to correct any tendency of the womb to lean, however slightly, in either direction. They were also used in case of prolapse (the condition in which the womb bears down on the vagina) and the stem was supposed to prop it up and relieve the pain and dragging sensations. A stem pessary is basically a mushroom-shaped object—a button attached to a stalk—yet a great number of pessaries of quite different shapes were classified along with them. Some of the 'pessaries' did not enter the uterus at all. They consisted of balls, or egg-shaped, spiral or saddle-shaped objects, which rested in the vagina. Over the course of the years, many of these pessaries had stems added to them.

Vocabulary certainly becomes a problem when trying to make any sense out of this somewhat macabre collection of devices and the literature that concerns them, Although, during the Renaissance, medical men did begin to define their terms, no one seems to have bothered to define the word 'pessary' in any useful way. The word itself is derived from the Greek, and in its original form it means a pebble or small stone. Some writers have pointed to the custom found among some groups of oriental farmers and travellers of putting stones into the uteri of their livestock and female camels to prevent unwanted births. However, it seems unlikely that the European IUD originated in this way. The key to its origin is to be found (if indeed it can be found at all), only by examining the very extensive literature on pessaries that was produced particularly in the nineteenth century.

Unfortunately in this literature, the word can have a great range of meanings. It depended only upon what the writer wanted it to mean. It encompasses anything from a mass of herbs pounded into a lump or inserted in a little bag, to an extremely wide variety of mechanical contraptions. Take for example the simplest shape—a ball. Doctors from the time of Hippocrates and Soranos used this shape as a simple measure to shore up a uterine prolapse. The ball pessaries used by the Greeks were made of string and wool, but later authorities used wood, ivory, metal and other substances. Although such a pessary was widely known as a form of treatment, it was known to Casanova as having quite a different use. He mentions the use of such balls as contraceptives. He acquired three of them, made of gold, and he seemed to think that soaking them in an alkaline solution added spermicidal power. He was wrong in this latter respect but he nevertheless says that he found them effective during a fifteen-year-period of use, and that they never became displaced during coitus.

It is sufficient for the ball to be at the base of the temple of love when the loving couple carry out the sacrifice. The antipathetic power given to this metal by an alkaline solution in which it has been placed for a certain time prevents all fertilization. But, says the friend, movement may displace the ball before the end of the libation. . . . This is an accident which need not be feared, provided one exercises foresight. . . .

Medical literature abounds in references to similar balls, yet no one ever seems to have suggested that they had a contraceptive use until 1931, when an American doctor referred to them as 'block pessaries' and called them a 'curiosity'. She said that they were now obsolete but that at one time they had been used as means of birth control. Cases were described in which women had suffered from internal damage, as a result of wearing such devices over long periods of time.

After the ball, perhaps the next most simple shape is the tube. The hollow leaden sounds used by Hippocrates were intended to cure uterine disorders, and Hippocrates was more precise than many of the doctors who followed him, for his oath explicitly states 'I will not give anyone a pessary to procure an abortion'. Devices of this form reappear over a thousand years later. The first reference we have found in the European medical literature dates from 1296 when Lanfranchi of Milan recommends the use of a stem 'if the cervical orifice is closed and does not permit the passage of sperm'. From that time onward, the literature contains many similar statements. Many of the doctors who wrote books describing their method made some reference to such devices, and gave explicit instruction on how to make them. It has been said by more than one author that some midwives and practitioners in the Middle Ages suffered serious penalties for their practice of inserting these stems into the pregnant uterus in order to procure abortion. However, with the prevailing confusion of the day, when only the very knowledgeable drew any fine distinction between abortion and contraception it is possible that the punishment was administered as much for the latter as the former offence.

By the seventeenth century, there are dozens of reports of pessaries in use all over Europe. A Dutchman, Hendrick van Roonhuyze described one in 1663, and at the Hotel Dieu in Paris, Barthelemy Saviard, a respected surgeon, who was with the hospital for seventeen years, advised patients to 'mis un pessaire de liege bien garni de cire, pour empecher la rechute . . .' and to use 'un pessaire d'acier, tel que je l'ay decrit allieurs'. Other doctors experimented with different shapes, and with different materials, sometimes covering a hard pessary with wax or soft leather to prevent pain or uneasiness. Some of the pessaries were themselves made of wax, and it escaped no-one that other ingredients could be added during the preparation. In this way, all of the traditional theories could combine in the method of treatment.

A good example of this thinking is found in the mid-seventeenth century when a popular writer comes to discuss uterine prolapse, generally known as the 'descent' or 'the falling down of the matrix'. Descent, great or small, was brought about by 'a frequent bringing forth of children, miscarrying, bringing away a dead child, some fall from on high, hard riding, or immoderate dancing'. However, most commonly, the condition was brought about by 'too much moisture in that part'. A drying diet and bleeding were first prescribed. Purges were forbidden, but vomiting thought helpful. A purge would draw 'humours' to the affected area whilst vomiting would take them away.

The next part of the treatment is true 'wandering womb' therapy, for the uterus was to be put into position and bathed with mollifying fomentations, after which 'Yea, apply stinking things to her matrix, as assafoetida, galbanum, castor and stinking pisse; but to the nose, hold sweet things, as musk, civet and amber'. After further treatment 'to dry up the slimy humour and expel the wind' a pessary is prepared from:

Emplastrum pro matrice pitch gummi laranne, trochisch de Gallia Moschata, the powder of red roses, red corall and acorns.

These ingredients are made into a mass with wax, and spread on a piece of leather, cut into a convenient form. There is no indication of what a 'convenient form' might be.

More specific, however, are the surgeons, and a good example is found in the work of Scultetus, whose seventeenth-century '*Armamentarium Chirurgicum*' went through many editions and was produced in many languages. Illustrated in the book is a stem pessary which looked exactly like any of those manufactured in the 1920s. Scultetus devotes some time to discussing the technique of using such a device and he recommends that the 'candle (which must have a basis)' be made of wax and assafoetida.

The technique started a controversy, even in those early days, for some people observed that such a stem interfered with conception. However, William Sermon in the *Ladies Companion* of 1671 affirms the opposite. Having described the necessary treatment, he says that the pessaries

'are never taken out (except they please); which pessaries keep the womb in its right place. So the women notwithstanding, do all their necessary employments and may as well be enjoyed by men in carnal conjunctions; do also conceive and carry their great bellies, and bring forth, which is affirmed by many authors, and not unknown of late to myself.'

'Aristotle' as always, had something to say on the subject. To the usual mixture of wandering womb therapy and pessary lore, he adds

'and put pessaries into the bottom of the womb, that may force it to remain. I know some physicians object against this, and say they hinder conception: but others, in my opinion, much more justly affirm, that they neither hinder conception, nor bring any inconvenience; nay, so far from that, that they help conception, and retain it. . . .

The controversy was unresolved, despite which the devices continued to be used. During the nineteenth century they reached the height of their popularity among doctors, and presumably among their patients, too. It is odd, and even a little frightening, to think that in such a recent period of history, this aspect of medicine was such an amalgam of Galenism, superstitition and sheer Victorian eccentricity.

A feature which made nineteenth-century gynaecology more eccentric than it might otherwise have been was the lack of women doctors. The *Lancet*, greeting the New Year of 1878, passed an observation on 'the vexed, and, as we cannot help thinking, somewhat contemptible movement, to transfer women from their true sphere, and violate the laws of decency, by making them medical practitioners'. On following the controversy a little further (through the correspondence columns, which were by far the most interesting and illuminating part of the journal) it emerges that one of the main fears of the elderly male practitioners was that the ladies would have to have some knowledge of the male genital apparatus, and would have to understand its functions, ailments and infections and the treatments necessary to cure them. Although this idea seems to have thrown the gentlemen into a state of shock they seem to have found quite decent and proper their own obsessions with the female system.

Indeed some of them were so obsessed with it that any and every female complaint was ascribed one sole cause—uterine disfunction. More and more pessaries were used, to right the problem. In the mid-century, there was a period when no operations at all were carried out in some hospitals. Where an operation might normally have been thought of, a pessary was used. Uterine conditions were probably the most popular medical topic of the day and apart from the practitioners, who described their own experiences and inventions, the students also gave thought to the problem. Enough theses were produced on the subject to suggest that it was the most important single aspect of the entire history of medicine.

The result was a staggering amount of cumbersome verbiage Most doctors considered the devices as a means of curing sterility and relieving uterine conditions. We have no way of knowing how many devices were actually in use. Still less do we know to whom or even when it finally became clear that an intra–uterine device would effectively prevent conception from occurring. But an indication was given in America as early as 1866, when W. D. Buck, the President of the New Hampshire State Medical Society commented in a paper called 'A Raid on the Uterus':

A distinguished surgeon in New York City, 25 years ago said, when Depuyren's operation for relaxation of the sphincter ani was in vogue, every young man who came from Paris found that every other individual's anus was too large, and proceeded to pucker it up. The result was that New York anuses looked like gimlet holes in a piece of pork. It seems to me that just such a raid is being made upon the uterus at this time. It is a harmless, unoffensive little organ, stowed away in a quiet place. Simply a muscular organ, having no function to perform, save at certain periods of life, but furnishing a capital field for surgical operations, and is nowadays subject to all sorts of barbarity from surgeons anxious for notoriety. Had Dame Nature forseen this, she would have made it iron clad. What with burning and cauterizing, cutting and slashing and gouging, and spitting and skewering, and pessarying, the old fashioned womb will cease to exist, except in history. The Transactions of the National Medical Association for 1864 has figured 123 different kinds of pessary, embracing every variety, from a simple plug to a patent threshing machine, which can only work with the largest hoops. They look like the drawings of turbine water wheels, or a leaf from a work on entomology.

Pessaries, I suppose, are sometimes useful, but there are more than there is any necessity for. I do think that this filling of the vagina with such traps, making a Chinese toy-shop of it, is outrageous. Hippocrates said that he would never recommend a pessary to procure abortion—Nay, he swore he never would. Were he alive now he would never recommend one at all. If there were fewer abortions there would be fewer pessaries, and if there were fewer pessaries, there would be fewer abortions. Our Grandmothers never knew they had wombs only as they were reminded of it by the stuggles of a healthy foetus; which, by the by, they always held up, and if a baby accidentally gets in by the side of the machinery and finds a lodgement in the uterus, it may, perchance, have a knitting needle stuck in its eyes before it has any. It is the easiest thing in the world to introduce a speculum and pretend to discover ulceration of the os, and subject a patient to this revolting manipulation once or twice a week, where there is, in fact, nothing the matter. By some practitioners, all diseases which occur in the female are attributed to the uterus. In this class are especially to be included all such as make of the abnormal conditions of the uterus a speciality.

The first American patent for a device to prevent conception dates from almost 20 years before Buck made this comment. It consists of a drawing headed 'J. B. Beers. Preventing Conception. No. 4729, patented Aug. 28, 1846'. At that time, it was not the practice to publish a full, written specification. Sometimes there was only a diagram, and sometimes a very brief description. In this case the description reads:

What I claim as my invention is the particular combination of a curved loop attached to a handle by a spring joint, as described and for the purpose above specified.

The British boasted less than the 123 American varieties, but nevertheless there were many different kinds of pessary available in Britain. A number of them were on display at a 'Conversazione' held by the Obstetrical Society of London in 1866. The catalogues of surgical-instrument makers were full of such devices throughout the nineteenth and the first decades of the twentieth century. A great deal of confusion has ensued, because depending upon the type, such devices were used both as contraceptives and as aids to infertile women.

All of the true stem pessaries, however, had one flat, disc-shaped portion which remained in the vagina, with the stem of the instrument passing through the cervix and up into the uterus. Quite different in their design were the true intra–uterine devices from which the modern forms of IUD are derived.

In 1909 a Dr Richter of Waldenburg in Germany published a paper which described a 'thread pessary' which was for contraceptive use only, and which rested entirely inside the uterus. How pleasant it would be to imagine that this particular year represented a turning-point in medical history and that from that date on, devices which were truly intrauterine came into their own. It was, of course, not to be. Richter's report attracted little attention. During the same decade, other doctors produced papers on their use of the stem pessary as a contraceptive device in normal healthy women. One had inserted the device in more than 400 cases. A French doctor, writing of his visit to America described the ease with which he had been able to purchase such devices in many American cities, including those in New England and even in Canada, where contraception remained illegal until very recently. He observed that the stem pessary was the principal contra-ceptive method used by the American Malthusians.

In the nineteen-twenties, Graefenberg was inserting his completely intrauterine contraceptive rings, some of which consisted of gut (not unlike those made by Richter), some of which also contained rings of silver or gold, as the metal showed the position of the device on an X-ray plate. But again, al-though it had been realized that all that was necessary for effective contraception was a foreign body in the uterine cavity there was no fall-off in the use of stems. Dr Pust produc-ed a rather different kind of stem long after he had learned

Two pictures showing poverty in London. Crime and unwanted children were two of the commonest features of London life a little over a century ago. When Disraeli described the 'two Englands' he was contrasting the life of the affluent middle-class with the sort of scenes portrayed in these two pictures.

10. **Field Lane about 1840**

11. **The Drunkard's Children**

12. The Oneida Community 'Children's Hour'. 'We are not opposed to procreation. But we are opposed to involuntary procreation. We are opposed to excessive and of course, oppressive procreation . . . we are in favour of intelligent, ordered procreation . . . We believe the time will come when involuntary and random procreation will cease, and when scientific combination will be applied to human generation as freely and successfully as it is to that of other animals . . .' *First Annual Report of the Oneida Community*, February, 1849.

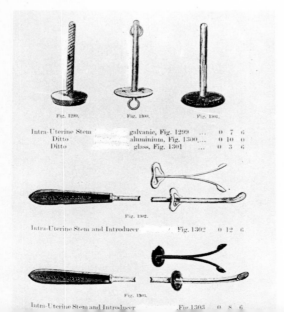

13. The changing face of the IUD. Some of the intra-uterine stems inserted into women in the nineteenth century with some of the applicators that were used to insert them.

of Richter's work. He retained the stem shape, with a button over the cervix, but made the 'stem' portion of gut and silk threads.

The whole IUD story presents a picture of confusion. Even in the nineteen-thirties, when intra-uterine contraception was being condemned as dangerous, most of the authorities seem to have had little idea of the difference between an intra-uterine foreign body and a stem pessary. Indeed, one of those who condemned the method seems to have been unable to distinguish between these two kinds of contraception and the use of a cervical cap. Much of the denunciation sprang from the fact that the devices were so little understood, and that even the practitioners of the time knew so little about them. Whether a device was an instrument to cure infertility or a contraceptive precaution was beyond them. Most of them guardedly announced that it was both, and charged large fees for its insertion or removal.

It is difficult for us now to imagine how much ignorance there was on sexual matters in the past even among doctors. But until very recently there was no organized corpus of medical knowledge. Every physician was very much a one-man band, and working by trial and error. This applied equally to other aspects of contraception. When Knowlton recommended the douche in the early part of the nineteenth century, his opinions were based on a very sketchy knowledge of reproductive physiology. He thought that it took a month for the ovum to travel the length of the Fallopian tube, and he saw menstruation as the preparation for conception rather than as an indication that conception had not taken place. Indeed for many years the menstrual cycle had been a subject of wonder or disgust, but it took a very long time for anyone to discover what it really involved. Some thought that it had something to do with the moon. By others it was treated as an illness. Jules Michelet—an historian of doubtful reliability—

E

recorded in 1859 that 'woman is forever suffering from the cicatrization of an interior wound which is the cause of whole drama. So that in reality for 15–20 days out of 28—one may almost say always—woman is not only invalided but wounded. She suffers incessantly the eternal wound of love.'

At the beginning of the eighteenth century biologists were attempting to understand the first principles of generation—how was a new individual formed and conceived and how did its development take place? They already knew of spermatozoa, which Leeuwenhoek and others had described and drawn, but little was established about the nature and purpose of these 'little animals'. Some classified them as a new species. Then too there was some knowledge of the ovarian follicles, which Regnier de Graaf had described in 1672. Two main schools of thought emerged, both affirming that spontaneous generation took place. One side was sure that the sperms were all that was necessary for conception. The other side was equally sure that the egg was the important material. It took some time for a third school to prevail with the notion that both substances were involved.

In 1824 Dumas and Prevost repeated some experiments which had been carried out by Spallanzani in the eighteenth century. They affirmed that when the spermatozoa were removed from semen, the filtrate lost its fertilizing power. The ovum was recognized in 1827 and the fertilization of frog spawn was also described in the same decade. But since almost all observations were made in animals, it is not surprising that most investigators regarded menstruation as being comparable to the 'heat' period seen in many animal species.

Such a theory was advanced by a Frenchman, Félix Archimède Pouchet, who was awarded a prize by the French Academy of Science in 1845 for his work on ovulation. He was one of the first to affirm that ovulation is spontaneous in women, that it is regular and that it occurs at a fixed time in the cycle. From his studies on mammals he announced:

Nous n'en doutons pas, avant peu les physiologists adopteront à l'unanimité que l'ovaire émet constammaent et spontanément les ovules qu'il secrétè . . . l'ovule est toujours émis a une époque fixe, qui est en rapport avec le rut, et il est émis au dehors independamment de toute fécondation. La fécondation offre un rapport constant avec l'emission de menstrues. Aussi, dans l'espece humaine, est-il facile de prié oiser rigoureusement l'époque intermenstruelle où la conception est physiquement impossible et celle on elle peut offrir quelque probabilité.

Unfortunately he was wrong in his final conclusion, which was that conception was most likely during menstruation and for the following twelve days, but he was outstanding in that he did regard his observations as providing a useful means of controlling conception. Thus he did not view his work merely as a scientific theory, or as the satisfaction of pure academic curiosity. Rather he thought that the information would influence the social order and would lead to 'great social and political changes in the nations'. Far from viewing this with any alarm, as most of his contemporaries would have, he was entirely optimistic about the kind of change which the control of fertility could bring. His findings were certainly adopted by several subsequent writers and there is also evidence that a number of doctors passed on the advice to their patients. The theory was adopted not only in France: it reached both Britain and the United States.

Some doctors and research workers had other ideas, and considered the possibility that the human body functions differently from the bodies of the lower animals. Their views do not seem to have been so readily accepted, but it is interesting to see that at least one doctor in England managed to come quite close to the truth. The London Medical Gazette of 1849 printed a paper by Dr Henry Oldham, the Obstetric Physician and lecturer in midwifery at Guy's Hospital.

Whilst lecturing on the problems he had encountered in inducing an abortion in a woman who had a contracted and scarred vagina, he observed:

You see, too, in the history of this impregnation another fact, that its DATE IS FIXED. Now I have taken some pains to be quite sure on this point: and I am well informed that the last day of her menstrual period was the 16th January—that sexual intercourse occurred on the 28th January— that it had not taken place for several weeks before, and has not been repeated since, and consequently she was impregnated twelve days after menstruation. This has an important experimental reference to the modern theory of genera-tion, which makes the menstrual period correspond with oestration in the lower animals, and limits the period of conception to a day or two before, and about eight days after the flux. During this time it is affirmed that an ovum has been spontaneously cast off from the ovary, and during the slow movement through the sexual passages, that it may be impregnated; but should it not be impregna-ted then the female cannot conceive until a day of two before the next menstrual or oestral time. The physical impossibility of preg-nancy during this interval is not blinked by the supporters of this theory. You see if this were true it would have a most practical bearing. It constantly happens that cases come before us where either from diseases of the uterus or pelvis, or sexual organs, or exhaustion from frequent abortions or protracted labours—that it would be most desirable to suspend for a time or altogether prevent pregnancy. And this might be done were this really a physiological law, and without imposing a much greater restraint on sexual indulgence than does the old Rabbinical law. But the truth is, that this theory has been prematurely shaped into a law, and it will not, I am sure, bear a practical test. I know of cases, which I have carefully enquired into, where impregnation has occurred at the respective times of ten days, twelve days and twenty-one days after the monthly periods; and while, on the one hand, I am quite ready to admit a greater disposition to impregnation shortly after a menstrual period, yet I know of no facts that disprove the opinion that the human female is susceptible of impregnation at any time between her monthly periods.

Slightly later, a French physician, Dr Avrard of La Rochelle, put forward a third theory, which differs from either of the others. He divided the cycle into three parts, called the 'menorrhagic, genesic and hypnotic periods'. According to him, fertilization could occur only during the genesic period, which he described as occurring 'after the excretory function of menstruation. However long the menorrhagic period lasts, the genesic period always ends on the fourteenth day after the onset of menstruation.' When considering amenorrhea— the absence of any menstrual flow—Avrard describes menstruation as 'the only way of ending a congestion which in many cases of amenorrhea, dissipates without flow. There is a physiological amenhorrea, that of nursing mothers.'

Neither Avrard nor Oldham seem to have created much interest with these revelations. Most doctors were far too busy refuting the absurd idea that menstruation and ovulation were in any way related. In 1878 a prominent medical man was postulating in the pages of the *Lancet* that menstruation was caused by the more rapid rate of growth found in female children as compared with males. This rapid growth, he said, slows during puberty but the body goes on producing blood at the same rate as before. The excess of blood in the body builds up such tension that when it reaches a certain limit, the delicate blood vessels of the uterus rupture and the excess blood is lost. This might have been a slightly more reasonable view if women had only one period, and that at puberty. Presumably the blood went on being produced at a rapid rate and the rupture of the vessels continued, apart from when, during pregnancy and lactation the blood was used to nurture the foetus or the baby. It did not escape their notice that such a process was quite unnatural. If a woman was constantly becoming pregnant and giving birth (as of course she ought to be) then the distasteful process stopped altogether.

By 1878 contraception was too disgusting a subject to soil

the pages of the *British Medical Journal*. Menstruation was almost as bad, but it did manage to sneak into the correspondence columns. The discussion began when one member asked if any of the others had information about the tendency of hams to rot, when prepared by a menstruating woman. In reply a physician observed that the hams did indeed rot, but only when the pig was female and was menstruating at the time of its slaughter; he was not aware that the condition of the cook had any influence. This kind of discussion went on for several months, one doctor after another adding his small bit of information, presumably culled from the local old wives. One even went so far as to suggest that the matter might be researched 'in lunatic asylums and prisons'.

Given this remarkable climate of opinion, it comes as no great surprise to find that the nineteenth century contains perhaps more than its share of eccentric ideas about the control of conception. The religious maniacs were much in evidence. Even in the eighteenth century, some sects had managed to find a religious excuse to practise outlandish customs, and the group founded by Eva Butler at Sassmannhausen is just one example. After the first initiation ceremonies, the female members of this group had to undergo a dangerous and painful operation on the Fallopian tubes.

A rather larger sect was the Skoptzies who originated in Russia. The name actually means 'the castrated' but they called themselves the 'White Doves'. The sect was an offshoot of another group who believed in flagellation. The Skoptzies first appeared in about 1757, and were condemned by the government for heresy. The cult members were sentenced to hard labour in Siberia. But this did not bring about any lessening of their fervour. Eventually one of the Tsars had the founder put into an asylum. The next Tsar had the man transferred to a hospital, but then a Councillor of State was converted to the sect, and the leader was freed. Soon there were

Skoptzies all over the country, and even at court. By 1873 there were more than 500 of them in Roumania conducting missionary work.

The Skoptzies were eager to fight against lax morals, and lived 'chaste lives' fasting and abstaining from liquor (and almost everything else, it seems). Their sexual doctrines were based upon the Bible, especially on Matthew 19: 12, which counsels: 'and there be Eunuchs which have made themselves for the Kingdom of Heavens' sake', and Luke 23: 29, 'Blessed are the barren'. They managed to discover quite a number of other texts in the same vein, and taking it all literally, the members undertook 'voluntary martyrdom' and mutilated their genital organs. The males referred to their genitals as 'the keys of hell' and the female organs were 'the keys of the abyss'. Converts seem to have been quite glad to lose them, though some fatalities were recorded from the procedure.

Mutilation of a less violent kind was thought desirable by some Malthusians who observed that infibulation (an operation to fix the foreskin over the end of the penis, which the Romans had used), was a simple procedure and offered an easy method of ensuring that the poor and undesirable males did not breed. Anthropologists were also discovering that some tribes applied a similar procedure to their women. Leicester Assizes were amazed during the trial of one George Baggerly to hear that in jealousy of his wife he had 'sewed up her private parts'. In 1894 the New York Academy of Medicine were told of a woman who had come from Germany and had been similarly infibulated. No one, except the doctor who reported the case (and she had apparently been examined by a number of doctors) had ever enquired about the holes through which a padlock was worn.

Male continence, a less painful expedient, was adopted by another religious group. This method resembles normal intercourse except that the male does not have an orgasm.

The couple remain in union for more than an hour, during which time the woman achieves satisfaction, but the man refrains from ejaculation. Detumescence is allowed to take place in the vagina. Such an activity is permitted by the Roman Catholic Church, but it is more often associated with the community founded by John Humphrey Noyes. The community was persecuted, and seven years after its foundation moved to Oneida in New York, which was then a frontier settlement. They practised a form of group marriage in which every man and every woman member were considered married to each other. The method of birth control seems to have been discovered by Noyes in 1844. It was of great importance to the community since any member was free to have sexual intercourse with any other. The community did not permit all of this sexual activity to be productive, and indeed they instituted a system of breeding in which Noyes and a committee were responsible for deciding who should have a baby, and who should father it. This was part of a eugenic system called 'stirpiculture' which was aimed at improving the stock. Noyes's basis of selection in the early days seems to have been piety, but later health and intelligence were emphasized. The leader himself fathered eight children after he was fifty-eight years old. The high standards of health and the low mortality rates found in the community have been commented upon by a number of writers.

Male continence was taken up by others, not necessarily for religious reasons. It has been associated to some extent with eastern mysticism, and the practice of yoga. It appeared under a variety of fine-sounding names – 'Karezza', 'Magnetation control' and 'Zugassent's Discovery' which may have made it sound, at the end of the last century and the beginning of this one, more attractive to a public which was becoming accustomed to contraceptives, abortifacients and cures for infertility, which were sold by quacks and given romantic sounding names.

Despite this background of hostile, confused and mistaken ideas, a number of significant contraceptive advances were nonetheless made during the nineteenth century. One of the most important is one to which we have not yet referred. It is the development of the occlusive pessary. We have traced the history of such an object from the Egyptian papyri but it is only within the last 150 years that real improvements were made, both in shape and in materials. There are two basic types of occlusive pessary still in use, the cervical cap and the vaginal diaphragm. The cervical cap is a small, high-domed device which fits over the cervix. The diaphragm is larger, flatter, and dish-shaped, usually with a spring contained in the rim. Other caps have been constructed, which combine the principles of both. For example the 'vault cap' is intended to close off the internal portion of the vagina, as well as the cervix.

The first nineteenth-century mention of the use of an occlusive method to prevent pregnancy seems to date from 1823, when in a paper on the harmful effects of withdrawal, a German doctor, C. W. Hufeland mentions:

Die meisten Bauerfamilien hatten nur 2 bis 3 Kinder, und dann nicht mehr. Bai genauer Untersuchung and siche, dass eine Hebamme dieses Geheimnis besass, Sie brachte den weibern unbewusst, zu ende des wochenbettes, einen fremden Körper vor dem Muttermund, welcher den Eingang verschloss. (Most of the farmer's families had only two or three children, then no more. By making closer enquiries it was found that the midwife knew the secret. Without the patient knowing, whilst the woman was laying in, after the birth, she placed a foreign body in front of the cervix which closed the entrance.)

The idea was further developed by 1838, when another German doctor, Friedrich Adolphe Wilde produced a treatise on gynaecology, which is of considerable importance. Wilde sensibly discussed the indications for contraception, and in reply to the prevailing ideas on morality, he observed that the avoidance of conception was better for a patient than having to undergo a dangerous operation, such as a caesarian section. He discussed magical methods and superstitions, and he even seems to have been conversant with the customs of Chinese priestesses, who ingested white lead, and who burned balls of herbs on their bodies as ways of trying to avoid pregnancy. Wilde knew about methods such as the condom, sponge and withdrawal, but he thought that they were all insufficiently effective. At the time when he was writing, before good rubber condoms were available, he may well have been right. The best advice he could give was that those women who wish to avoid bearing children should constantly wear a rubber pessary which has no opening, which completely covers the cervix, fits snugly, and which is taken off only during the menses. In order that it may suit every individual it must be made from a special model produced by taking a wax impression of the parts with the use of a vaginal speculum. He quotes the story about the midwife, which Hufeland told, as proof of the effectiveness of such a method. Wilde was far ahead of his time in discussing contraception. He understood, for example, that removal of the uterus or a part of the Fallopian tube was an effective way of making a woman sterile. Most doctors of the time thought that the same effect was achieved by removing the clitoris.

In the same way that the condom was 'reinvented' a number of times, so it was with the cervical cap. It is thought that an American doctor, E. B. Foote may have devised such a cap. However, this is not fully established for so effectively was Foote persecuted that the majority of his work was destroyed. The cap was certainly invented again in Vienna in 1908, when a gynaecologist called Kafka began to produce 'firm caps' made of metal and celluloid. The idea spread eastwards from Vienna, and in Eastern Europe this form of contraceptive is still called a 'Kafka cap'.

The cervical cap achieved considerable popularity, but the form preferred by most women was the diaphragm, popularly known as the 'Dutch cap' because the method, in its earliest days, gained great popularity in Holland. Holland was the first country to have any kind of family planning clinic, the first of which was opened as early as 1882. The work was organized by the 'Nienw Malthusiaanschen Bond'—the Dutch Malthusian League. The clinic offered infant welfare advice to poor women, and rather sketchy advice about contraception during its first months. The best that could be suggested at the time seems to have been a plug of soap. However, Dr Aletta Jacobs, the country's first female doctor, heard of the 'Mensinga pessary '(the earliest name used for the diaphragm) and added it to the list of services which were provided by the clinic.

The inventor, Dr Mensinga, was a German, and a professor of anatomy. He produced a book which stands out in the nineteenth century for its humane and sympathetic approach. The arguments which Mensinga used to justify contraception were not the usual Malthusian population fears, nor indeed, any other familiar philosophy. He quite simply talked about life and marriage, and even after a hundred years (although the language and phraseology is a little difficult to translate) the message sounds remarkably modern. He spoke of 'the true happiness of marriage' which was not built upon a discussion of physiology and physiologists' ethics, but on the health of both partners, and their true mental and physical harmony at all stages of life. He believed strongly that women should have equal rights in everything, and saw no reason why their lives should be made short and painful through bearing too many children. The main part of the book is a description of the cases he knew. He saw women who simply did not know what to do for the best, and women who actually expected to die in their next childbirth. He was horrified that some of them simply accepted that it would happen, and supposed that it was part of their lot. These were women who knew pain, and talked of the pain not only of birth, but also of losing the baby. An office worker's wife had had eight children, and only three survived. She sadly commented, of the five who died at birth 'They are in good custody'.

Emancipation and the status of women were subjects which Mensinga studied closely and felt deeply about. He also felt that the whole purpose of science was to help mankind, and one of the best ways it could do so was by fighting illness and death. The doctors ought to take a good look at what they were doing, and what they really could do to better the lives of their patients. Prudery and traditional arguments were not good enough when the *Centralblatt für Gynakologie* was reporting that a woman who had some physical impediment which made birth difficult had been subjected to Caesarian operations six times. He also spoke of those healthy women who had become desperate enough to try to induce a criminal abortion. Like many of his time, he looked to the Bible for advice and asked the medical profession if they had moved so far from the teachings and example of the prophet of Nazareth, that they would let all of these patients 'die by the side of the road'.

The second part of the book describes the diaphragm and how it is fitted and used. Mensinga goes into great detail, and discusses the length of time for which one appliance will remain safe, and the need for adequate medical help in checking and refitting. In the edition produced in 1892 he lists those works written in German which oppose and those which recommend contraception and also discusses the enormous number of letters that he has received. This leads him to add a section on 'Answers to Colleagues' Questions' where he reprints the kind of questions that are asked most often: 'Is the pessary not dangerous; will not the pessary increase the sexual appetite of a healthy woman; is the pessary preferable to the condom?' and a host of others. He also includes a note on the instructions given to the patients, and on the care and use of the diaphragm. He ends the book with a large number of tabulated case histories, and some detailed diagrams of the diaphragm, and how to position it for effective use.

Both caps and the condom were greatly improved by developments in rubber technology. The vulcanization process, first carried out in 1843, made it possible for such contraceptive devices to be made more reliable, and also to be cheaply mass produced. By the 1880s there were also spermicides in mass production. Throughout the earlier part of the century, a great variety of proprietary brands had been appearing. These included 'Female pills' of various kinds which were supposed to provoke an abortion, rather than being used as contraceptives. The first man to become actively engaged in producing and selling spermicidal suppositories was the chemist W. J. Rendell. In about 1880 he began to make up quinine and cacao-butter pessaries, which he distributed freely amongst the poor who lived around the Clerkenwell area of London, where his shop was situated. The results exceeded his wildest expectations, and soon the demand grew so great that producing the suppositories became a full-time job. Such pessaries were also recommended by several of the British birth control pioneers.

Thus, by 1880, caps, condoms, spermicides, intrauterine contraceptives and of course withdrawal, were all known and used. However, the discovery and improvement of contraceptive methods was not enough. The fight against traditional morality and the fight to inform the population that methods of birth control existed, was only just beginning.

CHAPTER SEVEN

The Fight for Acceptance

THROUGHOUT the nineteenth century one of the most controversial words that could be uttered, both in Europe and in the United States was 'Malthusianism'. Many of the believers in birth control described themselves by the term; their opponents regarded it as a synonym for all that is vile and unnatural. Yet the curious feature is that the man whose name the term commemorates was in no sense the founder of the movement.

Thomas Malthus would have been horrified at the idea that his name had become associated with 'preventive checks'. He was first and foremost a clergyman, and as such far too staunch an upholder of conventional morality ever for a moment to consider means which would allow couples to enjoy sexual pleasure without incurring its consequences. His only advice was like Jane Austen's: people should marry late, and should refrain from intercourse. His ideas on population, as we have seen, were not original, and he realized the fact, yet his writing did have the effect of sparking off a whole new study of population. His view that 'the realization of a happy society will always be hindered by the miseries consequent on the tendency of population to increase faster than the means of subsistence', became a subject of national concern.

His views were opposed by many, who reading them in the context of the time, saw them as an attempt to demonstrate that poverty was inevitable and that it was absurd to provide relief for the poor, since they could never obtain higher living standards. He was hated by the working class, who imagined his purpose as an attempt to exalt the rich and debase the poor. His arguments certainly were useful to landowners who discovered in them fresh excuses for clearing the peasants from the land, and enfencing the estates. The high-mindedness of many of Malthus's commentators contrast strangely with the realities of life. Enfencement and urbanization were part of the background of the industrial revolution, yet they also created what Disraeli described as 'the two nations'. One nation possessed more than sufficient wealth. The other was termed 'the industrious classes' a euphemism used in much the same way as 'less-developed. or 'developing' is today. All three terms hide the society's most characteristic features—squalor, want and poverty.

London's first Medical Officer of Health produced several descriptions of what the term really meant:

Courts and alleys with low, dark, filthy tenements, hemmed in on all sides by higher buildings, having no possibility of any current of air, and (worst of all) sometimes constructed back to back, as to forbid the advantage of double windows or back doors, and thus to render the house as perfect a cul-de-sac out of the court as the court is a cul-de-sac out of the next thoroughfare.

It was

no uncommon thing, in twelve feet square or less, to find three or four families styed together (perhaps with infectious disease among them), filling the same space night and day—men, women and children in the promiscuous intimacy of cattle. . . . Whatever is morally hideous and savage in the scene—whatever contrasts it offers to the superficial magnificence of the metropolis—whatever profligacy it implies and continues—whatever recklessness and obscene brutality arises from it—whatever deep injury it inflicts on the community—whatever debasement or abolition of God's image in men's hearts is tokened by it—these matters belong not to my office. Only because of the physical suffering am I entitled to speak, only because pestilence is forever within the circle; only because Death so largely comforts these poor orphans of civilization. . . .

He described others, even worse off 'renting the twentieth straw-heap in some lightless fever-bin . . . squatting among rotten soakage . . . breathing from the cesspool and the sewer'. Such were the living conditions for many. The only recreation of the day seems to have been excessive drinking, with a little bull-baiting and cock fighting to enliven the proceedings.

Although Queen Victoria herself has become a symbol of sexual restraint, during her reign London swarmed with prostitutes, many of them no more than children. The condition of children can be imagined from reading *The Water Babies* and from the lives of Dr Barnardo and the Earl of Shaftesbury. It would take a long book to document all of the evils of the time, but some idea of the priorities of the nation may be judged from the fact that Parliament in 1839 saw fit to allocate £30,000 for national education, and £70,000 for the building of the Royal stables and dog-kennels at Windsor.

Both of Disraeli's 'nations' were corrupt. Whilst the poor lived in such conditions the rich indulged in a remarkable degree of sexual licence, though little of it reached the surface. It is against such a background that we have to view the mouthings of the social philosophers and the medical profession of the day.

The views of the nineteenth century writers on birth control seem to be somewhat unreal. It is difficult to see how the prevention of births could be thought more immoral than allowing the living conditions of the population to remain so terrible. This emphasizes acutely the gap between the two nations. The richer section of the community (which included most of the writers) knew little of the poorer, and the majority of them simply did not care. Poverty was only mentionable when it was sentimentalized by writers like Charles Dickens.

Conversely, when one encounters some social thinker suggesting that infanticide would provide some relief for the poor, the idea seems particularly sadistic. Yet possibly those who made such suggestions were the more charitable. They may have done so in the realization that unless something could be done genuinely to offer new-born babies more of a life than a few short and painful years in the slums, then infanticide was a more humane remedy.

As history would have it, the most important thinkers of the day were those who managed to carve a pathway of sanity between these extremes. They were the followers of Bentham rather than Malthus or the Establishment, and it was one such man who started the world's first birth control campaign.

Francis Place (and perhaps more appropriately the birth controllers should have been called 'Placeians') was only too well aware of what living conditions were like for the majority. Poverty and suffering were nothing new to him for he was born in a private debtor's prison, of which his father was the keeper. After a hard and miserable childhood, he was apprenticed to a maker of leather breeches. He progressed well in this trade, but soon ran into trouble, being prominent in a strike for better wages, and also being one of the mainstays of the primitive trade union which had recently been organized. He knew what it was to be unemployed and to suffer near-starvation, and yet during all these tribulations he managed to read voraciously, and to acquire an education for himself.

Despite tragedy and hardship he was able to rise in society, and in 1816, by the time he was 46 years old, he had made a success in trade as a tailor, and had a large shop at Charing Cross. He handed this over to his son, and was then able to concentrate entirely upon radical politics. Even before he 'retired' he had worked hard for better pay and conditions for the workers, but after his liberation he involved himself greatly in the struggle for education. He was also involved in drawing up the Charter from which the 'Chartists' took their name, though he had little to do with the movement as such. His home became the meeting place for many well-known radicals, many of whom were in agreement with his ideas on birth control.

In 1822 he published his treatise *Illustrations and Proofs of the Principle of Population* in which the following idea is expressed:

If, above all, it were once clearly understood, that it was not disreputable for married persons to avail themselves of precautionary means as would without being injurious to health, or destructive to female delicacy, prevent conception, a sufficient check might at once be given to the increase of population beyond the means of subsistence.

Clearly this statement differs from the view of Malthus. To Place, his common sense and knowledge of working class life made it abundantly clear that 'moral restraint' was not a useful recommendation. It was quite simply unacceptable. In addition, it should become unnecessary since birth control measures ('precautionary means') would be more likely to become popular, and would achieve much better results. With the provision of birth control people would marry younger. In so doing they would achieve deeper relationships and would also avoid illicit sexual activities. Place even thought that this might lessen the incidence of veneral disease. The problem of child labour interested him too, and he thought, as many others had, that large families were one of its causes. Throughout the century there were many attempts to stop the practice of employing small children, or to make their labouring conditions more humane. Incredibly enough, the Shaftesbury Act forbidding the 'climbing boy' method of chimney sweeping was passed by Parliament as late as 1875.

In 1823 Place embarked on his campaign to publicize his ideas about birth control. He wanted to explain to the common people that there were reliable and harmless methods of contraception, and that conditions might be improved if they would limit the size of their family. He began by contacting a number of newspaper editors and having them publish the information in their columns. He also produced a series of leaflets, which became known as 'The Diabolical Handbills'. There were three versions of these leaflets, and in all of them the main reliance is upon the use of the sponge as a vaginal tampon, though withdrawal is also mentioned in one version. An uncirculated draft of a fourth handbill suggests that the tampon may be made of a variety of household goods —'lint, fine wool, cotton, flax or whatever may be at hand'. It is curious that there is no mention of the condom. Maybe Place thought that it was difficult to obtain outside London, or that it was too expensive.

The doctors consulted by Place seem to have given the matter some thought, for the handbills state that the sponge method 'has been successfully resorted to by some of our most eminent physicians, and is confidently recommended by first rate Accoucheurs, in cases where pregnancy has been found injurious to the health of delicate women'. Another handbill says that 'some respectable persons in the metropolis of this country, of both sexes, among whom are included many medical men of the first rank, have enquired after the means which are here unfolded'.

These comments suggest that at the beginning of the century sections of the medical profession were prepared to give the matter some thought. Their irrational hostility had not yet set in.

A large number of handbills were circulated, through various travellers and enthusiasts who knew Place, but how effective the information was in actually converting people to the practice of birth control is unknown. One package of leaflets had quite the opposite effect. It was delivered to a lady who was well known for her welfare work among the poor, and who was noted for showing great bravery during the Peterloo 'massacre' of 1819. The receipt of the package seems to have given her a shock, and she took some trouble to try to discover the origin of the leaflets. She imagined the papers to be part of a plot to discredit her, and that they must have been issued by the followers of Malthus. She wrote to the Attorney-General about the matter but no prosecutions followed. After waiting for some weeks, during which nothing happened, she wrote to ask Richard Carlile's advice on the matter.

In approaching him, she came near to the source of the hand-bills, for Carlile was a great friend of Francis Place. Originally he had been much opposed to the idea of contraception, but in time he changed his mind completely, and by 1825 had written a very outspoken book on the subject which was entitled *Every Woman's Book: or, What is Love?* Carlile had also spent some years in prison, though interestingly enough, it was not his birth control activities that made him fall foul of the law. His crime was blasphemy.

Bentham, Place and Carlile are important in the history of birth control for two reasons. Firstly, in their writings they describe contraceptive methods for anyone who wishes to read about them. That is, they provided the information. In addition, however, they provided the converts who were to keep the movement alive. They influenced the young people who knew them and talked with them. John Stuart Mill was arrested at the tender age of 17 for handing out birth control leaflets in a market-place, and it was another young admirer of Bentham's who can be truly said to have begun the birth control movement in America.

Robert Dale Owen (the son of Robert Owen) was educated in Europe and went to America when he was 24. He knew the views of the British movement and owned a copy of *Every Woman's Book*. It was his approval of this work that began his troubles. He was hated in many quarters and he suffered the insults of those who thought that the whole subject was degrading and filthy. He therefore wrote a booklet of his own in defence of contraception. It was called *Moral Physiology; or, A Brief and Plain Treatise on the Population Question* and was largely devoted to the socio-economic and eugenic justification of family limitation. The book went into a number of editions. Francis Place was quite delighted with it, sending copies to many of his friends. As with most writers of this period, the style is, (by modern standards), somewhat stilted. However, the belief that the availability of contraception would mean that women would be able to resort to all kinds of immoral behaviour (an idea still encountered today), was refuted in the following manner:

Truly, but they pay their wives, their sisters, and their daughters a poor compliment! Is, then, this vaunted chastity a mere thing of circumstance and occasion? Is there but the difference of opportunity between it and prostitution? Would their wives, their sisters, and their daughters, if once absolved from the fear of offspring, become prostitutes—sell their embraces for gold, and descend to a level with the most degraded? In truth, they slander their own kindred; they libel their own wives, sisters, and daughters. If they spoke truth—if fear were indeed the only safeguard of their relatives' chastity, little value should I place on a virtue like that! and small would I esteem the offense, who should attempt or seduce it.

He continues in a similar vein for some pages, and eventually he describes three methods by which conception might be prevented. He thought that withdrawal was the best. Unlike other writers of his time, he stressed that complete withdrawal was necessary for success; partial withdrawal was not safe, and he thought that it was quite feasible for almost all men to practise the method successfully. He knew of the sponge and the condom and mentions them in the early editions, but he also knew of cases where the sponge had failed. He therefore recommended waiting until more information about such a method had emerged. The condom was certainly effective, but it could be used only once, and it was very expensive.

Moral Physiology was described by Norman Himes as 'able and virtuous', but it added very little to contemporary knowledge of birth control. Its main importance is that it did take the subject across the Atlantic where it influenced America's second pioneer, Charles Knowlton. Knowlton's own work, *Fruits of Philosophy* is sometimes said to be the most important account of contraception since Soranos and Aetios. Apart from its discussion of the methods themselves the book is important for the enormous social influence that it was to have. It was to become the centre of attention in a number of legal proceedings both in America and in Britain.

The *Fruits of Philosophy* contains a justification of contraception and answers the common arguments against it. The usual ones (though seen in various guises), were that the practice pointed the way to immorality, and that it was against nature. On the positive side the book represents a departure from others on the subject, for the author recommends douching. Knowlton was 'quite confident that a liberal use of pretty cold water would be a never failing preventative'. All the same, he suggested that a variety of chemicals could be added to the water to aid the process and to help cure other conditions at the same time. Alum and 'astringent vegetables' were effective. The vegetables included white oak bark, hemlock bark, red rose leaves, green tea and raspberry roots. He also stated that the addition of zinc sulphate would help in cases where the woman suffered from a vaginal discharge, and that sugar of lead was useful if there was any tenderness. He thought that baking soda was a useful general additive, and he also mentioned vinegar—the first writer to do so since Aetios. He was certain that the use of a douche to prevent conception was his own original idea. He tells us that: 'Any publication, great or small, mentioning the syringe (or anything else that operates on the same principle) as a means of preventing conception—whatever liquid may be recommended, is a violation of my copyright.'

The douche itself is not a particularly useful contraceptive measure, especially when used as Knowlton recommended—'It is my opinion that five minutes' delay would not prove mischievous—perhaps not ten.' But it was the book itself that was to bring about social changes rather than its content. Knowlton was prosecuted three times, and served a prison sentence, but the work continued to circulate in both Britain and America. Although he originally restricted its sale, it is estimated that by 1881 over a quarter of a million copies had been sold. The popularity of the book seems to have been engendered by the legal proceedings which surrounded it—a situation not entirely unknown today.

In 1877 Charles Bradlaugh, a well-known radical and sometime Member of Parliament, and his colleague in the Free-thought movement, Mrs Annie Besant, decided to publish the *Fruits of Philosophy* for themselves. The book had been quietly circulating for 40 years, and it was in fact quite antiquated when compared to some of the works which had become available in the intervening years.

However, it had been the subject of a legal action at Bristol in the previous year. It is alleged that the proceedings were not so much to do with the content of the book itself, as with the fact that its pages had been interleaved with 'obscene pictures'. At that time any anatomical diagram of the genitals would easily have qualified as obscene. The London publisher was also prosecuted but he had pleaded guilty and was let off lightly.

Bradlaugh and Besant were extremely indignant over these proceedings. The work had been identified with the Free-thought movement over the 40 years. It had been recommended and sold by many of the leaders of the movement, all of

whom had approved it. If the book was obscene then the impli-
cation was that the activities of the movement were in a similar
category. To provoke a test case, they therefore published a
new edition 'honestly believing that on all questions affecting
the happiness of the people, whether they be theological,
political or social, fullest right of free discussion ought to be
maintained at all hazards'. They informed the police of the
publication, and of where and when they could be found
selling it.

When one considers the rather boring nature of the book,
the indictment is amazing:

The Jurors for our Lady the Queen, upon their oath present that
Charles Bradlaugh and Annie Besant unlawfully and wickedly
devising and contriving and intending, as much as in them lay,
to vitiate and corupt the morals as well of youth as of divers other
liege subjects of our said Lady the Queen, and to incite and encourage the said liege subjects to indecent, obscene, unnatural, and
immoral practices, and bring them to a state of wickedness, lewdness
and debauchery, therefore, to wit, on the 24th day of March, 1877,
in the City of London, and within the Jurisdiction of the Central
Criminal Court, unlawfully, wickedly, knowingly, willfully,
and designedly did print, publish, sell, and utter a certain indecent,
lewd, filthy, and obscene libel, to wit, a certain indecent, lewd,
filthy, bawdy, and obscene book, called 'Fruits of Philosophy'
thereby contaminating, vitiating, and corrupting the morals as well
of youth as of other liege subjects of our said Lady the Queen,
and bringing the said liege subjects to a state of wickedness, lewdness, debauchery, and immorality, in contempt of our said Lady
the Queen and her laws, to the evil and pernicious example of all
others in the like case offending, and against the peace of our said
Lady the Queen, her crown, and dignity.

The trial took place in June 1877 before the Lord Chief
ustice. In his summing up, he observed that 'a more ill-
advised and injudicious prosecution was never instituted' and
criticized the Solicitor General who had led the prosecution,
and who in so doing had imputed that the defendants had

harboured improper motives. The Jury was instructed that it had to decide whether the book was likely to deprave public morals. If it was, then the defendants were guilty, whatever their motives. After an hour and a half the Jury found that 'The book in question was likely to deprave public morals, but that we exonerate the defendants from any corrupt motive in publishing it.' The Judge interpreted this as 'Guilty' and imposed sentence. The sentence, however, was never served since a higher court discovered a technical error in the indictment. Bradlaugh and Besant were therefore acquitted. The right of publication had been vindicated.

The following year another case was brought to court. The trial of Edward Truelove had been postponed because of the Bradlaugh case, though Truelove's offence was similar. He had issued Owen's *Moral Physiology* and another inexpensive tract entitled *Individual, Family and National Poverty* by J. H. Palmer. After much argument, the jury failed to agree on a verdict and were discharged. A second trial followed, and despite his advanced years, Truelove was found guilty and sentenced to prison for four months. He was also fined £50. The sentence caused a storm in liberal and radical circles, where Truelove was acclaimed as a martyr. There were several petitions and attempts to lighten his sentence, but all were unsuccessful. The most important feature of both of these trials was the vast amount of public interest which they generated. The publicity which surrounded the proceedings was responsible for many people learning about the possibilities of controlling family size. The general public was eager to learn more about birth control and the sales of literature on the subject were vastly increased.

Once her own trial was over, Annie Besant produced a better and more instructive work which replaced Knowlton's booklet and brought more current information into circulation. The book was called the *Law of Population* and in it she discussed the safe period (which was not very safe), the condom and douche (which were distasteful), and withdrawal, about which she observed:

a few among the French doctors contend that the practice is injurious . . . but they have failed, so far as we can judge, in making out their case, for they advance no proofs in support of the theory, while the universal practice of the French speaks so strongly on the other side.

In the early versions the sponge was the method she seemed to think best, although in the later editions of the book when two new methods, the cervical cap and the soluble pessary had become available, these were listed as being preferable.

However interested the general public may have been to discover that family limitation was within easy grasp for all who cared to read a pamphlet, the medical profession as a whole remained unconvinced. In 1823 when the Diabolical Handbills had appeared, the *Lancet* acknowledged them as 'things . . . which are beneath our notice'. But one British doctor did hold different views. Dr George Drysdale wrote two books, *Physical, Sexual and Natural Religion* and *Elements of Social Science* both of which were produced under pseudonyms. Drysdale was mainly concerned with the urgent problem of population control, although there is a short discussion of methods that might be employed. A number of other short works of varying merit appeared. Although medical men were obviously aware of the social problems, and saw a great deal of maternal mortality, abortion and even infanticide, they still shied away from giving any possible place to birth control in their treatment. The 'Accoucheurs' that Place described must have been a dying or a silent breed.

The majority opinion of medical men may be judged by the views put forth in the *Lancet* in 1859:

It often occurs to me in reading cases where women, whose pelves

have become distorted by mellitis ossium, are delivered of dead or
mutilated children, that the question involves a consideration apart
from a medical one. If a woman is aware that her pelvis is so deformed that it is physically impossible that anything can pass through
it and retain life, why is she at liberty to continue connexion with
her husband when she knows that the inevitable consequence will
be the destruction of her child? Would it not be a merciful act to
place a penalty upon that woman's becoming again pregnant,
being morally on her part a case of murder? A woman knowing
this and persisting in sexual congress is really as guilty as the woman
who destroys her child after it is born.

But by 1868 the medical profession could no longer ignore
the subject completely. Bertrand Russell's father, Lord Amber-
ley, having read and appreciated Drysdale's book, spoke at a
political meeting in favour of small families. The incident
caused an uproar and a scandal. The *British Medical Journal*,
who printed a report of the meeting was sure that 'Our profession will repudiate with indignation and disgust such functions
as these gentlemen wish to assign it'. The journals felt it necessary to print even more signs of disapproval and the *Lancet*
positively rejoiced when a Dr Beatty raised his voice at the
annual meeting of the British Medical Association against
all 'beastly contrivances' and 'filthy expedients for the prevention of conception'.

Ten years later, it was Routh's turn. He graphically outlined
the opinions of the profession. Apart from the moral crime
involved, he thought that contraception was physically hazardous. He had obviously been reading the French literature on
the subject, for what he has to say follows fairly closely on
what continental authorities had also pronounced. Among the
hazards to female health from 'sexual fraudulency and conjugal onanism' are

'death, or severe illness from acute and chronic metritis, leucorrhoea,
menorrhagia and haematocele, histeralgia and hyperaesthesia of the
generative organs, cancer, in an aggravated form assuming in such

examples a galloping character so rapid is its course, ovarian dropsy and ovaritus. In cases where severe results are not observed, the organs become so charged that sterility results from their chronic disease. Lastly, mania leading to suicide and the most repulsive nymphomania are induced.

The males were likely to suffer from

general nervous prostration, mental decay, loss of memory, intense cardiac palpitations, mania and conditions which lead to suicide.

He admitted that the safe period had a use, although he thought that there were hardly any people in any *real* danger from conception. If the avoidance of conception were *absolutely* necessary, then recourse might be made to the method of Pouchet. However, even this information was to be used with the greatest caution:

Let it not be made an excuse or a cloak for fraudulency, for conjugal onanism is not only criminal in men, it must tend to demoralize women. If you teach them vicious habits, and a way to sin, without detection, how can you assure yourself of their fidelity when assailed by a fascinating seducer, and why may not even the unmarried taste of forbidden pleasures also: so that your future wife shall have been defiled ere you knew her?

Mr President and Gentlemen, as medical men we are often the guardians of female virtue. We are admitted into the closest confidences of our patients; we know the secrets of many a household. We are trusted, respected, nay, loved, for our considerate kindness to the sorrowful and the sick. Shall we now remain silent when attempts are made to introduce into our happy homes habits of immorality which are so vile in their character, so dishonourable in their development, so degrading in their practice? Let us protest as medical men, as moral men, as Christian men, against recommendations by whomsoever made, so filthy, so base, and so abominable.

It was against a background of opinion of this kind that the Malthusian League began its work.

The League, which had been first organized in the early

eighteen-sixties and had subsequently been disbanded was enthusiastically re-established after the Bradlaugh–Besant trial. In 1880 it formed a Medical and Scientific Branch, to try to gain some support from the medical profession. The difficulties which faced it in the beginning were far greater than most people would remember. C. V. Drysdale (George Drysdale's son) explained much later that it was hard

to realise the difficulties which confronted the League . . . faced by the smug conventionality and silence on the part of the comfortable classes [who were adopting family limitation on their own behalf] the opposition of the clergy, medical profession and economists permeated with Fabianism, and the hostility of the poor.

Despite its attempts, very few doctors were attracted by the League. An International Conference which took place in 1881 was attended by about forty doctors from various countries, and letters from sympathetic practitioners who were unable to attend were read out. They hoped that the conference would help to bring Neo-Malthusian doctrines to the notice of the medical profession. But British medical opinion was not favourably encouraged when a few years later, Dr H. Arthur Albutt, who with Drysdale took a leading part in the Medical Branch of the League, was struck off the Medical Register. The offence was yet another publication—this time one entitled *The Wife's Handbook*. The booklet was priced at sixpence and thus available to everybody. It contained a great deal of useful information on matters of general hygiene, pre-natal care, and the management of babies. It also contained a small chapter on 'How to prevent conception when advised by the doctor'.

The patient was advised to consult the doctor as to which was the best method in her case, but the choices described by Albutt covered the safe period (five days before and eight days after menstruation), withdrawal, douching and the Mensinga diaphragm (for the first time in an English book; presumably Albutt heard of it at the Conference). He also mentions the cervical cap, Rendell's pessaries, and an artificial sponge 'containing at its centre a friable capsule filled with slightly acidulated quinine solution'. In addition the booklet contained information on the retailer's addresses, together with some advertisements. Had Albutt charged ten shillings for the book, instead of sixpence, he would probably have continued in medical practice with the full approval of the General Medical Council.

The Malthusian League continued well into the nineteen-twenties though it was never a very large nor a very vocal organization. For most of its members, it provided a simple creed: 'overpopulation is the cause of poverty'. With this simple statement, a host of social ills could be explained.

In Britain in the second half of the nineteenth century the right to spread information about birth control was becoming firmly, if slowly, established. In the United States, however, the situation was quite different. Following the beginnings made by Robert Dale Owen and Charles Knowlton came a period of comparative silence. A few rather obscure publications appeared but they aroused little interest. As in Britain, birth control was taken up by freethinkers and radicals, but whereas the British radicals had been comparatively influential, their American counterparts were so radical that they were almost outcasts. For them, birth control was not an aspect of Malthusianism. Their primary interest was sexual reform, of which voluntary parenthood was simply an aspect. Much of their literary output appeared in their newspapers, which had names like *Lucifer* and *The Firebrand*. Their names were revealed only when they were arrested. Most of them are not at all well known, although Emma Goldman achieved some notoriety as an anarchist, and is remembered for her short espousal of Bolshevism.

A number of other publications were also available which offered bits of more or less useless information. *Aristotles*

Complete Masterpiece was published in New York in 1788. Several indigenous *Marriage Guides* and *Lectures on Chastity* appeared. In 1835 William Alcott observed that 'the world abounds in impure publications'. One wonders what they could have said. In 1847 A. M. Mauriceau, a self-styled expert produced the *Married Woman's Medical Companion*. The book seems to have been plagiarized largely from Robert Dale Owen whom it hardly mentions. However, it does point out that Owen was ignorant of 'Desomeaux's Method' also known as the 'French secret'. The secret would be revealed at a cost of ten dollars, and Mauriceau held the exclusive agency. There is no indication of what the secret was. Since Mauriceau seems to have come from France it could well have been the Pouchet version of the safe period. Alternatively it may have been some chemical substance to be used for douching. Another 'doctor', writing at much the same time recommended opium, prussic acid, iodine, strychnine and alcohol for their spermicidal powers. Unfortunately he omitted to offer any adequate instruction as to how such dangerous substances should be used.

In 1873 in the United States the dissemination of any information about birth control suddenly became illegal. The Comstock Bill was introduced to Congress in February of that year, passed by both houses, and signed by the President before the Session closed on 4 March. There were no speeches, practically no discussion and no public hearings. The Bill was stressed as 'a measure for the suppression of trade in and circulation of articles for immoral use'.

Anthony Comstock, Secretary of the Society for the Suppression of Vice had an effective way of obtaining support. After securing interviews with Congressmen and other influential persons he then showed them samples of the most disgusting publications which were currently in circulation. He chose articles which were both pornographic and outrageous although generally they had nothing to do with birth control. The Congressmen thus approached were naturally disturbed by the situation and were eager to prevent such items from being circulated, especially among young people. They also wanted to stop the unscrupulous from making huge profits from such practices. Had they considered the matter a little further they would probably not have wanted to stop the spread of scientific and medical information, but in their innocence they managed to pass a Bill which did exactly that.

State legislation followed rapidly, and some of it was even more suppressive. Comstock managed to acquire the power to enforce the new law. According to one biography, immediately after the Bill was passed, several of the Senators and representatives who had been prominent in its passage asked the Post Master to appoint Comstock as a special agent of the Post Office to enforce the new legislation. The Post Master agreed to do so, if an appropriation were made for his salary and expenses. Comstock refused the allowance on the grounds that if he accepted no salary the position would be kept out of politics. And thus it was that he was appointed to an office which he was to hold for forty-two years. However, it is also recorded that the Young Men's Christian Association paid him a hundred dollars a month 'to compensate him for the time lost from his business' (he was in fact a grocery clerk).

In 1910 a new Postmaster General insisted that Comstock should have a salary and become a government employee on a regular basis. His title of 'Special Agent' was changed to 'Inspector'. His duties covered 'investigation of all matters connected with the Postal Service' and 'alleged violations of law'. In addition he was 'when necessary to aid in the prosecution of criminal offences'. Postal employees were his subordinates. Inspectors were allowed to open 'pouches and sacks and examine the mail therein'. He was also able to 'make searches for mailable matter transported in violation of the law' and to 'seize all letters and bags, packets and parcels, containing letters which are being carried contrary to law on board any vessel or on any postal route'.

In New York State he had special power, relating to his position in the Society for the Suppression of Vice. The New York laws contained a quite remarkable provision which said that

The police force of the city of New York, as well as of other places, where police organizations exist, shall, as occasion may require, aid this corporation [the Society for the Suppression of Vice] its members or agents, in the enforcement of all laws which now exist or which may hereafter be enacted for the suppression of the acts and offences designed in Section 3 of this Act.

A further provision (which was repealed later) said that a half of all of the fines collected through the activities of the Society were to be given to its funds. The Society for the Suppression of Vice even acquired the power to arrest people. Comstock himself certainly enjoyed making arrests. In his books he describes in dramatic terms how he made some of his captures. One incident in Boston ends with the jolly exhortation 'Then ho for the Charles St. Jail!'

His books tell us a good deal about his mental condition. The Devil was a real creature and an active force. Obscenity was everywhere—'Light literature is then a devil trap to captivate the child by perverting taste and fancy . . . The love story and cheap work of fiction captivate fancy and pervert taste'. Interviewed as late as 1915 he declared that 'Existing laws are a necessity in order to prevent the downfall of youth of both sexes,' and that 'to repeal the present laws would be a crime against society and especially a crime against young women'. The interviewer was somewhat confused 'that Mr. Comstock should class contraceptives with pornographic objects which debauch children's fancies, for I know that the European scientists who advocate their use have no desire at all to

F

debauch children'. Comstock replied that he had no time for 'theorizers who do not know human nature . . . if you open the door to anything, the filth will all pour in and the degradation of youth willl follow'.

His biographer, the Rev. C. G. Trumbull, wrote that toward the end of his career:

Mr. Comstock today liked to dwell upon what he calls the wonderful goodness of God in those early days of the fight for purity. And it *is* a story of God's work, not man's, when we remember that it was an unknown clerk, twenty-eight years old, who had hardihood to go to the national capitol with the idea of getting his own convictions put into legislative action; that finding there two or three other bills pending in the same field, . . . he stuck to it till all were merged in a single bill . . .; and he prayed his bill through both houses . . . and that he returned home under appointment as a staff officer of a cabinet officer of the United States!

Anyone, however respectable and however pure their motives, was at any time liable to fall foul of Comstock's ideas since he could find 'obscenity' anywhere. No one was safe. The Freethinkers came in for special persecution, for according to Comstock 'infidelity' (atheism) was a grave offence. The National Liberal League roused him to new heights of rhetoric. It was founded in 1876 and one of its main objects was to repeal the Comstock Law. In a rather telling phrase he demanded 'Do infidelity and obscenity occupy the same bed?'

One Freethinker, Ezra Heywood, was a special target. Comstock took grave exception to Heywood's description of him as a 'religio-monomaniac, whom the mistaken will of Congress and the lascivious fanaticism of the Young Men's Christian Association have empowered to use the Federal Courts to suppress free inquiry.' Heywood said at his second trial:

Sad indeed is it that hitherto liberty has come mainly through martyrdom; that 'by the light of burning heretics' we track the bleeding feet of progress—civilization advancing from prison to prison, from gibbet to gibbet, from stake to stake. . . .

Even the aged were not free from the fear of persecution. Moses Harman, editor of *Lucifer* and the *American Journal of Eugenics* was sentenced to hard labour when he was over eighty. Nor were doctors beyond danger. Edward Bliss Foote advocated the prevention of conception in several publications, and produced a pamphlet called *Words in Pearl*. In response to a decoy letter, Foote mailed a copy of the booklet and in 1876 was indicted in New York. He was found guilty and fined $3,000 but the costs amounted to $5,000. His son, Edward Bond Foote who was also a doctor, held similar views but in his writing care for the law made him omit any details of techniques. So effectively was the elder writer's work suppressed that not a single copy of *Words in Pearl* is thought to exist today. .

Decoy letters were part of Comstock's way of life. As early as 1878 in Boston where he was trying to organize a branch of his society, a clergyman asked him:

Did you, Mr. Comstock, ever use decoy letters and false signatures; did you ever sign a woman's name to such decoy letters; did you ever try to make a person sell you forbidden wares, and then when you had succeeded, use the evidence thus obtained to convict them?

Comstock replied in the affirmative to all of the questions. But this is perhaps not surprising, when it is known that he would happily walk into a brothel, have the occupants parade naked before him, and then arrest them for indecent exposure.

Though Comstock's activities represent the extremes of bigotry he was, in a sense, merely reflecting the predominant attitude of his time. As in Britain, American medical opinion was strongly opposed to contraception. Physicians imagined a vast number of dangerous illnesses which were caused, or at

least made more acute by the use of contraceptives. In 1860
an American doctor claimed that:

local congestions, nervous affections and debilities are the direct
and indisputable results of coitus imperfecti, tegumente extaria,
ablutiones gelidae, infusiones astringentes, et cetera as commonly
employed by the community, who are so ignorant on all these
matters, and who are in fact substituting for one imaginary difficulty
in prospect, a host of ills that will leave no rest or comfort to be
found . . .

In 1883 the *Columbus Medical Journal* contained a communication entitled 'One of the Abuses of Carbolic Acid'. The
writer began by describing the danger of induced abortion,
and how often the doctor is called to treat women in its latter
stages. The reason women undergo abortion, he decides, is
'the effects of the terrible impression left on their minds by a
childbirth death. I really believe that two-thirds of the abortions produced every day are done more through fear of death
during childbirth, than through any other motive.' He describes 'the private chambers of married women' in which if we

take a peep into the little dark closet, . . . we see bottles of ergot,
cotton root, savin, oil of tansy, etc., to produce as they call it 'acci-
dental miscarriage'. And when these agents fail, how many times
will we find a 'reputable and prominent physician' receive a specified sum, and, sound in hand, enter that chamber and induce premature labour! We are all ready to acknowledge that this is the
darkest spot in our profession. These women are in reality the worst
set of patients the profession has to contend with. Still there is
another class, who in my opinion suffer more than these; they are
those who endeavor to prevent conception. If you have never
kept a record of the number of cases of 'nervous patients' you
treat annually, whose affection is induced by this one thing, do so,
and see how great will be your surprise at the end of the year . . .

He then describes a prostitute who used carbolic acid as a
douche. The inmates of the brothel all used it, to avoid both
pregnancy and venereal disease. ('I confess I was somewhat

embarrassed at my diagnosis, and had she not assisted me would have made an utter failure of it'). The ladies it seems, were accustomed to its rather unpleasant side effects, and would, when they became too painful, stop using carbolic acid and take doses of quinine, which dispelled the symptoms. From the context it seems that the doctor was a sympathetic person, but even so the idea of offering any other, safer form of contraception was nonetheless unthinkable.

A number of British doctors also wrote articles in American medical journals, expressing their opinions on the dangers of contraception, and exhorting the American branch of the profession to take a hard line. One such writer was Thomas Dolan of Halifax who managed to have the same paper published at least four times. Dolan opposed contraception on religious grounds and complained of the activities of the Neo-Malthusians 'openly teaching how fecundation may be prevented; and, worst still, means are provided'. His arguments were verbose and moralizing. When he did come to discuss the physical illnesses which were supposed to occur as a result of using contraceptives, he turned to what the French doctors had to say. 'The French language lends itself better than ours to an explanation of delicate subjects' he explained and so the contra-indications are quoted in French. According to Dolan, morals were as lax as during the fall of the Roman Empire, with infanticide and abortion being practised on a large scale. 'We are told', he informed his American counterparts,

that in your country the abortionist, male or female, practices the art most openly, and that it is a very lucrative trade. We are told that some of your women, who are too refined to adopt the other preventive checks have no hesitation in resorting to practices more heinous still, and more criminal.

Apparently the situation was no better in Britain. According to a consulting physician at Guy's Hospital in London, the married were regarding abortion as 'ordinary and proper' and one is cooly asked to induce abortion for the veriest trifles—because it interferes with the autumn holiday or the season, because of the disagreeables of pregnancy and labour, for trifling sickness, or because the husband, or both, do not like children.

Both Dolan and the Guy's consultant knew where to lay the blame:

This tone of mind is the natural outcome of such teachings as are conveyed in works like *Fruits of Philosophy* . . . it has . . . undermined the health and moral tone which was formerly characteristic of the English women.

The profession was called upon to make a stand.

We may be the saviours of our country. . . . We are offered for the philosphy of the Scriptures and the Gospels the newer philosophy of the sponge, the tampon and the vaginal douche, of which these are the fruits. The choice is before you.

After reading so many papers in the same vein it is refreshing to find that at least one doctor took a different view. In the *Michigan Medical News* of 1882, Dr O. E. Herrick discusses 'Abortion and its Lesson' and gives a new slant to the usual party line. He points out that abortion is becoming a more and more frequent occurrence.

The clergy have preached to, and warned their congregations against the evil practice; lawyers have drafted new laws upon it, and have sought to enforce existing ones against it; and doctors have discussed means for its prevention; but all with little or no avail. . . .

He sees the increase as a sign 'that the means used for its suppression is in part, or wholly, inadequate to the end. As physicians, we have nothing to do with the moral aspect of the crime; our province ceases with the consideration of its hygenics'. He attacks many of the familiar arguments.

It is not the unmarried, not the rich who adopt the solution most often, but poor women, for the poor lead healthier lives than the sedentary rich, and are more liable to conceive. The poor have stronger motives to want small families, and they do not have the enlightenment of the rich. Abortion is their only escape.'

He ridicules the moral argument. Of the 'duty to bear children', Herrick demands to know who ever thought of duty when begetting a child.

In most instances they simply thought of their unbridled brute passions, and at the supreme moment of coition were absolutely thoughtless and regardless of results . . . the idea of one's indulging in sexual union, because of his or her duty to society, 'nature's laws,' or 'holy purposes', is preposterous as well as ludicrous, in fact. If there were no more pleasure . . . than in shaking hands, I apprehend the next generation would be pretty small in point of numbers, even though duty were constantly knocking at the door of a dutiful people.

He deals a death blow to the treasured notion that all manner of ailments follow from the use of contraception by saying that of course the organs become congested during intercourse, and of course, the congestion subsides afterwards. If the act is unfinished, congestion subsides as soon as contact ceases, and if a syringe is used, it subsides more quickly

else why do we use a syringe in cases of congestion and inflammation. . . . It must be apparent to all physicians that this congestive pathology is a myth. Again, in reply to the claim that disease follows as a result of prevention, every gynaecologist in the country will bear me out in the statement that more than two-thirds of the diseases of women are either directly or indirectly caused by the partrurient state. . . . It seems then that married women are less liable, by two-thirds, to become victims of disease if they prevent conception.

Believing that no woman should become a mother if she was unwilling, he thought that contraception was a better remedy than abortion. He was the recipient of a large number of letters from other doctors asking about methods of birth control, and in reply to all of them his article summarized the means. Unfortunately the methods he knew were not as good as his arguments. He thought that the 'Comstock Syringe' was a fine thing 'called after Anthony Comstock, who prosecuted the manufacturers for sending the syringes with directions for using, through the mails. He was beaten, however, and has the honour of having a useful instrument named after him.' He also knew about withdrawal and the 'womb veil' by which he presumably means the cervical cap.

Herrick was outstanding in his time for his sheer common sense. There was not much of it about. Even at the end of the nineteenth century the *status quo* was still being carefully preserved. The President of the American Association of Obstetricians and Gynaecologists, Edward J. Ill gave his address in 1899 on 'The Rights of the Unborn' and in 1890 the President of the American Gynaecological Society had spoken on 'The Limiting of Childbearing among the Married'. Both papers were defensive in tone. The latter speaker seemed to find himself in some difficulty when dealing with the arguments for family limitation. However, he quoted almost every authority he could think of to justify large families. There should be eight or ten children, for he says 'There is no fold, howe'er tended, but one dead lamb is there'. And, of course, he could always use Abraham Lincoln's words: 'The Lord must love the common people. He made so many of them!'

CHAPTER EIGHT

The Breakthrough in Britain

IT is rarely possible to assign a precise date to any major change in the way that a population as a whole thinks about any important issue. The pioneers appear, perhaps half a century before their time, preaching their gospel but the reactionaries resist the new doctrine to the grave. Between these two extremes are the vast majority of the populace who change their minds only slowly but who do eventually come to embrace the new idea completely. So it was with the final acceptance of contraception by the majority of the population of Great Britain in the first half of the twentieth century.

A large proportion of the British middle-class was ready to practise some form of birth control immediately after the Bradlaugh–Besant trial. More and better opportunities were opening up for their children, but they needed money to take advantage of such changes. In an era of rising costs many of them knew that without family limitation coupled with hard work, a yawning gap would appear between their achievements and their aspirations. A rough indication of the seriousness and speed with which they took to the practice may be had by comparing the birth-rates of two London boroughs: Shoreditch, a poor area in the East End, and Hampstead, predominantly a middle-class area. In 1881 the birthrates were very comparable (31·2 in Shoreditch, and 30·0 in Hampstead). By 1911, however, the Hampstead birth-rate had fallen to 17·5, but in Shoreditch, where the working class had still not learned the 'secret,' the figure remained at 30·2.

A better indication of the effect of the trial can be found in a report on the declining birth-rate written at the outbreak of World War I by Ethel Elderton, a Fellow of the University of London. The report deals mainly with the north of England and describes a growing tendency toward small families. One of the main reasons given for this change was the circulation of birth-control propaganda. People were discussing the subject among themselves, and were taking advice from anyone who would give it. They were consulting their local chemists and buying contraceptive devices from the newly set up manufacturers. Apart from the use of withdrawal, many knew that condoms and pessaries were also obtainable. A surprisingly large number of people holding views either for or against birth control, linked this prevalence of family limitation directly to the activities of Annie Besant forty years before.

And the trend was general. The national birth-rate fell from 35·0 per thousand in 1878 to 14·9 in 1933. Such a significant fall did not escape the attention of those who remained opposed to the use of contraceptives. However, it seems in retrospect that those critics (and indeed those protagonists), who based their arguments on a consideration of the national birth-rate were to a large extent missing the point. Couples who accepted family planning as a part of their normal married life certainly did not do so because of any consideration of the national rate of population growth. Their motives were far more personal.

A good example of this 'demographic' (and largely irrelevant) way of thinking was provided by the Medical Officer of Health of Huddersfield. He began a paper on 'The Immorality of Family Restriction' by quoting the fearful fall in local births. There had been twenty-two fewer males and seven fewer females born in 1916 than in the previous year. He pointed out that the birth-rate had been declining for a number of years, and dated the beginning of this grave situation from

a vicious, anti-natural and immoral propaganda carried on here (as well as elsewhere) by two persons of different sex at the end of the third quarter of the last century. In imagination I can perceive the historian reviewing in the future the facts of our natural life, as from the date of Sedan to the close of the present war, ascribing many of our failings and weaknesses to the fruits of this pernicious philosophy. . . .

But, of course, predications of the future are always difficult. He was much concerned with the growth of the German and Austro-Hungarian Empires but he observed of Russia that 'Despotism gone, it seems impossible that so huge and heterogeneous an empire can hold together for even a single generation. Therefore it is not worth the while to waste attention in that direction.' The solution of our national problem was clearly the growth and survival of a bigger and better British race, and contraception could have no part in such a process. Rather, he recommended that 'a sense of nationality and love of the homeland be fostered' in the British people.

The need for continued opposition to contraception was felt, as we have seen, within the medical profession for a century. Curiously enough their public protestations do not seem to have had any profound effect on their own private lives. The 1911 census revealed that doctors had the smallest families of all occupational categories. For years they had persisted in this ambiguous attitude, managing to keep their own families small and planned, whilst refusing to inform their patients on how to do so. Branches of the British Medical Association passed resolutions condemning the spread of contraception, and the Association itself even went so far as to support a Parliamentary Bill intended to stop the sale of contraceptive devices. The Bill (which never became law) reflected the fact

that the onus for informing and educating the general public
in the practicalities of contraception had fallen to a large extent
on the commercial sector. It was the manufacturers and
chemists, the 'rubber shops' and the retailers who published
what information there was, and hence made it publicly available, at least to certain sectors of society.

It was in this situation, with a public on one hand eager to
know more about methods of birth control, and a medical
profession on the other determined to repress such knowledge,
that the first British birth control clinics were opened. The
Malthusian League in 1913 had produced a leaflet on contraception, but many of its members had realized that such methods
of publicity were inadequate. What was required was a place
for women to come to; a place where they would receive
advice and contraceptives as well. Such a step could not be
taken immediately, but the League did start to hold public
meetings in the streets. These meetings took place in the
poverty-stricken areas of London and large audiences were
attracted to them. For the first time the League was really
successful in addressing an audience altogether different from
the already converted middle-class.

However, the best that they could do at the time was to
circulate their leaflet at these gatherings and advise their
listeners as to where the nearest and best sources of contraceptives might be found. In addition it must be said that the
League's members were at a disadvantage. They continued
to adhere to their simple creed, and blamed every human evil
on population growth. They even explained the first World
War in terms of population pressures and pointed to the situation as a vindication of the doctrine of Malthus.

The end of the war brought vast social changes. In the midst
of emancipation and revolution, public opinion also changed
on many subjects. Birth control was one topic among many to
receive a great deal more public discussion than ever before.

Birth control organizations had the support of well-known people. H. G. Wells and Arnold Bennett were the Vice-Presidents of the Malthusian League. The Church and even the medical profession began to hold discussions. But all this was not fast enough for some. The greatest need was still for clinics. The League itself had decided to open its first clinic in 1917, but for various reasons the plan had to be delayed until 1921. By that time, the League's clinic was not the only one, nor indeed even the first, in Great Britain, for another London clinic had been opened a few months earlier by Dr Marie Stopes and her husband, Mr H. V. Roe, the famous aviation pioneer.

From the outset both the Malthusian League and the Society for Constructive Birth Control and Racial Progress (the organization which Marie Stopes had formed) were in agreement on one point. The answer to the problem of family limitation did not lie in the opening of large numbers of such private clinics. It was agreed that the Government and local authorities ought to be providing birth control services in their official clinics, alongside their maternal and child health services. As the two clinics were opened, both groups made it known that in their estimation there was no need for any other privately financed special clinics to be opened anywhere. They themselves were just showing the way. They felt that once one birth control clinic was established, authority would surely see the vast demand that existed for contraception, and would just as soon see the improvement in the health of working-class mothers and children that the means of contraception would provide.

In 1921 the two clinics themselves affected relatively few people if one considers simply the number of patients who attended, but the year was one of the most important in the whole history of birth control simply because of their very existence. It was also the year in which both the Establishment and the public were subjected to a considerable shock when the King's Physician, Lord Dawson of Penn, was invited to address the Church Congress in Birmingham. His address was not at all what they had expected. Lord Dawson had believed for some time that 'artificial birth control' was desirable on social, medical and personal grounds, and he condemned the traditional view that abstinence offered any kind of solution to the problem of unwanted children. He called upon the Church to revise its opinions in the light of modern knowledge and living conditions. 'Birth control is here to stay' he told them. The public response was enormous. Perhaps because of his position and because of the advance that birth control had already made among the middle-class, there was little condemnation of his views.

A change was even wrought in the pages of the medical journals. The *Lancet*, after so many years, suddenly discovered 'The gap in medical knowledge'. Steps were taken by the appropriate medical bodies to examine the current state of knowledge about birth control and to circulate more information about it. The *British Medical Journal* published a paper on practical contraceptive methods.

Thus, inasmuch as any such fundamental social change can be dated at all, the real breakthrough in contraceptive acceptance in Great Britain can be said to have occurred just fifty years ago. The courage of Lord Dawson in speaking his mind and of the two organizations who formed their beliefs into physical reality made an immense and lasting impact on the attitude of the British people. But the struggle was far from over.

Despite its campaigning and its clinic the Malthusian League in 1921 was in difficulties. Many people were coming to advocate birth control, but very few of the new birth controllers were in close agreement with the theories of the League. Some of the newcomers joined it, but many, like Marie Stopes, found it quite impossible to accept the League's limited economic arguments for the use of contraception. The character of the League was altered by the newcomers and in 1922 it changed its name to the 'New Generation League'. Even so it remained unacceptable to many.

The thoughts of Marie Stopes on the subject were a far cry from anything the Malthusians might have dreamed of. Although she did give some consideration to eugenic and social aspects of family limitation her overriding message was that of personal need. She saw birth control as a weapon in the struggle to save women from the bondage of unwanted pregnancies, and as a means of offering them freedom, sexual satisfaction and joyful motherhood. She hated to be thought of as an eccentric, and the phrase *constructive* birth control' was used by her to indicate that she was certainly not anti-baby or anti-child. She simply wanted to see mothers and children both happy and healthy.

There are already a number of books which deal with her life and trials, and she herself was a prolific writer. We cannot do her true justice in a few pages, but suffice it to say that even without her espousal of the cause of birth control, she would have earned a place in the history of the twentieth century. Her achievements as a scientist were noteable, and she was also well-known as a poet and playwright. For the majority of us however, it is in the field of birth control that her name is most familiar. Her first book, called *Married Love* was published in 1918, after her unsatisfactory first marriage. She wanted to spare others some of the misery and frustration which she had suffered through ignorance of sexual matters. *Married Love* was a runaway best seller, in great demand from the time of its appearance. It scarcely mentioned birth control at all, but before very long she found herself innundated with letters from her readers who wanted further information on this essential aspect of married life. She therefore produced a second volume entitled *Wise Parenthood* in which she recommended the cervical cap as being the best means of contraception. This was the method that she held to be the best available throughout her career as a birth controller, and the method which was usually prescribed at her clinic.

She was greatly helped in her endeavours by her second husband, H. V. Roe. The clinic was opened with his help, and financially supported by both of them. Roe had offered the financial backing to open a clinic at St Mary's Hospital in Manchester as early as 1917. His offer was very generous: £1,000 a year for 5 years and £12,000 on his death, but no institution could be found who would take it up. Four years later the following inscription was framed and hung upon the wall of the clinic in Holloway:

This, the first Birth Control Clinic in the British Empire, was opened on the 17th of March, 1921, by Humphrey Verdon Roe and his wife Marie Carmichael Stopes, in order to show by actual example what might be done for mothers and their children with no great difficulty, and what should be done all over the world when once the idea takes root in the public mind that motherhood should be voluntary and guided by the best scientific knowledge available.

This clinic is free to all, and is supported entirely by the two founders. Those who have benefitted by its help are asked to hand on a knowledge of its existence to others and help to create a public opinion which will force the Ministry of Health to include a similar service in Ante-Natal and Welfare Centres already supported by the Government in every district.

The clinic occasioned great interest; her books were widely read, and an enormously successful public meeting held at Queen's Hall. According to Marie Stopes, her success was in some measure a '*reaction from* Malthusianism'. She was somewhat scathing about the League, its small size, its conservatism and the 'handicap' of its economic policy. She imagined birth control being brought, largely by her efforts, to a position

14. Francis Place (1771–1854), who started the birth control movement in Britain in 1823. *By courtesy of The National Portrait Gallery.*

TO THE

MARRIED OF BOTH SEXES

OF THE

WORKING PEOPLE.

———◆———

THIS paper is addressed to the reasonable and considerate among you, the most numerous and most useful class of society.

It is not intended to produce vice and debauchery, but to destroy vice, and put an end to debauchery.

It is a great truth, often told and never denied, that when there are too many working people in any trade or manufacture, they are worse paid than they ought to be paid, and are compelled to work more hours than they ought to work.

When the number of working people in any trade or manufacture, has for some years been too great, wages are reduced very low, and the working people become little better than slaves.

15. The Diabolical Handbills. These are two pages from a small pamphlet which qualify for a place in history as being the first leaflets ever produced in a campaign to educate the public about birth control. The leaflets were circulating in England during the year 1823.

When wages have thus been reduced to a very small sum, working people can no longer maintain their children as all good and respectable people wish to maintain their children, but are compelled to neglect them;—to send them to different employments;—to Mills and Manufactories, at a very early age.

The misery of these poor children cannot be described, and need not be described to you, who witness them and deplore them every day of your lives.

Many indeed among you are compelled for a bare subsistence to labour incessantly from the moment you rise in the morning to the moment you lie down again at night, with out even the hope of ever being better off.

The sickness of yourselves and your children, the privation and pain and premature death of those you love but cannot cherish as you wish, need only be alluded to. You know all these evils too well.

And, what, you will ask is the remedy?

How are we avoid these miseries?

The answer is short and plain: the means are easy. Do as other people do, to avoid having more children than they wish to have, and can easily maintain.

What is done by other people is this. A piece of soft sponge is tied by a bobbin or penny ribbon, and inserted just before the sexual intercourse takes place, and is with drawn again as soon as it has taken place. Many tie a piece of sponge to each end of

The appeal made by Place is frankly economic and the problem is stated quite simply; he observes that the solution 'is short and plain : the means are easy'.

16. 'Arrest them all—The laws of decency must be respected!' The attitude of Comstock's generation to a large working class family is in sharp contrast to their denial of the use of any form of birth control.

where it could be considered in its essential medical and physiological aspects and taken away from 'the controversial cult of economics and party politics'.

She founded the Society for Constructive Birth Control and Racial Progress (the CBC) in the same year. Its declared objects were first:

to bring home to all the fundamental nature of the reforms involved in conscious control of conception and the illumination of sex life as a basis for racial progress;

and second:

to consider the individual, national, international, racial, political, economic, scientific, spiritual, and other aspects of the theme, for which purpose meetings will be held, publications issued, Research Committees, Commissions of Enquiry and other activities will be organised from time to time as circumstances require and facilities offer.

The CBC was to undertake a great deal of pioneering, and to meet prejudices head-on. But one clinic did not solve the whole problem, nor did it very quickly change the opinions of the medical profession or the members of the public who opposed the practice. Even the doctors who favoured birth control did not necessarily agree with Marie Stopes. As in all movements, personalities played an important part, and a good many of them found it difficult to agree with her methods. Her books were described by one specialist, well known for his advocacy of birth control, as 'practical handbooks of prostitution'. Many doctors did not approve of the clinic because normal cases were not seen by a gynaecologist, but simply fitted with a cervical cap by a nurse. Only abnormal patients were referred to such a specialist.

Eventually the Marie Stopes Clinic was moved from Holloway to a more central location in Whitfield Street, just off Tottenham Court Road in London where it remains, still giving a valuable service today. The original clinic was sold to a manufacturer, who used it as a retail outlet for contraceptives. Nor was he the first to enter such a market. Norman Himes commented on the 'commercialization of contraceptive instruction' and observed that a considerable body of literature was available from shops and through advertisements in newspapers and journals. A quick check through the sources he quotes showed us that most of the businesses he mentioned are still there today, and still occupying the same unaltered premises, in many cases. Despite disparaging remarks about the 'rubber shops' which may be heard even now from the 'respectable' side of the contraceptive business, the contribution which they made towards informing the public over the years must have been enormous.

The CBC pioneered many new ventures and among the most interesting was the early use of mobile clinics. Today, there are many strangely-located family planning centres, some on boats and some in vans, but Marie Stopes was certainly the first to think of having a clinic in a mobile caravan. The first caravan took to the road in 1927, going first to Bethnal Green where it was parked outside the public library. It then ventured on more rural trips around the South of England, and was for some time engaged in work in the valleys of South Wales. A second clinic toured the North of England. The mobile clinics had the dual function of helping and instructing patients and also contacting and teaching contraceptive techniques to the local medical staff. Naturally, such an activity was not allowed to continue without opposition, and the northern clinic was destroyed by fire. This led to a court case, as did so many incidents in Marie Stopes's career. However, such destruction made her even more determined to carry on, and a new caravan was soon fitted out and took over the work.

The other clinic to be opened in London in 1921 was the East Street Welfare Centre for Pre-Maternity, Maternity and

Child Welfare. It began its work in Walworth on 9 November of that year and it functions there still. The Welfare Centre represented the Malthusian League's long awaited dream. Its opening was finally made possible through the generosity of two supporters, Mr John Sumner who bought the house and let it to the League at a very low rent, and another benefactor who gave £350 to defray the expenses of the first year's running costs. The clinic was to perform all of the normal functions of a welfare centre, with the addition of a birth control service. Both the League and Marie Stopes reiterated that they were still opposed in principle to the opening of private clinics. This one was simply intended as a model for the authorities to learn from. The League insisted that it was the function of the Government to provide a full medical service, and that they were merely showing them how to do it.

They were not very successful in their enterprise. Despite many efforts to popularize their services, especially those to do with maternal and child health only twenty women appeared between December 1921 and May 1923 to ask for ante-natal advice. Only seven of these ever returned to take advantage of the birth control clinic. Few women took advantage of the well-baby clinic either. These services were already provided at the official clinics which women were accustomed to attending. From July 1923 the ante-natal and baby clinics were regretfully abandoned. The Committee deplored having to take this step but they had financial problems, and were hard put to it to provide money to keep any services in operation. The clinic was saved only by severing its connections with the Malthusian League in September 1922 and establishing an independent Committee to run it. Sumner again came to the rescue and gave the Committee the premises on a rent-free basis. He also donated a generous sum to the funds.

Not all the women who attended the clinic were women

who had large families. Some had small families and wanted their children to have better health, homes and education. 'It isn't fair on the children to have any more' was frequently heard. Many of them had long records of induced abortions. The doctors reported improvement in the health of such patients, once contraceptives were used instead.

Workers at the clinic soon discovered that the more tragic the woman's history, the more difficult it was to help. Patients were encountered who had had as many as thirteen children, (nine living), and two miscarriages. One such woman was pregnant at her first visit, and never returned. Another aged 33 had seven children, four of whom were living, and she had had four miscarriages. She became pregnant again, having failed to use her pessary, and a letter sent to try to encourage her to come back was returned with the single word 'deceased' inscribed on the envelope. Many such women could rarely visit the clinic, could not afford to pay for supplies, and were so ill and broken that they sometimes failed to use the supplies which were given to them.

However, the clinic staff did have some success. In a group of thirty-two mothers who had more than seven children, half of them succeeded in avoiding pregnancy for at least three years, and many passed the menopause without becoming pregnant again. Of the remaining half only three returned to say that they could not use the appliances they had been given.

By 1924 the Walworth Woman's Welfare Centre, as it had then become, was working well and many of the doctors who visited it were sufficiently impressed to think of starting something similar in their own locality. The Committee began to see possibilities of gentle expansion, and in April 1924 it changed its name again, this time to The Society for the Provision of Birth Control Clinics. During the next seven years, sixteen more clinics were opened under its auspices. The North Kensington Women's Welfare Centre opened in

November 1924, in an overcrowded and poverty-stricken part of that area. By 1927 this centre was taking many new initiatives, and made the first systematic attempt to follow up 'dropouts'. They managed to trace about 100 women who had failed to return to the centre and gathered some illuminating information in the process. It was soon discerned that one of the real needs was to find cheaper, simpler and more effective contraceptives.

The first centre to open outside London was at Wolverhampton, where in May 1925 the pioneers began work in two small and inconvenient rooms, which were only tolerated because they were so cheap. During the industrial dispute in the collieries in the following year, the Wolverhampton workers were able to set up in a temporary centre at Cannock Chase where 164 miner's wives were given free treatment. These women came in crowds, starving and ill and already with large families.

Other clinics became established as fast as possible. Soon they were functioning in Cambridge, Manchester, Shoreditch, Glasgow, Aberdeen, Oxford, Birmingham, Rotherham, Newcastle, Ashington, Exeter, Nottingham, Pontypridd and Bristol. The Bristol clinic opened in 1931 and dealt with 106 patients during its first six months. Walworth, the first, had seen 14,527 women during its first ten years. During this same period the Society's clinics together had dealt with well over 30,000 patients. The tide was most certainly turning.

Not surprisingly, the doctors and workers at these centres soon felt the need to come together occasionally and discuss their common problems. North Kensington initiated the first such conference, and after holding two similar meetings the parent body organized a larger one in 1930, to which other specialists were invited, A second body, the Birth Control Investigation Committee was also formed on the initiative of the workers in North Kensington and Cambridge. This

Committee was started in 1926 with the aim of bringing together a group of distinguished and impartial persons who would have differing specialities and views, but who would all be interested in furthering knowledge on various aspects of birth control. The Committee began a detailed study of statistical material gathered by the clinics, and a great deal of this analysis was presented at the 7th International Birth Control Conference at Zurich in 1930. But this statistical work was only one of the many interests of the Committee.

The group obtained the co-operation of Dr C. P. Blacker and the Eugenics Society and took the much-needed step of starting research which would make available new, or at least improved, methods of birth control. A gift from Mr C. F. Chance made it financially possible for Dr John Baker of Oxford University to undertake research into the chemical nature of spermicides. This work resulted in the production of 'Volpar' (a contraction of *Vol*untary *Par*enthood)—a spermicide which was harmless but effective, and which was soon mass-produced and hence made easily available.

A further organization which was rather similar to the Committee was the International Medical Group for the Investigation of Contraception, formed at the Population Conference held at Geneva in 1927. This group's annual reports were edited and published by Dr C. P. Blacker, who was Secretary of the Committee and Chairman of the Group. Emphasis in these reports was placed on topics of statistical and scientific interest concerning the use and effectiveness of contraceptive methods, and upon research which might lead to the development of better ones.

The diversity of these organizations is important since each worked in its own area and sphere of interest. At the same time. despite all their aims to remain non-political and to keep birth control as a non-party issue, the desire to see advice and treatment made available at Government clinics was not likely to become a reality unless the Government was drawn into the struggle. The Ministry of Health had to be convinced.

Birth control was an issue which interested many of the rank and file members of the Labour party, though they were quite unimpressed by the Malthusian League and certainly rejected most of the thoughts of Malthus himself. However, once birth control was freed from this Malthusianism many people found that it was a cause which they could support. In 1923 the Women's Co-operative Guild resolved 'That this Congress urges upon the Ministry of Health and local Authorities the advisability of information in regard to birth control being given at all maternity and child welfare centres in the country'. Working-class organizations and many well-known Labour leaders were also drawn closer into the fight when two libertarian communists were arrested in London and prosecuted for selling copies of Margaret Sanger's *Family Limitation*. The pamphlet was held to be obscene and was subsequently destroyed.

Various deputations pressed their demands upon the Minister of Health who happened to be a Roman Catholic. He was not much in sympathy and either rejected their requests or side-stepped the issue by saying that welfare centres already had a directive that if a patient should avoid pregnancy on medical grounds, she was referred to a private practitioner or a hospital. This rule was of little practical use, however, since those who really needed advice could not afford a private practitioner. Even if they could, the chances of him knowing anything about birth control were rather remote. Hospitals, of course, were crowded and busy. They were unable or unwilling to meet such needs. Eventually the Ministry decided to allow the Welfare Centres to refer such women to the Medical Officer of a Birth Control Clinic (although there were less than twenty in the whole country), and some centres began to take advantage of this service for their most hard-pressed patients.

In the teeth of the struggle the Worker's Birth Control Group was set up to bring pressure to bear on Parliament and to gain support within the Labour party. The Ministry had to be made to see birth control as an essential aspect of public health. There followed a period of intense work, and resolutions were passed by many groups favouring birth control. At the head of this struggle were Mrs Dora Russell, Mrs Stella Browne and Mrs Frida Laski. The activities of this group and the other similar bodies led to startling changes in public opinion, and by 1926 a resolution was passed in the House of Lords calling upon the Government to remove all obstacles to the introduction of birth control services into the existing maternal and child welfare clinics.

The local authorities were not opposed to the idea that this service should be made available through their facilities. Indeed, some of them had already tried to introduce birth control services, but had discovered that in so doing they fell foul of the Ministry's regulations. However, the more progressive councils (and Shoreditch was among them), took an active part in trying to change the Ministry directives and asked other councils to put pressure on the Ministry of Health. Local authority representatives were also present at a large conference convened at Central Hall, Westminster, in April 1930. This Conference represented a powerful lobby of public opinion for it was organized by the Society for the Provision of Birth Control Clinics, the Workers' Birth Control Group, The National Union of Societies for Equal Citizenship and the Women's National Liberal Federation. Delegates came from 35 public health authorities, the 16 maternal and child welfare centres and 132 other organizations.

A resolution was passed, with only three dissenters, calling upon the Minister of Health to: 'recognize the desirability of making available medical information on methods of birth control to married women who need it'. The work which began in 1921 showed positive results three months after the passing of this resolution. In July 1930 the Minister issued Memorandum 153 MCW, a document outlining the revised policy of the Government with regard to the provision of birth control advice by local authorities. The memorandum gave permissive authority to allow such advice to be given to several categories of women: those who were normally in attendance at a maternal and child welfare centre; those who were nursing and expectant mothers; and women who were attending a gynaecological clinic for medical treatment.

In the same year, the public were surprised to hear the resolution which had been carried by the Lambeth Conference of Bishops. Ten years earlier the Anglican Church had been as opposed to contraception as the Roman Catholic. Now it suddenly recognized that there was a moral justification for birth control. In a part of their discussion the bishops declared:

Nevertheless, in those cases where there is such a clearly felt moral obligation to limit or avoid parenthood, and where there is a morally sound reason for avoiding complete abstinence, the Conference agrees that other methods may be used, provided that this is done in the light of the same Christian principles.

It was in 1930 too that an extremely important new organization appeared. In August of that year the National Birth Control Council (now known as the Family Planning Association), was founded. The Malthusian League had been disbanded at the end of 1927. Its members agreed that birth control was now well accepted and that the League could suspend its activity. It could be reformed if the need ever arose but the Council effectively took over the campaigning and propaganda work. Its function was to centralize and co-ordinate the work of the five existing organizations, for there was still a vast amount to be done. Yet its very foundation represents a great achievement. The nine years which passed from the opening of the first two clinics had been years of hard fighting. The pioneers at Walworth, and Marie Stopes herself, had been pelted with eggs; the clinic premises had been damaged and the windows smashed. The founders of the Manchester clinic were called in the Press 'overdressed, well fed and badly bred', and were described as flaunting cigarettes between painted lips and pushing birth control down the throats of the poor. The League of National Life was formed to oppose the birth controllers, although most of its outputs of information was somewhat unconvincing. And many members of the medical profession still remained unpersuaded.

When Lord Dawson spoke out he succeeded in startling the medical profession into a line of serious discussion, but their deliberations were painfully slow. In 1923 *The Practitioner* produced a special number devoted to birth control. Female emancipation had wrought changes and

contraceptives has now become a commonplace of conversation at women's clubs and mixed tea-tables. This attitude, which was at first merely defiant . . . became frankly practical, material, and utilitarian. Women of unblemished virtue espoused the cause, and eagerly advocated it on the highest moral grounds, summoning to their aid a wealth of intimate detail to which no man has ever dared to aspire. The floodgates of special knowledge being thus unlocked the stream would seem at the moment to be carrying all before it.

The Practitioner had found that the books being written by such women contained practical information but also possessed aspects of which doctors might disapprove. The special edition was designed to help the doctor decide how best to deal with the subject. There were, for example, vexed problems such as whether degenerate members of society should be sterilized. However, most practitioners had more immediate need of knowing quite simply what to advise when confronted by an enquiring patient. Unfortunately there was little discussion about normal couples, although the editor did consider birth control as a valuable weapon against the use of abortion. Oddly enough, he thought that birth control would never be taught to male medical students. The schools for women would doubtless teach it 'for women are more practical and less hypocritical'. (And this only about 40 years after the profession had thundered about the possibility of women practising medicine at all.)

Although in principle the special edition was a good idea the papers in it are a great disappointment. Only one of the contributors, Norman Haire, seems to have any practical experience. The other learned doctors read as if they were still opposed to the idea of contraception, or, at best, completely confused about the whole subject. Sir Maurice Abbot–Anderson the Princess Royal's Physician, entitled his contribution 'Birth Control as seen by an Open Mind' and he managed to find eugenic justifications for the practice. He thought that the sponge or a 'Malthusian pessary' (i.e. a cervical cap), were the least harmful means of achieving it. The intra-uterine device was categorized as 'a barbarous weapon' and an abortifacient. The writer clearly has his feet firmly placed in the nineteenth century. He suggests that the use of contraceptives may render a woman insane, and ends by regretting that he

cannot now go more deeply and scientifically into other general harmful effects of the constant use of contraceptives, but I should regard this paper as quite incomplete if I did not definitely lay stress on the point that it is an established fact that complete sterility may result therefrom.

Most of the other papers are about as encouraging. The doctors managed to justify contraception for lunatics, and seemed sure that any normal person who tried to space his family would end up by becoming one. Some railed against the 'rubber shops' and wanted to have them closed down. They 'advertise and sell contraceptive appliances together with books and literature of an objectionable erotic character. They are a very grave moral danger'. Another contributor had been reading

a popular periodical devoted to the interests of dog fanciers, and noticed in a prominent position of the advertisement column a series of small announcements whereby books on birth control were advertised in the same type and style side by side with books on whelping and puppy rearing, including 'valuable recipes'!

This led the writer to wonder whether 'this so-called "sex education" of the masses is to the ultimate good of the community. . . . Furthermore, where is it going to end?'

It was clearly stated that 'eugenic ideals' were being prostituted to the lowest type of commercialism. Doctors were worried that since the 'Flower of the nation's manhood' had been depleted by the war, the fit people who were left should restrict their fertility whilst 'derelicts' who could not afford books on family planning, and who in any case were illiterate, were breeding as fast as they liked. The loss of their only sons was said to have brought the lesson home to the middle-class who had accepted family planning earlier. Mothers who played bridge and golf rather than accepting maternal responsibility now regretted their folly. Small families were all very well, but the 'seed of Malthusianism . . . will be as difficult to check . . . as it is to eradicate poppies from the fields of Flanders'.

Anyone looking through the ninety-six pages in the hope of finding a little practical information might have found it hard to do other than agree with the persuasive pens of the 'experts', and might even have decided to restrict sexual intercourse to 'about eight days' a month, for one writer assured everyone that they would not conceive after the 17th day following menstruation. This procedure was safer than risking one's health by using 'contracepts'. Contraception was equated with masturbation and everyone knew the grave diseases which followed such a practice. Those who had studied the subject deeply were equally sure that variations in sex-play such as oral-genital contact were also dangerous though few writers would even mention such a dreadful activity.

Norman Haire wrote the longest paper in the issue, a consideration of 1,400 case histories. His ideas changed over the years as he gained more experience, but at the time of writing he was opposed to intra–uterine methods, and recommended the Mensinga diaphragm. He pleaded for more study by the medical profession, for 'only thus may it [contraception] be rescued from the hands of quacks and charlatans and non-medical doctors who write erotic treatises on birth control conveying misleading information in a highly stimulating form'. One is left somewhat bewildered as to how Dr Haire managed to find any of these publications either stimulating or erotic (a criticism, it will be recalled, that was also aimed at the *Fruits of Philosophy*). Perhaps we are accustomed to taking so much for granted now, but most of the publications were very mundane little pamphlets with a simple explanation of contraceptive technique, and perhaps some justification of the use of birth control.

Some were written by well-known figures. The 'non-medical doctor' is, of course, a reference to Marie Stopes. Her writing is sometimes a little ornate but it hardly qualifies as being in the erotic category. Even allowing for certain eccentric beliefs which she held, her work was far more sensible than anything produced by the medical men of the time, who all found much more to say about moral principle than medical practice.

Roman Catholics, of course, stood out strongly as opponents of contraception, and were often engaged in battle with the birth controllers. The Church has not changed to any great degree, although nowadays the fighting is far less militant and tends to be as much between Catholics as against outsiders.

In the nineteen-twenties, though, there were pitched battles. The *Catholic Medical Guardian* regularly published papers by leading opponents of contraception, which in retrospect seem either funny or pathetic. One doctor, also noted for his championship of the League of National Life, discovered a new (contraceptive-induced) disease in which the uterus was enlarged and softened and the patient suffered unpleasant discharges and heavy, painful periods. The woman looked 'drawn and anxious' 'through the fear of the failure of the contraceptive method and the fear of pregnancy'. Instead of seeing that the woman was offered a more reliable method this particular doctor made the patient stop using any contraceptive method at all. He called his newly invented complaint the 'Malthusian uterus'.

Today the *principle* of family planning is no longer opposed by the Catholic Church. The opposition is to the use of artificial methods to achieve such an end. One can perhaps be excused for wondering just how great an advance is this.

In Britain the pioneers had to fight against medical, religious and private opinion. But at least there were no prohibitive laws to hinder them further. In America the prevention of conception had been illegal since 1873, and various European countries enacted similar laws during the present century. France and her colonies made contraception illegal in 1920. Like many countries, including Britain, she too was suffering from a new wave of that peculiar dread of depopulation which occasionally sweeps across Europe. But the law did little to stimulate population growth. The French Malthusians were flung into dissarray and intelligent discussion virtually ceased, but the main result of outlawing contraception was a massive rise in the number of illegal abortions. Nazi Germany similarly attempted to stimulate population growth, and achieved no greater degree of success.

The failure of such campaigns to stimulate population

growth may sometimes cause one to speculate that massive birth control campaigns, if tackled from the wrong standpoint, may similarly be doomed to failure. Fertility is so deeply personal that couples will control the number of their children according to their own desires. They are not readily influenced by legality or by the needs of the State. Demographers and politicians may regard a particular birth-rate as a desirable national aim, but this has little effect on a woman who wants a lot of babies, or a woman who regards even one pregnancy as a personal tragedy. Conversely, when contraception is withdrawn illegal abortion is the sad resort of many unfortunate women, and it was the effect of such operations upon poor women in New York City that brought the American nurse Margaret Sanger into the fight for birth control in the United States.

CHAPTER NINE

From National to International

MARGARET Sanger played, in the American birth-control movement, a rather similar role to that of Marie Stopes in the British. For this reason it is almost impossible to avoid comparing the two women and certainly they were very similar in many ways. They both had the energy and initiative to achieve a great deal, but at a more personal level, neither was an easy woman to get along with. However much they may have been motivated by high ideals and humanitarian principles, each tended to regard birth control and its advocacy as her own personal property. Both ladies were fond of publicity and liked to take the major credit for whatever was achieved, despite the fact that other, less well-known and self-seeking people may have been responsible for the greater part of the work. Neither of them could tolerate any organization which she could not completely dominate. To some extent the history of birth control has been distorted by books and articles which have tried to make saints of these two women. They were far from saints. They worked hard and their achievements are remarkable but the contribution of the women who worked day after day in clinics like North Kensington was every bit as important, though never so well publicized.

Margaret Sanger's own contribution sprang partly from compassion and partly from radicalism. At the beginning of this century, any American doctors who wanted to add a chapter on birth control to their textbooks of gynaecology discovered that they were unable to do so. Pages of such books were sometimes left completely blank—an eloquent protest against the powers of the censor. The spoken as well as the written word was also repressed, and so great interest was aroused when the nearest American equivalent to Lord Dawson of Penn's speech was given by the President of the American Medical Association, Dr. A. Jacobi, in 1912. In the same year the President of the British Medical Association also endorsed birth control, but his American counterpart was far braver. Not only did he face the disapproval of his colleagues and of the public, but he was also in danger of falling foul of the Comstock law.

Dr Jacobi was the grand old man of American pediatrics. He was well known for his fondness of children. It therefore came as a shock when he suggested that

It has become an indispensable suggestion that only a certain number of babies should be born into the world. As long as not infrequently even the well-to-do limit the number of their offspring, the advice to the poor—or those to whom the raising of a large family is worse than merely difficult—to limit the number of children, even the healthy ones, is perhaps more than merely excusable.

I often learn that an American family has had ten children, but only three or four survived. Before the dead ones succumbed they were a source of expense, poverty and morbidity to the few survivors. For the interests of the latter and the health of the community at large, they had better not have been born.

It was within this climate of repressive but changing opinion that Margaret Sanger began her propagandist work for the cause of contraception. As with Marie Stopes, her life has been well documented by many other authors. They point out that as a nurse in New York her curiosity about birth control was first aroused when she worked among the poor. For many women abortion was an all too frequent outcome of pregnancy, and many of them begged her to tell them the secret used by the rich to limit their family size. Most of these

G

poor women looked at her in disbelief when she said that she knew of no secret, and that as far as she could judge, the answer lay in the few simple methods which anyone could use: the condom for example, or withdrawal. This then was the compassionate stimulus for her early work.

But at the same time Mrs Sanger and her husband mixed both with the radicals and the anarchists of New York. She herself was a socialist and took part in the activities of the Labour movement. She marched with the 'Wobblies' (The Industrial Workers of the World), and was bitterly opposed to the prevailing social order. In 1914 she began to publish a magazine called *The Woman Rebel* and determined to make it as 'red and flaming as possible'. In strident tones, the *Rebel* proclaimed that 'the marriage bed is the most degenerating influence on the social order'. It enumerated the 'rights' claimed by the 'Rebel Women'. They were the right to be lazy; the right to be an unmarried mother; the right to destroy; the right to create; the right to love; and the right to live. A woman's duty was 'To look the whole world in the face with a go-to-hell look in the eyes; to have an ideal; to speak and act in defiance of convention'.

The aim of the paper was to 'stimulate working women to think for themselves and build up a conscious fighting character'. The *Rebel* announced that the law pertaining to contraception would be defied—hardly the kind of talk which would make the average legislator listen sympathetically. It printed a prose poem enthusing and rejoicing in the Bomb—the Anarchist's bomb, a potent symbol of the movement, and it also presented contributions with titles like 'A Defense of Assassination'. The paper took its ideas and its style from other radicals, including the notorious Emma Goldman, but it went even further than she did in its demands. It attacked all of the usual radical targets, and vilified men like Rockefeller. Apart from the paper itself, Mrs Sanger produced a small pamphlet called *Family Limitation*. Neither the magazine not the pamphlet were the kind of literature that Comstock could tolerate. It was soon announced that she had violated no less than nine federal statutes. The day before the trial was due to be held, Margaret Sanger fled to England.

It was in England that she met the Drysdales and learned, for the first time, the story of the Malthusian League. She is said to have fallen in love with Havelock Ellis. Certainly it was he who encouraged her to concentrate upon birth control to the exclusion of the other radical causes which she had espoused. It was also he who supervised her studies at the British Museum. She met Marie Stopes, although what transpired between them is uncertain. Marie Stopes wrote *Married Love* in 1914, and if she had not finished it already, it must have been in the final stages at the time of their meeting. According to Margaret Sanger, Dr Stopes thought that the book would 'electrify England', although it seems odd that if Marie Stopes really did hold such an opinion, she refrained from publishing the book for another four years. Mrs. Sanger also claimed that Dr Stopes knew nothing of birth control at all, and that it was she who taught her all about it. The two were friendly in these early days, but later Mrs Sanger seems to have become unwilling to acknowledge other workers, an idiosyncracy which leads to a number of embarrassing passages and a certain amount of inaccuracy in some of her books.

During Margaret Sanger's absence from America, other radicals and members of the birth-control movement continued their work. The remarkable Emma Goldman who had been lecturing for years decided to discuss contraception more openly than before. She was both fined and imprisoned for circulating birth-control literature. Others were arrested for distributing a pamphlet which she had prepared called *Why and how the poor should not have many children*. Another campaign was started by a periodical called *The Medical Review of*

Reviews. Some 'sandwich' men selected from among the poorest members of the community walked about the city bearing banners inscribed with such sentiments as

I am a burden to myself and the State. Should I be allowed to propagate? Would the prisons and asylums be filled if my kind had no children? I cannot read this sign. By what right have I children? I must drink alcohol to sustain life. Shall I transfer the craving to others?

William Sanger, Margaret Sangers' first husband, was arrested and brought to trial late in 1915. One of Comstock's decoys had managed to trap him into giving out a copy of *Family Limitation.* Comstock caught a chill at the trial and died a few days later, but his death did not mean any relaxation of the law. However, there was growing an increasingly large lobby who felt that the law ought to be changed. They also felt that disruptive tactics and the creation of martyrs was not the best way of achieving such reform. It would be better to make a concerted effort to bring about a change by more reasonable means. In March 1915 the National Birth Control League was organized by a group of Liberal women, the best known of whom was Mary Ware Dennett. They demanded a change in the law

The League specifically declares that to classify purely scientific information regarding human contraception as obscene, as our present laws do, is itself an act affording a most disgraceful example of intolerable indecency.

Information when scientifically sound, should be readily available. Such knowledge is of immediate and positive individual and social benefit. All laws which hamper the free and responsible diffusion of knowledge among the people are in the highest degree pernicious and opposed to the best and most permanent interests of society.

The National Birth Control League attracted many professional people. Three of its legally qualified members drafted amendments to both State and Federal laws. The League also prepared petition slips, which were circulated to the electorate, demanding changes in legislation at both levels.

Mrs Sanger returned to America shortly after her husband's trial and found the League organized and hard at work. One cannot say exactly what happened when she met the League, since the accounts given by the two sides disagree. One version suggests that she was asked to become a Committee member, but 'She declined, stating that she did not think it wise to be officially a part of any organization, as she was likely to go to jail, and she did not want her mishaps to involve the activity of others, also that she felt it to be her particular function to break the laws rather than to spend effort at that time in trying to change them.' Mrs Sanger's own story recounts that Mrs Dennett told her she could expect no help from the League since they disagreed with her methods and that a law-abiding organization, specifically formed to change the laws, could not support one who had broken them.

In fact, Mrs Sanger did not go to prison for her earlier offences and the outstanding Federal indictments were dropped. It has been suggested that a letter to President Wilson, written by Marie Stopes and signed by eight other notable British citizens may have had some influence on this decision. The letter pointed out that

We in England passed, a generation ago, through the phase of prohibiting the expressions of serious and disinterested opinion on a subject of such grave importance to humanity, and in our view to suppress any such treatment of vital subjects is detrimental to human progress. Hence, not only for the benefit of Mrs Sanger, but of humanity, we respectfully beg you to exert your powerful influence in the interest of free speech and the betterment of the race.

After the case had been dropped, Mrs Sanger continued to

break the law. Again she was arrested, but again she escaped without punishment.

Others were less lucky. Among them was a young man named Van Kleeck Allison who edited a paper called *The Flame*. After handing out contraceptive leaflets in Boston he was brought before a Roman Catholic judge who took a serious view of such an offence and sentenced him to three years imprisonment. Fortunately for him the case attracted a great deal of publicity and the young man was released after serving only two months. The Birth Control League of Massachusetts was founded as a direct result of the proceedings. But Mrs Sanger seemed bent upon further defiance, and her next act was to try to open a birth-control clinic. She had been impressed with those she had seen in Holland and had learned something of their workings from the Dutch, although Aletta Jacobs who had started the work there had not been impressed with Mrs Sanger and had snubbed her rather pointedly.

The clinic was opened at 46 Amboy Street, Brownsville, on 16 October 1916. The work was shared by Margaret Sanger and her sister Ethel Byrne, who were nurses, and two social workers, Fania Mindell and Elizabeth Stuyvesant. The news spread fast and soon a long queue of women had collected. Some were pregnant and hoping for abortions, but others were eager to learn how to avoid pregnancy altogether. The clinic worked for ten days before the vice squad appeared and removed the staff. Once in prison, Ethel Byrne went on hunger strike and was pardoned after she had served 11 days. She had become so ill that she seemed about to die. Margaret Sanger was released on bail, and promptly reopened the clinic. The police rearrested her, equally promptly, and charged her with 'maintaining a public nuisance'. She served thirty days in prison, a lenient sentence compared with those served on others such as Van Kleeck Allison, and it was the only term in prison that she ever did serve. The case had a notable consequence in that the judge of the Court of Appeals interpreted the phrase 'for the cure and prevention of disease' to be applicable to any disease at all. Previously it had been taken to refer solely to venereal diseases. The change was an important one for the future of the movement.

On her emergence from prison the New York Birth Control League was founded and a new journal *Birth Control Review* also appeared. This latter work was performed in co-operation with a fellow radical, but the venture was short lived. Soon there were quarrels, for both parties were eager to dominate the enterprise and neither was willing to take second place. The split caused a great deal of unpleasantness and led to Mrs Sanger making a complaint to the District Attorney. This action was taken very badly in radical circles, and brought a complete break between Mrs Sanger and any other radical sympathisers.

By this time there were many small birth-control organizations, but none of them were strong or very well financed. Many attempts were made to change State legislation, but all were doomed whilst the Federal legislation stood. The Voluntary Parenthood League was formed in 1919 to concentrate specifically on Washington. It consisted of many of the members of the old National Birth Control League and its policy was similarly to change the law and permit the free dissemination of information.

Two years later, in 1921, Margaret Sanger had found more support, and with financial help from prominent people she managed to continue publishing *Birth Control Review*. She was also able to organize a conference formally to establish the American Birth Control League. As President, she then took a curious policy in advocating a bill which would permit doctors only to disseminate both advice and contraceptives. This policy led to heated antagonism, for Mrs Dennet and her League who had been advocating the removal of all restrictions

were now amazed to see Mrs Sanger, who had preferred breaking laws to changing them, coming out in favour of keeping
birth control classified with obscenity and allowing information to be given only to those who requested it from a
doctor.

It has been seriously suggested that the slowness with which
professional people became involved in the fight and the length
of time it took to change the laws (the last sting of the Comstock laws was removed as recently as 1966) was in no small
measure due to Mrs Sanger's efforts. Her revolutionary lean-
ings, her noisy law-breaking and her emotional statements ('I
have dedicated my life to this *fight*') together with her appeals
(which of course made good newspaper copy) asking people to
prepare for the 'long fight' and 'overthrow tyranny' were
repellent to professional men, most of whom were quiet,
conservative, law-abiding and usually quite ignorant of the
issues involved. Her manner of presentation only succeeded in
convincing those who had influence that it was probably a
good policy to keep the whole business illegal.

The more informed members of the medical and legal
profession were not opposed to birth control itself. Many co-
operated with the more conservative Voluntary Parenthood
League. Indeed, there were judges on its National Council, and
the League knew of situations prior to 1919 where judges had
dealt sympathetically with the cases which had come before
them, where the defendants had large, unsupportable families.
One judge suggested that such a defendant should be allowed to
learn about birth control, and added 'Theodore Roosevelt, with
his anti-race suicide talk, has done more harm in this country
than any other living man'. Judge Wadhams of New York
was confronted by a woman, guilty for the second time of
burglary. She had a husband suffering from tuberculosis and
six children. The judge passed suspended sentence and commented:

Her husband is not permitted by the authorities to work because of his being ill with tuberculosis. It would be dangerous for him to work on children's garments. It might spread consumption to the innocents. There is a law against that. As a result of this law, the husband has had no work for four years. Nevertheless, he goes on producing children who have very little chance under the conditions to be anything but tubercular and themselves growing up, repeat the process with society. There is no law against that.

But we have not only no birth regulation in such cases, but if information is given with respect to birth regulation, people are brought to the bar of justice for it. There is a law they violate. The question is whether we have the most intelligent law on this subject we might have. . . . I believe we are living in an age of ignorance, which at some future time will be looked on aghast.

In 1923 the New York Birth Control Clinical Research Bureau was opened as a Department of the American Birth Control League. Although later the clinic was better known as the Margaret Sanger Research Bureau, in the early days her influence was not altogether helpful, in that doctors and many others viewed the Bureau as a source of propaganda rather than a medical service. This happened despite the influence of those doctors who had by now come out in favour of birth control. These included the distinguished and influential gynaecologist Robert Latou Dickinson. Even Dickinson was somewhat wary of Mrs Sanger. He too disliked her radical background.

Dickinson was a prolific author and undertook a great deal of work to try to obtain medical endorsement for birth control. After the first World War, he began to consider such controversial subjects as artificial impregnation, the safe period and 'sterilization without unsexing'. In 1924 he retired from practice and became the Secretary of the National Committee on Maternal Health. This committee began in 1923 and was the only organization at the time which had a completely medical leadership. It maintained full-time offices with salaried staff and laid emphasis on research and upon publication rather than on the opening of new clinics. It was instigated by Mrs Gertrude Minturn Pinchot, and it attempted to relate birth control to marriage problems in general, and to such topics as sterilization, abortion and sterility.

The study of contraception by this committee had the sponsorship of the New York Obstetrical Society, the Academy of Medicine, and the American Gynaecological Society. A long article called 'Contraception, a medical review of the situation' was produced by Dickinson and was ready for distribution in 1924. First, however, he was concerned to find out whether he was breaking the law, and if so what the consequences would be. However, the postal authorities informed him that his publications were non-commercial, and furthermore, since both the author and the recipients were medically qualified, they could find no cause for an action.

Of Dickinson's other books the standard work on contraception for many years was his *Control of Conception* (which was dedicated to Charles Knowlton). His studies on *A Thousand Marriages* and *The Single Woman* both broke new ground. They suggested that masturbation was normal, and that celibacy was the greatest perversion of all. He was a great advocate of sex education and produced drawings and models which are still used today for teaching in many parts of the world. *Human Sex Anatomy*, an atlas which contains many of these drawings, was published when he was 73 years old. Even at such an age he was still extremely active and concerned with disproving what he called 'The Dramatic Five'. These were old-fashioned assumptions concerning the process of conception, such ideas for example as the 'descent of the uterus in orgasm', the 'fish mouth gasping of the os', and 'the insuck of semen'. His own drawings and observation directly refuted many such theories.

The Bureau continued its work, keeping carefully in line with the 'medical' justifications for contraception as redefined by the judge at the Sanger trial. However, it gained little stature until 1929 when a squad of policemen arrived at its doors, arrested the staff and seized some files which contained patients' case-histories. This action brought immediate reaction from the public and from doctors, since it violated the private relationship between a doctor and his patient. The case was eventually dismissed and the files were directed to be returned to the Bureau but some files were never seen again. Many of these related to Roman Catholic patients and the available evidence strongly suggests that the whole incident was engineered by the Church authorities.

In 1928 Mrs Sanger was forced to 'resign' from the American Birth Control League. 'Conservatism', she said, made it 'intolerable.' (She had in fact disagreed with the other members of the League who challenged her somewhat unusual ideas.) However, in 1929 she took control of the Bureau and also founded the National Committee on Federal Legislation for Birth Control. By this time a good deal of headway had been made, at least in the United States itself. The struggle was no longer entirely uphill. During the nineteen-thirties clinics were opened rapidly, and though legal skirmishes continued, considerable victories were won. For example, Dr Hannah Stone was allowed by a judge to import a package of birth control devices which were intended for scientific research; and slightly later a court gave permissive assent to the import of contraceptive literature.

With the climate of opinion in America becoming more liberal Margaret Sanger was able to spend more time on her other great interest—the organization of birth control at an international level. She travelled extensively, addressing meetings and visiting influential people. She was made President of the Birth Control International Information Centre, a body with headquarters in London. The centre had been organized by Gerda Guy and Edith How-Martyn, both of whom

gave their time and money generously in their efforts to promote birth control. Asia was the main focus of the Information
Centre's interest, and Mrs How-Martyn herself travelled
widely in the area and succeeded in befriending Mahatma
Gandhi. In September 1935 he wrote to her

Dear Sister . . . I am sorry to have to inform you that what . . .
has been reported of me about birth control is wholly imaginary.
I am quite at one with you that woman is the greater sufferer in this
matter, only the remedy suggested is worse than the disease. You
will see an article of mine in the forthcoming issue of the Harijan.
Already I am perceiving the harm it does in India. I still go out for
my walk to the Ashram every alternate day & when you come
again we must meet & have the same walk. Yours sincerely,
M. K. Gandhi.

Edith How-Martyn answered, and carefully annotated the
letter (as she always did): 'Returning to India Nov. M. S. also
coming. Hope to see him.'

However, it was Mrs Sanger who arrived at Wardha in
January 1936 and settled down to the task of convincing the
Mahatma. Unfortunately he refused to be convinced. For him,
sexual union was sinful, except when its purpose was to create
a child. One biographer has recorded that Margaret Sanger
was shocked by his attitude, but that Gandhi was equally
shocked by her 'dreadful earnestness'. 'When the long conversation was over, he was drained of energy. He had been
defending "bramacharya", the very essence of his life, against
a redoubtable opponent, and he was deeply troubled'. So
exhausted was the Mahatma that he had to be taken to hospital
in Bombay, where he arrived in a state of collapse. Whilst in
hospital he felt 'as though I wanted to see a woman'. Having
sought chastity for thirty-seven years, and indeed having achieved it, he was horrified and full of disgust at what had happened. He produced a spate of articles, reiterating the need for
chastity and the sinfulness of birth control.

The attitude of Gandhi and his followers towards contraception was an important one for it affected to a considerable extent the later acceptance of contraceptive policies in India. The doctrine is also a subtle one and not what it at first sight appears to Western observers. We shall return to this point later, but first we must go back and consider the origins of the birth control movements which were organized on an international scale.

The efforts of the Birth Control International Information Centre were very successful in many countries, largely because even before the second World War a great many people had already come to the conclusion that birth control had something to offer. They were ready to organize clinics and campaigns to inform those who remained unconvinced. Interest was also aroused and information exchanged through the medium of conferences. Indeed the first such Conference had been held in 1900 when the Malthusian Leagues met in Paris and formed their own international body, the Federation Universelle pour la Régeneration Humaine. C. R. Drysdale was the President, and three similar meetings were held at Liège, the Hague and Dresden before the outbreak of the first World War. After the hostilities an International Neo-Malthusian Conference was held in London in 1922.

When Margaret Sanger became interested in the international movement, several important meetings were organized and financed by her efforts. For example, the World Population Conference in Geneva in 1927 was organized by Mrs Sanger with assistance from Edith How-Martyn and Clinton Chance. Although Clinton and Janet Chance are probably best remembered for their work in the Abortion Law Reform Association, they also did a great deal for the birth-control movement. In addition Janet Chance was a notably sensible pioneer of sex education and marriage counselling.

However, the Geneva meeting did not turn out quite the

way Mrs Sanger had planned. Others who held different views, religious, political and social, managed to keep her in the background and ensure that she never had an opportunity to speak. The Conference attracted scientists and demographers who were happy to discuss population and related problems, but any discussion of the solution to such problems was ruled out of order. Nevertheless the efforts of Mrs Sanger and her friends were recognized at the end of the meeting when the President, Sir Bernard Mallet, said:

I cannot sit down without an expression, perhaps too long delayed, of admiration for the work of Mrs Sanger, and recognition to her husband, whose genial presence and generous hospitality have done so much to smooth away difficulties.

As a result of the Geneva Conference, two new organizations were formed. The first was the International Medical Group for the Investigation of Contraception, to which we have already referred. The other is the International Union for the Scientific Study of Population, a body which is still in existence.

We have mentioned that in 1930 yet another conference was held, this time at Zurich. But this meeting was quite different. It was primarily a gathering of the birth controllers, and an enthusiastic international group discussed the current situation. Their enthusiasm reflected the fact that in the decade before the second World War birth control was spreading to many lands. The struggles and achievements of this period have never been properly documented.

For example, the fight against Catholic opposition had begun in Ceylon in 1931, and after Edith-How Martyn had toured the island in 1936 a birth control clinic was opened. In China there were clinics in Peiping, Shanghai, Canton and Nanking. There had also been enthusiastic work in Germany, until the Nazi Government outlawed birth control. Despite

Gandhi's disapproval, contraception was also established in India.

The sub-continent is very large and varied, and it was obviously impossible to organize any movement on a national scale. However, there were State organizations and there were also Malthusian Leagues, of which that in Madras was a particularly active example. Apart from recommending the known contraceptive methods, this League researched into the literature and unearthed a large collection of 'traditional' contraceptives of unknown and doubtful effectiveness. These were published in leaflet form and circulated. We can only assume that the leaflet was intended to reassure the population that birth control was nothing new and to encourage them to ask for something more useful. They also opened a clinic, but found that few people would come forward to ask for advice. The same problem was encountered at the clinics opened by the Government of Mysore in 1930. When they were visited by the British Family Planning Association's Organizer for India, Mrs Rena Datta, in 1939, she found that there was still much to be done in educating the people toward an acceptance of family planning.

Most of the effort which had gone into contraceptive programmes was suddenly and effectively stopped by the outbreak of the second World War. Many countries found that there were no contraceptives available, and the organizers found themselves otherwise occupied. In Britain, for example, most of the premises used as clinics were soon made into evacuation centres and both the doctors and the layworkers were involved in some capacity on the war effort. By 1946 therefore, the family planning movement was in a very disorganized condition. In some countries it had ceased to exist altogether; in others the work resumed, but the clinic staffs found that they had largely to begin all over again.

In a luckier position were the neutral countries such as Sweden. The pioneering work there had been done by Mrs Elise Ottesen-Jensen and, over a relatively short period of years, the organization which she founded had managed completely to alter both legislation and public attitudes. Her fight had been not only for birth control, but also for a liberalization of attitudes towards sex education. The first postwar steps towards an international birth control organization were taken by the Swedish movement when Mrs Ottesen-Jensen invited anyone interested in family planning to attend the 1946 Annual Conference of the Swedish Association in Stockholm. The invitation drew a number of foreign delegates and an interim International Committee was formed, as a basis toward building something more permanent.

The next stage of the work took place in England. The Family Planning Association which had come into being just before the war was trying to get its own clinics established. In addition a small group of workers was also trying to re-establish old international links, and to form new ones. The two bodies were drawn together. Using the time-honoured procedure a conference was held at Cheltenham in 1948 and this meeting was particularly significant. It led to the establishment of the International Committee on Planned Parenthood, which several years later became the International Planned Parenthood Federation. Although it grew rapidly, the Federation was neither large nor influential in its early days, but nevertheless, the international spread of family planning did continue. The late nineteen-forties and early nineteen-fifties saw the emergence and re-emergence of many organizations devoted to the spreading of propaganda and the opening of clinics in many areas of the world.

The problem of population growth gave a new impetus to the family planning movement. In many countries in the immediate post-war period death rates fell dramatically. Improved medicine, better methods of food distribution, and

17. Marie Stopes 1880–1956. The well-known pioneer of family planning in Britain. She was loved and hated—but her ideas were certainly discussed. When she died, *The Times* said 'Dr Marie Stopes can fairly be said to have transformed the thought of her generation about the physical aspects of marriage and the role of contraception in married life.'
By courtesy of the Trustees of the British Museum.

18. Margaret Sanger 1883–1966. An American nurse who became known for her work as an international pioneer of birth control. Mrs Sanger fought against the laws which prohibited even the circulation of information about birth control, and opened the first clinic in America. Here she is seen with her sister, Ethel Byrne, when they and their helpers appeared in court following the opening of the Brownsville Clinic. *By courtesy of Planned Parenthood World Population.*

19. New York in 1916. Margaret Sanger opened the short-lived Brownsville Clinic in this area, in an attempt to counteract some of the misery that she saw around her. *By courtesy Planned Parenthood World Population.*

20. **Eight presumably 'wanted' children** sit on top of an exhortation to limit the size of one's family. *By courtesy of Planned Parenthood World Population.*

the spread of insecticides made an immediate impact upon public health. The 'population explosion', which so rapidly became a talking-point, was not caused by families having more children than before but simply by the sudden extension of the average life-span which was granted to mankind in the less-developed countries. Such a development gave rise to a new argument for birth control—the 'demographic argument'. If the prolongation of life is made possible, then man can be said to have achieved a considerable measure of 'death control'. However, unless these efforts are balanced by a corresponding control of births, then population growth takes place at an alarmingly accelerated speed.

The birth controllers thus found themselves accepted as never before, and armed with increasing justification for the practice of contraception. However, the 'demographic argument' finds little favour in the mainstream of the movement today (at least in the Western world). Similarly, eugenic arguments were tarnished by being incorporated as a part of the Fascist doctrine of Hitler and others. The third (and in many ways the oldest) justification for birth control, the philosophy expressed by Margaret Sanger and Marie Stopes, is therefore the one generally found in the forefront at the present time. Birth control's main justification remains its importance to maternal and child health, and its existence as one of the rights of women. The parallel with early Egyptian and Jewish thinking is obvious.

The tendency for the developed countries of the West to try to export birth control campaigns, and to view such an enterprise as an area in which Western expertise may be particularly valuable, has grown considerably in recent years. However, its value is somewhat limited by the fact that so many Western notions about birth control are inevitably flavoured by the course of its history in Western societies and by the philosophy which they have come to accept. In some Asian countries the governments have now taken on the responsibility for implementing family planning programmes, but it should be borne firmly in mind that their prime reason for doing so was not an overriding concern for maternal or child health. Obviously it would be wrong to suggest that there were *no* such ideas in currency, but the principle reason was that the force of the demographic argument is actively felt and easily seen in a country that is poor that has a population increasing at a rapid rate.

Such an action was forced upon the Government of India although it was in no sense an easy action for them to take. Problems both of a cultural and of a technical nature confronted them, even though the Indians themselves had been, at various stages in their past, no strangers to birth control. The great Vedic erotic lyrics contain recipes which are not so different from the recipes found in the classical works of our own culture; and whilst we had, at times, various forces at work in society which placed its members beyond the risk of pregnancy, India, too, had similar customs.

However, the prevailing cultural pattern in India may well be one of the main factors which act even now against the spread of birth control in the sense that we know it. When Gandhi spoke to Mrs Sanger, he spoke as a sage in his own cultural environment. He did not understand why she should want anyone to use artificial methods of birth control, any more than she could understand that he could be serious when he said that 'brahmacharya' was both possible and laudable.

Space forbids us to give here any detailed examination of Indian cultural and sexual attitudes. Sadly, there has been very little study of this rather important aspect of life, and what has been said so far seems to have been mistranslated and misunderstood. Brahmacharya is usually rendered simply as 'abstinence from sexual intercourse', yet in the way that the word is currently used, and in the way in which Gandhi used it, it had a far more positive meaning. It meant the sublimation of the sexual impulse into creative work for the community, for either a long or a short period, Nor does brahmacharya necessarily mean total abstinence from sexual intercourse. According to the sage, Manu:

There are sixteen days and nights in each month, with four distinct days neglected by the virtuous, these are called the natural season of women. Of those 16, the first four, the eleventh and the thirteenth are reprehended. The ten remaining nights are approved. That makes ten possible nights per month, or six for the virtuous.

But Manu also said: 'He who avoids conjugal embraces on the six reprehended nights and on eight others is equal in chastity to a brahmachari.' Such a practice would be scarcely conducive to maximum fertility. In fact, Indian ideals ('chastity is the highest law') are scarcely comprehensible to the West, and the difficulties encountered in making the population of that huge country accept artificial means of birth control may in some measure lie in this lack of understanding.

When independence was achieved birth control was considered to be desirable by the National Planning Commision of the Indian National Congress. They recommended that contraceptive advice should be given on economic grounds. But the Minister of Health at the time was the Rajkumari Amrit Kaur, a close disciple of the Mahatma, who had been present at the Sanger interview. Rajkumari opposed birth control on religious grounds. She also thought that it would be unacceptable to the majority of the peasant population, and that conditions in the villages were too unhygienic to permit the adoption of methods which might be used elsewhere. She maintained that attempts to do so might be harmful to health.

Because of her objections, it was decided in 1950 to hold a trial with the ryhthm method. Dr Abraham Stone directed the work under the auspices of the World Health Organization.

Despite the use of strings of beads as visual aids, all that was demonstrated was that the method was not practicable.

Ultimately family planning did gain a wider official acceptance and became a national programme, but the problems were still formidable. Leaving aside the fact that there may be as little as one so-called hospital and half a dozen dispensaries in an area the size of Yorkshire, the greatest difficulty was in finding feasible methods. One worker summed it up when she observed

whenever we were faced with a patient who desperately needed advice . . . it seemed quite useless to give them a cap, or even Volpar. . . . They were mostly living under conditions where there was no privacy for bathing, and also they would never come back regularly for supplies. Moreover even Volpar is very expensive to distribute on a large scale. . . . If one had a practical simple method to suggest it would be so much easier to approach the local authorities. . . . What is needed is some substance that is easily available in the villages. . . .

Attempts continued with the use of such 'conventional contraceptives' as caps, spermicides and the condom. At one point there was an attempt to popularize the use of a home-made spermicide made of rice flour and salt, but this met with no success whatsoever. Moreover, it was a rather unwise suggestion, since salt is not without danger. Some women did indeed suffer a vaginal irritation. Fortunately sterilization has made great headway, and many men and women have accepted the operation. Male sterilization—vasectomy—is more usual and more popular, since it a far simpler and less painful operation.

Incidentally, the very popularity of vasectomy is another example of the difference between Indian and Western attitudes. Indian men have found it easy to accept, and centres to carry out the operation have been set up in unusual though central locations, such as railway stations. Such a move has caused little comment in India, although the step was greeted with gloom, alarm and even disgust in the West. Similarly, the small amounts paid as expenses have given rise to moral speculations and accusations of bribery. When a Minister suggested that transistor radios should be given, or that the whole country should accept brahmacharya for a time, he was again guilty of scandalizing Western liberal opinion.

However, whatever the attitude to sterilization in the two cultures the problem of effective contraceptive methods for India still exists. A true contraceptive is a *reversible* means of birth control, but vasectomies cannot always be reversed. The introduction of intra-uterine devices from 1965 onwards gave some cause for optimism although even this technique was found to be not without its difficulties. And the problem applies not only to India, and indeed not only to the developing nations in general. Whatever the level of national development (and however it is judged), the world-wide need is still felt for more means and more effective means of family limitation.

In Chapter Two we suggested that in the history of contraception there is no new thing under the sun. All the possible approaches that might be used to avoid pregnancy (and the basic methods amount to no more than twelve) have been thought of many years ago. What has advanced is our technology, and our ability to make any particular method work. The Egyptians used a crude spermicidal mixture; we now use spermicides which are extremely effective at killing sperms. Soranos and the Jewish rabbis recommended a woollen tampon; we now have rubber caps and diaphragms, which are still far from perfect, but which are a much more effective form of occlusive pessary. Fallopius, though his main concern was not contraception, described a sheath made out of linen; modern sheaths are made of rubber or even plastic. As time has progressed we have seen technical improvements and indeed the history of these improvements has formed a large part of the substance of this book.

But one of the most effective means by which we limit fertility today had to wait for an extremely long time before the breakthrough occurred that made it an effective contraceptive method. It had to wait until 1956 to be precise. For at least 2,000 years before that date the search had gone on for a reversible sterilizing substance that could be taken by mouth. We have traced the development of this search from the Greek herbals and the Jewish cup of roots through the medieval potions provided by La Celestina and her friends and the preparations that the Barren Does found so unpalatable, to much more recent times. That the search was such a long one proves two things: firstly that the need for a simple oral contraceptive has been acutely felt for a very long time, and secondly that the problem of finding such a substance is by no means simple. The development of the contraceptive pill had to wait until a good deal was understood both about the nature of the reproductive system, and about the nature of a group of chemical substances known as the steroid hormones.

Although some work had proceeded earlier in the century, the history of the pill is generally regarded as having started in 1950. It was in that year, almost by chance, that Margaret Sanger met Gregory Pincus, the Director of the Worcester Foundation for Experimental Biology. The details of this now famous meeting never seem to have been recorded and the full story will never be known. However, it seems that Mrs Sanger was unsatisfied with the reliability of the contraceptive methods then available. She explained the situation to Pincus, and asked him if it might be possible as the result of an experimental investigation to devise some means of limiting fertility which was completely (rather than only partially) effective, and as applicable to women as it was to his experimental animals. Although Pincus had not originally been involved in the problem of controlling fertility, it rapidly became apparent to him that perhaps the most effective means of preventing conception would depend upon the prevention of ovulation by the use of some orally active substance. That is to say he started to consider the problem of whether any substances existed which if taken by mouth would prevent an egg from leaving the ovary, and hence prevent the possibility of it being fertilized.

The obvious clue was found when he considered what happens during pregnancy. It was generally agreed that when a woman is pregnant she does not ovulate, probably because her blood contains large quantities of a chemical substance called progesterone. Progesterone belongs to the class of substances known as hormones—materials which act as chemical messengers in the body. During early pregnancy the progesterone is produced by an organ known as the corpus luteum, an area that is derived from the region of the ovary that the ovulated egg has vacated.

In the closing years of the nineteenth century it had been suggested that the corpus luteum prevented any further ovulations during pregnancy, but it was not until the third decade of the present century that biochemists succeeded in isolating progesterone from the tissues which produce it. Hormones are present in the body in extremely minute quantities, and in the original extractions literally tons of sow ovaries —obtained from the slaughter house—had to be processed to obtain only hundredths of an ounce of the hormone. For this reason hormones like progesterone were extraordinarily expensive before the second World War. However, experimental work was carried out on the precious materials and one result was that in the rabbit at least, progesterone administered in appropriate amounts was found to inhibit ovulation.

Fortunately for scientific research, and even more fortunately for the development of contraceptives, steroids do not occur exclusively in animal tissues. Some are also found in plants. For this reason it is possible that some of the old herbal contraceptives that occur in the folk lore of so many civilizations may have some sort of real basis. By chance, a plant may have been discovered which genuinely did have a contraceptive action. Indeed more recently investigations have shown that a number of plant species have a contraceptive action when tested in the laboratory. In some parts of the world there are bureaux set up whose job it is to screen large numbers of plant species with a view to identifying or even extracting the (so far unknown) contraceptive materials.

However, the search is a long one, for the number of species that do have such properties is very few. The problem is complicated by the fact that although some plants contain steroids, they are not exactly the same type of steroid as those occuring in animals. Sometimes the animal itself may convert them during the process of digestion, but more often it involves a more complex piece of chemical manipulation to convert an inactive plant steroid to an active animal hormone.

Nevertheless it can be done, and one of the best-known stories in the history of organic chemistry is concerned with how it was done in the case of progesterone. In 1940 Professor Russell Marker, then working in Pennsylvania, discovered a means of converting a particular plant steroid into progesterone. However, the plant itself was rare, and Marker set out almost single handed to obtain a large enough supply to make the production of progesterone a commercial proposition. His travels took him to the jungles of Veracruz in Mexico where he found a black root called by the Mexicans 'cabeza de negro—the black headed one', which proved to be a fairly rich source of the starting material. However, he failed so markedly to interest American drug firms in his progesterone-producing process that he was left with only one alternative—to produce it himself. He set up his own factory in Mexico

City and with the help of unskilled labour he went to work. Within three years he had produced over four pounds of the hormone which previously had been obtainable only in such tiny amounts. With this development the use of progesterone in medicine became more feasible than it had been in the past, and it was to progesterone that Pincus turned for his original contraceptive pill.

First, however, it was necessary to establish that progesterone was effective when taken by mouth. Normally, when given for medical purposes, it was injected. In collaboration with Dr Min-Chueh Chang, also of the Worcester Foundation, Pincus found that progesterone was active if given by mouth both to rats and rabbits, and that in the majority of cases it inhibited ovulation in both these species. However, its effect on women were not readily understood. It seemed as though it might be difficult to obtain a large enough number of volunteers to investigate its action properly.

Fortunately, the problem was solved by another chance meeting, this time with Dr John Rock, a gynaecologist at Harvard University. For a quite different purpose Rock had been giving a mixture of progesterone and the other important female sex hormone, oestrogen, to a group of nearly 100 women. By witholding the oestrogen it became possible to study the effects on these volunteer subjects of progesterone alone. In order to disturb their menstrual periods as little as possible the dosage was started on the fifth day after menstruation, and it was continued for a 20-day period. Even in the very first trials the 20-day régime, which was to become so familiar to many millions of women throughout the world, had already been envisaged.

The results of these first trials were extremely encouraging. In the vast majority of cases the drug prevented ovulation from occurring. However, its action was not perfect. Some women still produced eggs. The method was therefore not sufficiently effective to be used on a large scale. But during the mid-nineteen-fifties chemists had been extremely busy producing not only progesterone itself but also a vast array of other substances which had rather similar chemical structures to it. Many of these were completely synthetic compounds. They did not appear in the body at all and yet some of them had actions similar to, and even more powerful than, the natural hormone. Pincus and his team undertook a systematic study of the substances—over 200 of them—which were then available.

Because of their resemblance to progesterone these products were known as 'gestagens'. Of all the gestagens investigated he found that three of them might be suitable for his purposes. They were active when taken by mouth and extremely powerful inhibitors of ovulation. One of them, a gestagen called 'norethynodrel' was to form the basis of the first large-scale trial of the contraceptive pill, a trial which was carried out in Puerto Rico in 1956. However, the gestagens when used alone suffered from one of the same troubles as progesterone itself. They gave a rather poor control over menstruation. Bleeding tended to be irregular and sometimes would occur unexpectedly during the middle of the cycle. Although some women would tolerate such an inconvenience for the sake of remaining free from pregnancy, to others such irregular menstruation was clearly distressing. The problem was overcome by combining the gestagen with another synthetic compound, this time a synthetic oestrogen. The oestrogen–gestagen combination gave good control of bleeding during the cycle and extremely good control over ovulation. It was a combined pill of this type (marketed commercially under the name Enavid), that proved to be so remarkably effective in the Puerto Rican trial.

From these beginnings, in the space of only fifteen years, a colossal industry has been built up which would have been quite impossible to imagine when steroids were obtained only from animal sources. It is difficult even to estimate the number of pills which are taken each year. In the middle of 1966 there were about 10 million women throughout the world using oral contraception. Even if they were not all using them continuously the world's annual consumption of contraceptive pills must have been, even then, well over 1,000 million. The figure today can hardly be any smaller.

At the time of writing this book there are several dozen different brands of oral contraceptive available. The most popular are still of the combined type. They consist of a mixture of any one of perhaps ten different gestagens combined with one of two synthetic oestrogen compounds. Often a particular firm produces a range of pills which all contain the same components but combined in different amounts. This is because women vary somewhat in their responses to different hormones. Some women respond better to a pill in which oestrogen is the predominant component. For others a pill with a higher content of gestagen produces less of a disturbance to their normal body chemistry.

Although the combined pill was the first on the market, and although it is by far the most popular, it is by no means the only form of oral contraception which is currently available. Indeed today the 'Pincus pill' is often called the 'first generation' oral contraceptive. Subsequent generations are already in use, and others are at this moment being tested on experimental animals. The first modification of the combined pill was introduced in 1963. It is a pill known as a 'sequential'. The adherents of sequential contraceptives point out that during a normal menstrual cycle the hormone levels in a woman's blood are changing. She does not maintain a constant ratio of progesterone and oestrogen. Before ovulation there is relatively little progesterone. Afterwards, both progesterone and oestrogen are circulating together.

Accordingly, sequential pills are of two types. The first type, which are taken for the first fifteen days of the cycle, consists of oestrogen alone. The second set of pills, which are taken for the next five days, contain both oestrogen and a gestagen together. In this way sequential contraceptives are supposed to mirror a woman's normal cycle more closely, at the same time ensuring that she does not conceive.

But even sequential pills are in a sense 'first generation'. Within the last five years we have seen the appearance of pills which contain only a gestagen, and a gestagen at a very low dose. Conversely there are oestrogen-only pills, to be used *after* exposure to the risk of pregnancy. In addition, because a substance taken by mouth is rapidly broken down by the body, there has been a return to injectible contraceptives designed to give prolonged protection against pregnancy. Even this does not exhaust the possibilities, for female methods are not entirely monopolizing the field, Work is also progressing on a pill for men, though so far progress is not very advanced. The possibility of immunization against pregnancy is also being seriously considered.

These are a few of the trends of the future, and it is towards the future that this book must now turn. The history of contraceptives has been a history both of methods and of attitudes—a message written between the lines of every chapter. And we shall find that the interlocking of these two aspects is just as important when we look forward as it was at any period in the past.

CHAPTER TEN

Tomorrow Always Comes

IMAGINE a newly discovered contraceptive potion, a twentieth-century' cup of roots' which unfailingly prevented conception when either a woman or her husband drank it, as long as they followed the directions on the bottle. Let us assume that it is completely safe, having no harmful effects on either partner; that its effects are immediately reversible; and that it is extremely cheap. Clearly it seems like a perfect contraceptive preparation, the fluid that has been sought for the last few millenia. However, there are just two other points about the potion: it can only be obtained from a doctor (though doctors are delighted to prescribe it), and because the body quickly breaks it down, a dose has to be taken every four hours. Bulk supplies are shipped to every government in the world. The biologists, demographers and family planners responsible for its discovery and its testing breath a sigh of relief and sit back to await reports of a declining birth-rate in all those countries where population pressure is a problem.

How long must they wait? We would suggest a very long time indeed. 'What has gone wrong?' they might ask after five years. 'Why is the world not using our perfect contraceptive?' The answer is that for the vast majority of the world's population the potion is not only imperfect—it is totally unacceptable.

The perfect fluid is of course a myth. No such wonder drug exists. We have invented it simply to show that the obvious characteristics of a 'perfect' contraceptive (effectiveness, reversibility, safety and cheapness), are not in themselves enough to make it acceptable to large numbers of people. At least as important are the facts that it must be very readily available and that using it must cause the very minimum of interference with the user's normal everyday life.

We have traced the changing attitude of the medical profession towards family planning from the time of Ancient Egypt. Sometimes their attitude was favourable, sometimes utterly hostile but slowly, over the last half century, contraception has become firmly established as an aspect of medicine. It is the doctor who a woman in Europe or America usually approaches if she wishes to obtain some form of contraceptive: a cap, a pill or an intra-uterine device. Family planning clinics are often located in hospitals and this serves to strengthen the tie.

Clearly there are advantages in this system, although ironically enough the advantages often have little to do with birth control itself. It is in any woman's interest to be examined several times during her reproductive life by a gynaecologist. Such an examination may reveal the existence of cancer of the cervix which can be effectively treated if it is caught early enough though untreated its consequences can prove fatal. Prolapse and other abnormal conditions of the uterus can also be detected and treated. However, a very large part of the family planning programme at any clinic can be, and indeed is, carried out by people who are specially trained but who are not medically qualified. Certain aspects of contraception are therefore ceasing, at least partly, to be the exclusive concern of the doctor.

Instead of sending his wife to the clinic, the husband may go to his local retailer, and obtain a supply of condoms with which to plan the family that he desires. Indeed the condom is probably the most widely used 'artificial' means of contraception to be found in almost any nation on Earth. In addition, certain spermicidal preparations can also be bought over the counter. The authority of a doctor is not required. It is clear then that already certain aspects of family planning can safely be left to para-medical auxiliaries and other aspects do not require even that amount of expertise. With the very greatest respect for the medical profession, such a trend should be actively encouraged. Indeed many medical men would agree. We have already discussed the enormous difficulties inherent in trying to bring adequate medical services to vast areas of Asia, where the number of trained doctors is pathetically small compared to the size of the population. In addition, there is a natural reluctance among many people both in the East and the West to consult a doctor or visit a hospital even when they are sick. To do so when they are well, in order to discuss a subject that many of them feel is private and difficult to talk about, is asking too much of most of them, even if the relevant doctors were immediately to hand.

For many millions of people the use of any form of contraception is an imposition; it is a deviation from their normal pattern of activity. In order to persuade them to use some sort of birth control, the effort involved with it must be cut to an absolute minimum. For example, our 'wonder potion' could be quite unsuitable for any widespread use. Only those couples for whom pregnancy would be a major disaster would contemplate a four-hourly dosage even during the day, let alone the situation at night. The example was deliberately chosen to be ridiculous. But for large numbers of women throughout the world even the effort of taking a pill every day is also beyond them. Either because of indifference or sheer forgetfulness many women who at least pay lip service to birth control are incapable of using an oral contraceptive successfully.

There are two consequences of this line of argument: a contraceptive must be easy to use and preferably should be long-acting. Hence much thought is being expended on the possibility of long-acting preparations containing sex hormones which are released slowly into the bloodstream, and which, by one means or another, inhibit conception. Similarly, the widespread use of IUDs which (ideally) need to be inserted only once, and which give a relatively high degree of contraceptive protection has been advocated by specialists for some time. Indeed such programmes are currently in operation. Both of these contraceptive materials after their initial insertion should, when the present technical difficulties have been resolved, give long-acting protection without any further effort on the part of the woman concerned. However, their obvious drawback at present is that their initial application still requires the presence of a doctor. The shortage of such men therefore limits their availability.

There are two ways of easing the situation. The first is to put a greater degree of responsibility into the hands of the non-medical assistants. The application of neither of the above methods is beyond the capabilities of a trained assistant, and indeed some moves are now being made in this direction. In addition, a much greater effort must be made to improve the 'traditional' methods that anyone should be able to obtain readily, and use without any form of medical advice. It may be encouraging in this direction to see that condoms made of plastic rather than rubber (resulting of course in a marked lowering of cost), have made an appearance and are being given away in some developing areas to anyone who will use them. We may also be about to witness a considerable improvement in the effectiveness, and in the ease of use, of certain types of spermicide. No one would suggest that the active research being devoted to such refined contraceptives as 'morning-after' pills should not be greatly encouraged, but at the same time a very strong case can be made for an improvement in what might be described as 'household' methods. And this is still true even though, as we noted in the last chapter, some attempts to do so have been abject failures.

In addition to an improvement in 'simple' methods themselves, vast efforts must also be made to distribute the improved product to a very large population. The distribution outlets usually available in Western nations (the doctor, the clinic, the pharmacist, the barber or the mail-order house) are vastly inadequate, for reasons already described, to meet the problem in developing nations. The outlets must be on a far wider scale, and this in itself is not without difficulties. We have already noted some Western reactions to the setting up of distribution centres at railway stations. But our Western attitudes must to some extent be repressed. The only important consideration is whether such a distribution plan can be successful, not whether it fits in with our pre-existing values.

And this brings us on to the last topic that should be discussed here. It is a subject that we have hinted at and alluded to in other chapters. It is the problem of whether the population explosion can be arrested at all, and if it can then what means can be effective in arresting it.

It is relatively easy to think about the contraceptives that might be developed in the future. Now the whole subject has become a matter of biological research. Such a biologist is not usually found among the ranks of birth controllers, but he is none the less an important individual who knows a great deal about the physiology and biochemistry of human reproduction. It is his job to devise ways in which its various phases may be interrupted by chemical or other means. It is certainly easier to consider the facts than it is to reach a firm conclusion about the effect of scientific developments on different societies. Will, for example, people who are assured of effective contraception, necessarily continue to order their lives in the same way? They could well decide that marriage is irrelevant, and could institute a new kind of society with a completely changed code of ethics. The study of human attitudes is not an exact science, and the attitudes themselves

H

are in a constant state of change. The general concensus has obviously altered radically in recent times, for only forty years ago a doctor who was thinking about the possibility of oral contraception wrote that:

Should it become possible to sterilise women temporarily at will by internal medication, the most urgent task would be that of working out a method of distribution of these drugs which would make them available where indicated for reasons of hygiene, and at the same time safeguard against the enormous danger presented by them to sexual order and morality, and to life and culture in general.

Such a statement seems even comical today, but we quote it to show how quickly an accepted idea and a norm can be completely replaced. When we come to consider the population problem, the way that people think and the changes in their thinking assume an even greater importance.

First it must be said that few problems have given rise to so much confusion. Almost daily the newspapers and other mass media report the latest pronouncements of the 'experts'. But one does not need to be an expert to realize that recently we seemed to be on the verge of a depopulation scare in Europe, whilst the population of many other parts of the world grows much too fast for comfort. Naturally, there are different ways of saying it. Some tell us that the ever-growing family of man is like a bomb, and point out that the exploding population is far more dangerous than any of the weapons currently stockpiled in the world's armoury. Others have likened it to an express train, rushing on faster and faster out of control. Some suggest to us, even more picturesquely, that if immigrants from Mars arrived in space-ships at the rate that the world's population increases, we should soon take some action to stop them.

Of course, many see the political implications in all this and say that we should stop giving aid to countries that do not take immediate action to halt population growth. Some even claim that a number of countries are by now in such at hopeless state that we should cut them off completely. Admittedly it is a new problem and we have come to discuss it only recently. Until the last two decades we had no idea of what a huge human growth rate had come upon us. We are still only coming to that realization. So far we have taken virtually no action to stop it.

We make this statement notwithstanding the fact that today people talk blithely of 'population control' and 'population policies'. The assumption usually underlying such discussions is that the 'control' is to be achieved by family planning. Let us assume for the moment that this is true and enquire just how much work is being carried out in this direction. We find that there are a few government-sponsored programmes but for the most part the whole problem is left in the hands of the private sector. Incredible as it may seem, the danger that we are told is the gravest that currently faces us, is left to voluntary organizations to solve. They are mostly family planning associations, and viewed in the light of the world problem they are usually extremely small, for which reason they reach relatively few people. In addition, there seems to be a great deal of confusion about the activity and scope of these organizations, and what it is that they are trying to achieve. They have the philosophy of the founders of the movement; they are interested in maternal health, child care and human rights. They justify their existence by combating illegal abortion and offering a road to material prosperity to couples who take advantage of their services.

But let us examine their underlying assumption that family planning means population control. The position gives cause for alarm for it is obviously false.

Family planning is concerned with individual couples, not with an entire population. Birth controllers have for many years adhered to the message that 'every child should be wanted'. They have nowadays managed to manoeuvre themselves into the belief that in preventing 'unwanted births' one is somehow managing to institute control over the size of an entire nation. But what of the couples who genuinely 'want' three children, or thirteen. They may well succeed in avoiding a fourth or a fourteenth but this will contribute little to the control of population growth.

So far as we know, no one has ever seriously discussed a real programme of population control. The reason, one must suppose, is that such a programme would be highly unpopular if not totally unacceptable. Taken to its logical extreme it will include not only rigidly controlling the total size of the population and permitting no growth whatever, but also deciding on its age and sex structure. Presumably, control over such factors as distribution, quality and even racial composition, would also have to be examined. Birth control considers only the population added by births. It has no direct effect upon mortality and migration.

For this reason it is not surprising that the aims of current government programmes are somewhat vague. In India it is hoped that the annual birth-rate will be reduced from 40 to 25 per thousand as soon as possible. Such an aim is largely meaningless, although it sounds impressive. The birth-rate was probably a lot higher than 40 to begin with, and for a country like India even 25 per thousand would represent a very massive growth of people. And there can certainly be no logic behind the idea that allowing couples to have the number of children they want will in some mysterious manner stabilize the population. The mere availability of contraceptives is entirely compatible with high fertility. As someone once remarked, 'family planning means that if we are going to breed like rabbits we should do it on purpose'.

Are we saying then that the provision of effective means of birth control has no part to play in limiting the size of nations, especially in those parts of the world where they are growing most rapidly? Far from it. Birth control clearly has an enormously important role if we do not propose to sit back and wait for the 'natural checks' of the Malthusians to take over the situation, with results that can only be considered disastrous. Certainly contraception must be adopted and adopted on a massive scale. The problem is how to induce its adoption in societies which are at best disinterested and at worst completely indifferent to their circumstances.

We have already seen the negative side of this problem. To have any chance of acceptance contraceptives must be cheap, easy to use and available everywhere. Without all of these provisions we have no hope of success. But even with them we have still only just begun. Having developed a product which might not be totally unacceptable we are still faced with the entirely different problem of having it accepted. It may well be that the population wants no form of birth control at all. In that case, no method however trouble free, has any chance of being adopted unless steps are also taken to alter the national attitude.

At the moment few workers in the field seem aware that they are facing this twofold difficulty. Any lack of acceptance is interpreted as a rejection of the specific method being offered. People who want a lot of children or 'as many as God sends' are termed 'resistant'. People who resist are ignorant, or have a problem brought about by 'cultural values'. In dealing with them family planning employs a blanket policy called 'education'. Education in this context consists of 'mass communication' and is carried out mostly through films, posters, leaflets lectures and so on. The aim is quite simply to make a woman decide how many children she wants, and to make her choose some means of contraception to assist her in this enterprise.

If this seems to be an uncharitable indictment of what after all are well-meaning efforts we must also point out that the situation in less developed countries is getting worse and not better. Even more difficult to accept is the certain knowledge that there is going to be no rapid improvement. It is quite possible that the medical and scientific advances of which we are justly proud will ensure that more people will manage to survive for a longer period in unspeakable conditions and failing health. They will not die as before. Instead they will be condemned to remain half alive with nothing to hope for. Such a view is not a popular one and it contrasts very sharply with many of the enormous numbers of books and papers produced by family planners on the subject. One of the most striking aspects of this output of words is how very easy almost everyone manages to make the problem sound. After all, we have created a few better and more effective contraceptive methods. We in the West have already managed to change our society from high to lower levels of fertility. Surely others will soon follow our example.

One point that is usually glossed over is that even if fertility control were instituted tomorrow on a global scale the less developed countries would still have all the problems which they face today, and these problems will remain for many years to come. The high rates of fertility and survival of the last and present generations mean that the children already born, and those being born now, will leave them with a dilemma for many years. Though fertility control is of the very highest importance in resolving this dilemma it offers no immediate solution. Great efforts towards improvement in every other aspect of development and desirable social change must also be undertaken if education, employment and the amenities of life are to be made available to more than a privileged few.

The decreasing fertility that we are all so anxious to see will therefore ease the situation but only over a long period. In the short term it is not without its drawbacks. For example, many writers tell us that the burden of dependants will be eased with the introduction of effective means of birth control. However, in many areas child labour is still so common that by the time an infant reaches what we call 'school age' he is actually at work and helping the family economy. Viewed in the longer term, as such infants grow up, there would be fewer members of the reproductive age group, and eventually it is hoped, fertility would stabilize at a lower level. But the interim period will be difficult. Constant encouragement and more tangible financial support would be essential to induce and maintain the necessary change of attitude—a change which is crucial to the whole exercise.

When we look back at the demographic transition in the West, many assume that the process can be easily repeated elsewhere, and that the lessons lie in our own history. But can we really learn from the past? It seems doubtful. If we look back at the description of London in the nineteenth century, it would be very easy to substitute the names of Indian cities and to imagine that the description were written today. However, the economic conditions in the two nations are different. In addition, though the conditions in the cities may well be the same the people are also different. It is in this context that we must return to 'cultural values', and that we must speculate about the possible role of education.

In coming to deal with the problems of less developed societies two schools of thought have emerged. One side postulates that the society should first accept birth control and then, we are assured, the adoption of 'modern' attitudes will follow. The other school maintains that unless and until 'modern' attitudes are engendered, birth control will not be accepted at all. Once they are created then contraception will naturally spread. Neither school appears to have thought about the problem in depth. The assumption is that modern attitudes are better than traditional ones, and that the change is both possible and desirable. In fact such a change is going to be tremendously difficult. The values and ideas held by the majority of Asians, for example, are very different from our own, and if anything even more strongly embedded.

Many specialists would have us believe that Asian traditions are on the wane, and that people are no longer affected by old-fashioned concepts such as caste. But the strength of such a notion may be judged by examining a group like the Sikhs, probably the most progressive group in India. Five hundred years ago their founder, Guru Nanak, rejected the caste system, yet today, after a turbulent history and a great deal of migration and social change, even the Sikhs in Great Britain give some consideration to caste when choosing a marriage partner. Many of these marriages are still arranged in the traditional way.

When we look at a society such as India we automatically start from the assumption that its members must want the things that we want. We seek ways to make their lives and activities similar to our own. But we make the mistake of supposing that our values are universally valid. Certainly they are when we are dealing with the élite of the country but this is hardly surprising. Many of them were educated in Western countries, some of them are more British than the British. However, they actually know very little about the way of life of the common man. Birth control campaigns based upon the intuition of such people seem doomed from the start. They will commend it and immediately obscure the real issues by putting up a smokescreen of well-meaning propaganda.

Indeed, in a country like India the whole discussion of 'attitudes' is something of an irrelevancy. Is it reasonable to suppose that either before or after the introduction of a simple measure like birth control the requisite set of desired modern

attitudes would be created? This would mean that vast numbers of people would have to begin to think rationally, and
to take an objective view of material advancement. It would
mean breaking up the family system, and abandoning traditional ways of life. Tools and training would largely have to
supersede religion. Caste relationships would have to change
and vanish. The future and materialism would have to replace
the past and the Law of Karma.

One cannot suppose that changes of this kind are remotely
near. Gandhi himself sought social change, but even he was
unable to achieve so much. His attitudes were modern at
their roots but clothed in Hinduism, and even this approach
and the reverence and esteem in which the Mahatma himself
was held were insufficient to make much impact. Modernism
strikes at the very basis of Hindu society where traditional
attitudes are at their strongest.

Another difficulty arises from the enormous difference
between what we suppose Asian attitudes and values to be,
and what they actually are. Asia presents an image of flower-
power, non-violence and an overriding obsession with spiritual
rather than material values. Naturally, we suppose that such
ideas would give rise to a society with compassion, charity
and love. In practice it shows few such characteristics. Its
members are obviously unmoved by sickness and misery.
Very few Indians do much to alleviate the conditions suffered
by their countrymen. Those who do are usually members of
minority groups, such as Christians and Parsees. For the
majority it seems only too easy to act crudely and to exploit
their fellows. What is even more incredible to us is that they
feel no guilt whatever whilst doing so.

Such then is the population dilemma, and it is an enormous
one. We do not propose to offer a solution here, nor did we
set out to do so. However, we must make some brief comment
on where we believe the solution to lie. It is unthinkable that

the situation should be allowed to continue year after year getting progressively worse. There must be steps that can be taken that would at least slow down the trend. And indeed there are, although it will be perhaps ten years before their effects can become apparent.

Only the government of a nation is in a position to dictate any real policy of control. As we have seen, the policy must be subtle. An all-out plan to arrest the rate of increase tomorrow would certainly have its effect, but only because of the number of people killed in the resulting protest riots. The government holds the purse strings. It gives rewards and inducements to those citizens who best serve its interests. It is by this means that the society survives. When the need is for more citizens and for more soldiers, family allowances are raised, taxes are levied on bachelors and medals are given for motherhood. We saw the ill-fated attempts that the Emperor Julius among others, made to stimulate the population growth in Rome by similar means. Conversely, when the emphasis is on a declining birth rate the reverse legislation may be employed. Raising the legal age of marriage; increasing the cost of a marriage licence; withdrawing child allowances and even imposing a tax on the third and every subsequent child: easing taxation on spinsters and bachelors; withdrawing travel and educational concessions for State employees who have an excessive family. All these are procedures that a government can implement in order to make childbearing less attractive. They are all true population control measures. They are in principle independent of any family planning scheme.

But clearly to make some of them work contraceptives must be made available (and free if necessary), to anyone who feels that it is sufficiently to his benefit to adopt such measures. And the key lies in this last statement. The scheme must be to the direct and immediate benefit of the individual and his family. Although the government sees the programme in national terms—it aims towards a nationally desirable objective—it is pointless to preach a message to the citizens at this level. For him the reward must be personal, and sufficiently appealing to compensate for the change in his behaviour.

The notion can be extended. Rewards can be given to those who volunteer for sterilization and abortion, provided that sufficient medical facilities are available to ensure that such operations can have a real impact on the population size. If too few are performed then the programme is not cost-effective. The money is better spent in other directions.

None of these ideas is new; we claim no originality. But their widespread adoption by the governments of the developing nations would most certainly be a new departure. It is true that tentative steps are being made in certain parts of the world. But the increase in the number of mouths to be fed is far from tentative. Programmes should be, indeed must be, extended and accelerated or any benefit that might accrue will be more than swallowed up in the rate of population increase. The world has become almost deaf to such pleas. They have been repeated so often that the Western world at least has learnt to live with them. But anyone who has seen the problem for themselves must surely realize that even in the Western hemisphere we will not be able to live with them for very much longer.

A LIST OF SOME OF THE MORE IMPORTANT WORKS CONSULTED

AETIOS OF AMIDA, *The gynaecology and obstetrics of the VIth Century A.D.* Translated from the Latin edition of Cornarius, 1592 ... by James V. Ricci. (Philadelphia: The Blakiston Company), 1950.

ALBUTT, Henry Arthur. *The wife's handbook: How a woman should order herself during pregnancy, in the lying-in room, and after delivery, with hints on the management of the baby, and on other matters of importance, necessary to be known by married women.* (London), 1886.

ANSTRUC, Johannes, *De morbis venereis.* (Paris), 1783.

ARIÈS, Philippe, *Histoire des populations Françaises et leurs attitudes devant la vie depuis le XVIIIe siècle.* (Paris: Self), 1948.

ARISTOTLE (pseudonym), *Aristotle's compleat master-piece ... displaying the secrets of nature in the generation of man ... to which is added, a treasure of health; or, the family physician.* (London), 1723, etc.

——, *Aristotle's master-piece compleated, in two parts. The first concerning the secrets of generation ... the second being a private looking-glass for the female sex ... treating the various maladies ... incident to women.* (Glasgow), 1782.

——, *His book of problems. In Aristotle's works compleated ... containing ... I The compleat master-piece ... II His compleat and experienced midwife ... III His book of problems ... IV His last legacy. ...* (London), 1733.

AUSTEN, Jane, *Letters to her sister Cassandra and others.* Edited by R. W. Chapman. (Oxford: The Clarendon Press), 1932.

BALSDON, J. P. V. D., *Roman women: their history and habits.* (London: The Bodley Head), 1962.

BANKS, J. A., *Prosperity and parenthood: a study of family planning among the Victorian middle classes.* (London: Routledge and Kegan Paul), 1954.

BANKS, J. A., and BANKS, Olive, *Feminism and family planning in Victorian England.* (Liverpool: Liverpool University Press), 1964.

BARDIS, P. D., 'Contraception in ancient Egypt', *Indian Journal of the History of Medicine*, 1967, 12: 2, pp. 1–3. Also printed in *Centaurus*, 1968, 12, pp. 305–7.

BAUER, A. W., 'Kritik der konzeptionsverhütungsmittel,' *Med. Klin*, 1930, p. 957.

BEATTY, Thomas Edward, Address in midwifery, delivered at the thirty-seventh annual meeting of the British Medical Association. *British Medical Journal*, 7 August 1869, 449, pp. 137–43. See also the *Lancet* of the same date.

BECK, Joseph R., 'How do spermatozoa enter the uterus?' *St Louis Medical and Surgical Journal*, 1872, 9, p. 449.

BEERS, J. B., United States Patent, Number 4729. 'Device for the prevention of conception', 28 August 1846.

BELL, G., *Nuba fertility stones, Sudan Notes*, 1936, 19: 2, pp. 313–16.

BERGERET, L. F. E., *Des fraudes dans l'accomplissement des fonctions génératrices, causes, dangers, et inconvénients pour les individus, la famille, et la société; remèdes.* (Paris), 1877.

BERGUES, Hélène, and others, *La prévention des naissances dans la famille; ses origines dans les temps modernes.* (Paris: Institut National d'Etudes Demographiques, Travaux et documents, No. 35: Presses Universitaires de France), 1960.

BERNSTEIN, E. L., 'Who was Condom?' *Human Fertility*, December 1940, 5, pp. 172–5 and 186.

BESANT, Annie, *The law of population: its consequences, and its bearing upon human conduct and morals,* (London: Freethought Publishing Company), n.d., 1878–9?

BITSCHAI, J., and BRODNY, M. Leopold, *A history of urology in Egypt.* (Cambridge, Mass.: Riverside Press), 1965.

BLANCHARD, Raphael, 'La diminution de la natalitè aux Etats Unis et ses causes,' *Bull. Soc. Franc. Hist. Med.*, 1910, 9, pp. 299–307.

BONSER, W., *Medical background to Anglo-Saxon England.* (London: Wellcome Historical Medical Library), 1963.

Boswell's London Journal 1762–1763. Edited by Frederick A. Pottle. (London), 1950.

BOUDEWYNS, M., *Ventilabrum medico-theologicum.* (Antwerp), 1666.

BRIANT, Keith, *Marie Stopes: A biography.* (London: Hogarth Press), 1962.

BROWNE, F. Stella, 'Die geburtenregelung im heutigen England,' *Neue Generation.* (Leipzig) 1926, XXII, pp. 233–5.

BROWNE, Sir Thomas, *Pseudodoxia epidemica: or, enquiries into very many received tenents, aud commonly presumed truths.* (London: T. H. for E. Dod), 1646.

BUCHHEIM, Liselotte, 'Abortus, konzeptionsverhütung uns menschenwerdung im alten Ägypten,' *Deutsche Ärzteblatt*, 1964, 61: 45, pp. 2371–5.

BUCK, W. D., 'A raid on the uterus'. (Extract from an address by the President of the New Hampshire State Medical Society.) *New York Medical Journal*, 1867, 5, pp. 464–5.

CABANÈS. *Les indiscrétions de l'histoire.* (Paris), 1903.

CAM, Joseph, *A rational and useful account of the venereal disease.* (London), n.d. (about 1740).

CARLILE, Richard, *Every women's book; or, What is love? Containing most important instructions for the prudent regulation of the principle of love and the number of a family.* (London), 1828.

CARSTENS, J. H., 'Final word on the stem pessary for amenorrhea, dysmenorrhea, sterility,' etc., *Journal of the American Medical Association*, 1909, 53, p. 1730.

CASANOVA DI SEINGALT, Giacomo Girolamo, *Memoires* . . . (Paris: Librarie Garnier Freres), n.d. (There are many other editions.)

Casti Connubii: Encyclical letter of His Holiness Pope Pius XI on Christian marriage in view of the present conditions, needs, errors and vices that affect the family and society. (London, New York, Sheed and Ward), 1933.

CHAVIGNY. 'Appareils anticonceptionnels', *Annales de Médicine Légal.* (Paris), 1924, IV, pp. 42–4.

CULPEPER, Nicholas, *A directory for midwives; or a guide for women in their conception, bearing and suckling their children.* (London: P. Cole), 1651.

DAVÉO, J. P., and PRAT, L., 'Corps étrangers anticonceptionnels et leurs conséquences,' *Bulletin de la Société de Gynecologie et d'Obstetrique.* (February 1939), 28, pp. 87–91.

DAWSON, Bertrand (Lord Dawson of Penn), 'Love, marriage, birth control,' being a speech delivered at the Church Congress at Birmingham, October, 1921. London, 1922.

DEFOE, Daniel, *Conjugal lewdness; or, Matrimonial whoredom. A treatise concerning the use and abuse of the marriage bed.* (London, T. Warner), 1727.

DENNETT, Mary Ware, *Birth control laws: Shall we keep them, change them, or abolish them?* (New York: Frederick H. Hitchock, The Grafton Press), 1926.

DICKINSON, Robert Latou, 'Contraception: A medical review of the situation: First report of the Committee on Maternal Health of New York', *Obstetrics and Gynaecology*, November 1924, 8, pp. 583–604. Also printed in *Transactions of the American Gynaecological Society*, 1924, 49, pp. 95–119.

——, *Human sexual anatomy: a topographical atlas.* (Baltimore, Williams and Wilkinsons), 1933.

——, and BRYANT, Louise Stephens, *Control of conception: An illustrated medical manual.* (London, Ballière, Tindall and Cox), 1938.

DIGBY, Sir Kenelm, *Nouveaux secrets experimentez pour conserver la beauté des dames, et pour guérir plusieurs sortes des maladies.* (The Hague), 1700.

——, *Choice and experimented receipts in physick and chirurgery.* (London), 1668.

DINGWALL, E. J., 'Early contraceptive sheaths', *British Medical Journal*, 1953, (I), pp. 40–1.

——, *Male infibulation.* (London), 1925.

DIOSCORIDES, *The Greek herbal of Dioscorides.* Edited by Robert T. Gunther, New York, Hafner, 1959.

DOLAN, T. M., 'Demographic considerations of the evils of artificial methods of preventing fecundation and of abortion production in modern times', *Transactions of the Ninth International Medical Congress.* (Washington D.C.), 1887. pp. 210–18.

DUEHREN, 'Le médecin Condom, a-t-il existé?' *Médicine International*, (Paris), April/May 1901.

FEDERSCHMIDT, Lamentationen über geburtenrückgang im Griechischen und Römischen altertum. *Blatter für Volksgesundheitpflege*, 1918, XVIII, 11/12, pp. 111–12.

FELDMAN, David M., *Birth control in Jewish law: Marital relations, contraception and abortion as set forth in the classic texts of Jewish law.* (New York: New York University Press; London: University of London Press), 1968.

FERDY, Hans, 'Contribution à l'étude historique du "coecal-condom",' *Chron. Méd.* (Paris), 1905, XII, pp. 535–7.

FONTANUS, Nicolaus, *The woman's doctour: or, an exact and distinct explanation of all such diseases as are peculiar to that sex. With choise and experimentall remedies against the same.* (London, J. Blague and S. Howell), 1652.

FRANZ, Adolph, 'Des frater Rudolphus buch De officio cherubyn', *Theologische Quartalschrift*, 1906, lxxxviii, pp. 411–36.

FRYER, Peter, *The birth controllers*. (London, Secker and Warburg), 1965.

Gabrielis Falloppii Mutinesis Physici et Chirurgici nostrorum temporum eximii de Morbo Gallico liber absolutissimus . . . (Batavia), 1564.

GESENIUS, Heinrich, *Empfängnisverhütung*. (München, Urban and Schwarzenberg), 1970.

GEBHARD, Bruno, *Medical pioneers of contraception. I Charles Knowlton M.D., 1800–1850, II Robert Latou Dickinson M.D., 1861–1950.* Reprinted from the *Ohio State Medical Journal*, Vol. 58, March/April 1962.

GIRTANNER, Christoph. *Abhandlung über die venerische krankheit.* Göttingen, 1788.

GRAUNT, John, 'Natural and political observations upon the Bills of Mortality'. (1662). Reprinted in C. H. Hull, *Economic writings of Sir William Petty.*

GUY DE CHAULIAC, *Chirurgia Magna* . . . *nunc demum suae primae integritati restituta a Laurentio Jouberts* . . . (Lyons), 1585.

——, *The questionary of cyrurgyens.* (London), 1542.

HECHTER-SCHULZ, Karl, 'Fertility dolls', *Anthropos*, 1966, 61, pp. 516–28.

HELBIG, C. E., 'Ein condom im altertum', *Reichs-Medizinal Anzeiger*, 1900, XXV.

——, 'Zu dem schrifttume über den condom', *Reichs-Medizinal Anzeiger*, 1907, XXXII.

HERRICK, O. E., 'Abortion and its lesson', *Michigan Medical News*, (1882), V, pp. 7–10.

HIMES, Norman E., *Medical history of contraception.* (New York, Gamut Press), 1936 (1963).

——, 'Forerunners of the modern condom', *Janus*, 42e. annee, 1938, pp. 1–6.

HIPPOCRATES, *Oeuvres complètes d'Hippocrate.* Translated by E. Littré. (Paris, Ballière), 1851.

HOLINSHED, Raphael, *The firste volume of the chronicles of England, Scotlande and Irelande, conteyning the description and chronicles of England from the first inhabiting unto the conquest. The description and chronicles of Scotland, from the first originall of the Scottes nation till the years 1571. The description and chronicles of Yrelande, from the first originall, untill the yeare 1547. (The laste volume . . . con-*

teyning the chronicles of Englande from William Conquerour untill this present tyme.) 3 vols. (London), 1577.

HOLLWEG, 'Uber intrauterinpessar', *Therap. Monatschr.*, 1902, 16, pp. 463–66.

HOPKINS, Keith, 'Contraception in the Roman Empire', *Comparative Studies in Society and History*, October 1965. VIII: 1, pp. 124–51.

HOW-MARTYN, Edith, and BREED, Mary, *The birth control movement in England.* (London, Bale), 1930.

HUFELAND, C. W., 'Von dem recht des Arztes über leben und tod', *Journ. Pract. Heilkunde*, 1823, 66: 1, pp. 1–28.

HURT-MEAD, Kate Campbell, *A history of women in medicine from the earliest times to the beginning of the nineteenth century.* (Haddam, Connecticut, The Haddam Press), 1938.

HUXLEY, Julian, 'Material of early contraceptive sheaths', *British Medical Journal*, 1957, (I), pp. 581–2.

ILL, Edward Joseph, 'The rights of the unborn', *American Journal of Obstetrics and Gynaecology*, 1899, XL, pp. 577–84.

INSTITORIS, H., and SPRENGLER, J., *Malleus Maleficarum.* Edited by the Reverend Montague Summers, London, Rodker, 1928.

INTERNATIONAL MEDICAL GROUP FOR THE INVESTIGATION OF BIRTH CONTROL. "Annual Issues", edited by C. P. Blacker. Published: No. 1, 1928; No. 2, 1929; No. 3, 1930; No. 4, 1931; No. 5, 1934.

JACOBI, Abraham, 'The best means of combatting infant mortality', *Journal of the American Medical Association.* 8 June 1912, LVIII: 23.

JAKOBOVITZ, I., 'Artificial insemination, birth control and abortion', *Hebrew Medical Journal*, 1953, XXVI, part ii, pp. 183–169.

JOHNSON, Ben, *Epicoene.* (London, D. Midwinter), 1739.

KASS, Norman, 'The Talmud on contraception', *Hebrew Medical Journal*, 1961, 34: 1, pp. 257–1.

KEFERSTEIN, 'Verurtheilung eines praktischen Arztes wegen fahrlässiger körperverletzung im 5 fällen durch einlegen eines von ihm erfunden besonderen intra-uterin-pessars als frauenschutz', *Centralblatt für Gynäkologie*, 1902, No. 23. pp. 609–12.

KELLY, Webb J., 'One of the abuses of carbolic acid', *Columbus Medical Journal*, 1882–3, I, pp. 433–6.

KNOWLTON, Charles, *Fruits of philosophy; or, the private companion of young married people.* There have been a great many editions. That published by Charles Bradlaugh and Annie Besant was published in London by the Freethought Publishing Company, and it is undated. (About 1876 ?)

LAMBETH CONFERENCE 1930: Encyclical letter from the Bishops with resolutions and reports. London, 1930.

LANGDON-DAVIES, John, *A short history of women*. (New York, Viking Press), 1927.

LEACH, Edmund, 'Virgin birth', *Proceedings of the Royal Anthropological Institute*, 1966, 39–49.

LE PILEUR, L., 'Les préservatifs de la syphilis a travers les ages. *Annales des Maladies Veneriennes*. (Paris), 1907, ii, pp. 501–27.

LEVY, Claude, 'Quelques exemples de 'birth control' au XVI, XVII, et XVIIIe. siècles', *Concours Méd*. 1957, 79, pp. 2376–80.

LIEBAUT, Jean, *Thresor des remèdes secrets pour les maladies des femmes*. Paris, R. Fouet, 1597.

LINKNER, J., 'Die empfängnisverhütung im lichte der geschichte', *Med. Welt*. (Stuttgart), 1962, Nr. 49, pp. 2635–8.

McCANN, F., 'The effect of contraceptive practices on the female sexual organs', *Catholic Medical Guardian*, 1927, V, pp. 48–61.

McKAY, W. Stewart, *The history of ancient gynaecology*. (London), Ballière Tindall and Cox), 1901.

MARCUSE, Max, *Die Ehe: ihre physiologie, psychologie, hygiene und eugenik. Ein biologisches ehebuch*. (Berlin, Marcus and Weber), 1927.

MARTI-IBANEZ, Felix, 'The medico-pharmaceutical arts of "La Celestina", *International Record of Medicine*, April 1956, 169: 4.

MAUDE, Aylmer, *The authorized life of Marie Carmichael Stopes*. (London, Williams and Norgate), 1924.

MAURICEAU, François, *Aphorismes touchant la grossesse, l'accouchement, les maladies, et autres dispositions des femmes*. (Paris, L. D'Houry), 1694.

——, *Des maladies des femmes grosses et accouchées*. (Paris, The author), 1668.

MENSINGA, W. P. J., *Über facultative sterilität. I. Beleuchtet vom prophylactischen und hygenischen standpunkte für practische aerzte. II. Das pessariam occlusium und dessen applikation*. (Neuweid and Leipzig), 1882.

MICHELET, Jules, L'amour. Paris, 1858.

MOÏSSDES, M., 'Le Malthusianisme dans l'antiquité Greque', *Janus*, 1932, XXXVI, pp. 169–79.

MOORE, S. G. H., 'The immorality of family restriction', *Medical Officer*, 1918, XX, p. 145.

MURRAY, Margaret, *The witch cult in Western Europe*. (Oxford, Oxford University Press), 1921.

NOONAN, John T., *Contraception: A history of its treatment by the Catholic theologians and canonists*. (Cambridge, Mass. Harvard University Press), 1965.

NOYES, Hilda Herrick, and NOYES, George Wallingford, 'The Oneida community experience in stirpiculture', *Eugenics Quarterly*, December 1967. 14: 4, pp. 282–90.

OLDHAM, Henry, 'On the induction of abortion in a case of contracted vagina from cicatrization', *London Medical Gazette*, July 1849, p. 45.

OHNESORGE, V., 'Schädigungen durch silkwormsterilette', *Münchener Medizinische Wochenschrift*, March 1927, 74, pp. 419–20.

OWEN, Robert Dale, *Moral physiology; or, a brief and plain treatise on the population question*. Many editions from 1831 onward.

PAYNE, Robert, *The life and death of Mahatma Gandhi*. (London, Bodley Head), 1969.

PERRY, W. J., 'Theology and physiological paternity', *Man*, 1932, article no. 218.

PIERPOINT, Raymond, Ed., *Report of the Fifth International Neo-Malthusian and birth control conference, Kingsway Hall, London, July 1922*. (London, Heinemann), 1922.

PLACE, Francis, *Illustrations and proofs of the principle of population . . . including an examination of the proposed remedies of Mr. Malthus, and a reply to Mr. Godwin and others*. (London), 1822.

POUCHET, Felix Archimedes, *Théorie positive de l'ovulation spontanée et de la fecondation des mammifères et de l'espèce humaine, basés sur l'observation de toute la série animale*. (Paris), 1845.

The Practitioner. Special issue on birth control. 1923.

PUST, 'Ein brauchbarer frauenschutz', *Deutsche Medizinische Wochenschrift*, 20 July 1923, 49, pp. 952–3.

PYKE, Margaret, 'Family planning: An assessment', The Galton Lecture, February 1963. Printed in *The Eugenics Review*, July 1963, 55: 2.

RALEIGH, Sir Walter, *The works of Sir Walter Raleigh, political, commercial and philosophical.* Edited by Thomas Birch. (London), 1751.

RAWLS, R. M., 'Status of the intrauterine stem pessary', *American Journal of Obstetrics and Gynaecology.* February 1921, 31, p. 449.

RENTOUL, Alex C., 'Physiological paternity and the Trobrianders', *Man*, 1931, article no. 162.

Report of the conference on giving information on birth control by Public Health Authorities. (London), (1930?)

REYNOLDS, John P., 'The limiting of childbearing among the married', *Transactions of the American Gynaecological Society*, 1890, XV, pp. 3–24.

RICCI, James V., *The development of gynaecological surgery and instruments.* Philadelphia, Blakiston, 1949.

RICHTER, R., 'Ein mittel zur verhütung der Konzeption', *Deutsche Medizinische Wochenschrift*, 1909, XXXV, pp. 1525–7.

ROBINSON, Victor, *Pioneers of birth control in England and America.* (New York, Voluntary Parenthood League), 1919.

'ROGER PHEUQUEWELL ESQ.' (Pseudonym), *A new description of Merryland.* (London), 1741.

ROUTH, C. H. F., *The moral and physical evils likely to follow if practices intended to act as checks to population be not strongly discouraged and condemned.* (1879) A reprint from the *Medical Press and Circular*, October, 1878.

SANGER, Margaret, *Family limitation.* (London, Bakunin Press), 1920.

——, *My fight for birth control.* (New York, Farrar and Rinehart), 1931.

——, *Proceedings of the World Population Conference, held at the Salle Generale, Geneva, August 19–September 3, 1927.* (London), 1927.

——, and STONE, Hannah, 'The practice of contraception. An international symposium and survey', from the *Proceedings of the Seventh International Birth Control Conference, Zurich, September 1930.* (Baltimore), 1931.

SAVIARD, Barthelemy, *Nouveau recueil d'observations chirurgicales . . . Avec quelques remedes particuliers, dont il s'est servy au traitement des maladies qui le composent.* (Paris, J. Collombat), 1702.

SAXONIAE, Herculis, *Luis Venereae perfectissimus tractatus ex ore Herculis Saxoniae.* Batavia, 1597.

SCULTETUS, Johannes, *The chyrurgeons store-house: furnished with forty-three tables cut in brass, in which are all sorts of instruments . . .*

with an exact description of every instrument. Together with a hundred choise observations of famous cures performed . . . faithfully englished, by E. B. (London, J. Starkey), 1674.

SERMON, William, *The ladies companion; or, the English midwife. Wherein is demonstrated how women ought to govern themselves during the whole time of their breeding children, and of their difficult labour. . . . Together with the diseases they are subject to . . . Also the various forms of the childs proceeding forth of the womb.* (London, E. Thomas), 1671.

SIMON, Sir John, *Reports relating to the sanitary condition of the City of London.* (London, J. W. Parker), 1854.

SMITH, Elizabeth, *The compleat housewife; or, accomplish'd gentlewoman's companion: Being a collection of receipts . . . in cookery . . . to which is added a collection . . . of receipts of medicines.* (London), (1726?)

Society for the Provision of Birth Control Clinics, Birth control and public health: A report on ten years' work of the Society for the Provision of Birth Control Clinics. (London, The Society), 1932.

SORANOS OF EPHESUS, *Soranos Gynecology*, translated with an introduction by Owsei Temkin. (Baltimore, Johns Hopkins Press), 1956.

STOPES, Marie Carmichael, *Contraception (Birth Control), Its theory, history and practice: A manual for the medical and legal professions.* (London, G. P. Putnam's Sons), 1931.

——, *A new gospel for all peoples.* (London), 1922.

——, *Wise parenthood, a sequel to "Married Love", a book for married people.* (London, Putnam), 1919.

STRANGELAND, Charles Emil, *Pre-Malthusian doctrines of population: A study in the history of economic theory.* (New York, Augustus M. Kelley), (1904), 1966.

STREICH, Artur, 'Zur geschichte des condoms', *Arch. für. Gesch. d. Med.* 1929, XXII, pp. 208–13.

TALBOT, P. A., *Some Nigerian fertility cults.* (London, Oxford, Oxford University Press), 1927.

TURNER, Daniel, *Syphilis. A practical treatise on the venereal disease.* (London), 1717.

TURNER, Robert, *De morbis foemineis: The woman's counsellour; or, the feminine physitian, enlarged, Modestly treating such occult and secret diseases, as are incident to that sex . . . Also a supplement*

*touching agues and feavours, usefully applicable to both sexes. Where-
unto is added, the man's counsellour, healing of ruptures, and particular diseases belonging to men.* (London, J. Streater), 1686.

WILDE, Friedrich Adolph, 'Das weibliche gebär-unvermögen. Ein
medicinisch-juridische abhandlung zum gebrauch für, practische
geburtshelfer, aertze, und juristen'. (Berlin, In der *Nicolai'schen
Buchhandlung*), 1838.

ZIRKLE, C., 'Animals impregnated by the wind', *Isis*, 1936, 25: 1,
pp. 95–130.

Index